On the Logic of the Social
Sciences

Studies in Contemporary German Social Thought
Thomas McCarthy, General Editor

On the Logic of the Social Sciences

Jürgen Habermas

translated by Shierry Weber Nicholsen
and Jerry A. Stark

97 - 1038

The MIT Press
Cambridge, Massachusetts

Fourth printing, 1991

This work originally appeared in German as a special supplemental volume of the journal *Philosophische Rundschau* in February 1967. It was published in book form in the volume entitled *Zur Logik der Sozialwissenschaften,* © 1970 Suhrkamp Verlag, Frankfurt am Main, Federal Republic of Germany.

Printed and bound in the United States of America by Maple-Vail, Inc.

Library of Congress Cataloging-in-Publication Data

Habermas, Jürgen.
  [Zur Logik der Sozialwissenschaften. English]
  On the logic of the social sciences/Jürgen Habermas; translated by Shierry Weber Nicholsen and Jerry A. Stark.

  p. cm.—(Studies in contemporary German social thought)
  Translation of: Zur Logik der Sozialwissenschaften.
  "Originally appeared in German as a special supplemental volume of the journal *Philosophische Rundschau* in February 1967"—CIP t.p. verso.
  Bibliography: p.
  Includes index.
  ISBN 0-262-08177-6 (hb)   ISBN 0-262-58104-3 (pb)

  1. Social sciences—Methodology. I. Title. II. Series.
H61.H2513 1988   300'.72—dc19   88-583

Contents

Introduction

Thomas McCarthy

When it first appeared in 1967, *On the Logic of the Social Sciences* challenged the existing division of labor between the sciences and the humanities: "While the natural sciences and the humanities are able to live side by side, in mutual indifference if not in mutual admiration, the social sciences must resolve the tension between the two approaches and bring them under one roof." At that time discussions of the methodology of science were still dominated by logical positivism. Kuhn's pathbreaking work, published a few years earlier, had only begun to make itself felt among philosophers of natural science; in the philosophy of social science it was, and was to remain for some time to come, only a distant rumbling. Thus Habermas's main concern was to challenge the hegemony of "empirical-analytical" conceptions of social science, to show, in particular, that access to the symbolically structured object domain of social inquiry called for procedures similar in important respects to those developed in the text-interpreting humanities. In making this point, he was already able to draw upon insights developed in the phenomenological (Schutz), ethnomethodological (Garfinkel, Cicourel), linguistic (Wittgenstein, Winch), and hermeneutic (Gadamer) traditions, and on this basis to mount an argument that anticipated in all essential respects the subsequent decline of positivism and rise of interpretivism.

If this were all there were to the story, *On the Logic of the Social Sciences* would be primarily of historical interest as a striking anticipation of contemporary developments. But there is more. Habermas argued just as forcefully against swinging to the opposite extreme of "hermeneutic idealism," which has since achieved something of a counterhegemony in the philosophy of social science (but not, of course, in the practice of social research). The point was—and is—to bring explanatory and interpretive approaches "under one roof," as Max Weber had already seen. Thus we have here not only an anticipation of the retreat of positivism, but a critique-in-advance of the absolutizing of interpretive approaches that followed. If social research is not to be restricted to explicating, reconstructing, and deconstructing meanings, we must somehow grasp the objective interconnections of social actions, the "meanings" they have beyond those intended by actors or embedded in traditions. We must, in short, view culture in relation to the material conditions of life and their historical transformation.

With this in mind, Habermas goes on here to examine functionalist approaches, in particular, the structural-functionalism of Talcott Parsons. He finds that the attempt to conceive of the social system as a functional complex of institutions in which cultural patterns are made normatively binding for action does furnish us with important tools for analyzing objective interconnections of action; but it suffers from a short-circuiting of the hermeneutic and critical dimensions of social analysis: "In the framework of action theory, motives for action are harmonized with institutional values.... We may assume, however, that repressed needs which are not absorbed into social roles, transformed into motivations, and sanctioned, nevertheless have their interpretations. Either these interpretations 'overshoot' the existing order and, as utopian anticipations, signify a not-yet-successful group identity; or, transformed into ideologies, they serve projective substitute gratification as well as the justification of repressing authorities." Habermas argues that if the analysis of social systems were fully to incorporate these dimensions, it could no longer be understood as a form of empirical-analytical science on the model of biology; it would have to be transformed into a historically oriented theory of society with a practical intent. The form such a theory would take is that of a "systematically generalized history" that reflectively grasped the formative process of society as a whole, reconstructing the contemporary situation with a view not only to its past but to its practically anticipated future as well. This is, in fact, what the classical social theorists were after—from the natural history of civil society of the Scottish moralists, through Marx's historical materialism, to Weber's theory of rationalization.

And yet, Habermas maintains, they were unable to grasp the methodological specificity of such a theoretically informed and practically oriented history; instead, they tried repeatedly, and in vain, to assimilate it to the strictly nomological sciences of nature.

Habermas finds in psychoanalysis the most suggestive model for reconceptualizing and reintegrating the explanatory and interpretive, functionalist and narrative elements required for social theory. Anticipating the extended discussion of Freud in *Knowledge and Human Interests* (which was published in the following year), he views psychoanalytic theory as a general interpretive scheme of psychodynamic development, whose application to the narrative reconstruction of individual life histories calls for a peculiar combination of interpretive understanding and causal explanation, and whose corroboration depends in the last analysis on the successful continuation of those same life histories. In an analogous way, critical social theory undertakes a narrative reconstruction of the self-formative process of society, with a view to its successful continuation: "In place of the goal-state of a self-regulating system, we would have the end-state of a formative process. A hermeneutically enlightened and historically oriented functionalism ... is guided by an emancipatory cognitive interest that aims at reflection.... The species too constitutes itself in formative processes, which are sedimented in the structural change of social systems, and which can be reflected, that is, systematically narrated from an anticipated point of view."

Since publishing *On the Logic of the Social Sciences*, Habermas has considerably expanded upon a number of its key elements. Thus, for example, symbolic interactionism and ethnomethodology, functionalism, and systems theory have come in for extended discussion in later writings. And although Habermas could write in 1982 that he still found the basic line of argument correct, he has altered his position in a number of important respects. The idea of founding social-scientific inquiry in a theory of language, which already existed in germ in *Knowledge and Human Interests*, came to dominate his work on universal pragmatics and rational reconstruction in the later sixties and early seventies. Toward the end of the 1970s he started the turn that culminated in *The Theory of Communicative Action*, a turn marked by the warning that methodology and epistemology are no royal road to social theory. Rather, questions concerning the logic of social inquiry can fruitfully be pursued only in connection with substantive questions—the theory of communicative action is not constructed in a methodological perspective. Despite these changes and developments, and despite the altered context of contemporary discussions in the philosophy of social science, the present work has somehow retained its power and fascination. Perhaps this is because it avoids the one-sidedness that still marks the views of the principal protagonists, and unlike them finds something of value in all of the major contending approaches to social inquiry, something worth preserving and reconstituting. Perhaps it is because Habermas here anticipates so many of the issues and themes that occupy us today, and does so with a sharpness that has not been surpassed. Or perhaps it is because Habermas's earlier sketch of a critical theory of the present—in the form of a systematically generalized narrative constructed with the practical intent of changing things for the better—has lost none of its appeal, even when viewed in the light of his later, more emphatically theoretical undertakings.

Translator's Note

I would like to thank Arden Nicholsen and Jeremy J. Shapiro for their help in the preparation of this translation. Both of them read drafts of the manuscript and offered many valuable suggestions and criticisms.

Shierry Weber Nicholsen

Preface

This review of literature pertaining to the logic of the social sciences
was written in the mid-1960s, when analytic philosophy of science,
with its program for a unified science, still largely dominated the
self-understanding of sociologists.[1] It contributed to the basic
changes in that situation that took place in the following decade.
My discussion not only continued Adorno's critique of positivism
but also directed attention to the spectrum of nonconventional
approaches—including the later Wittgenstein's philosophy of language, Gadamer's hermeneutics, and the phenomenological ethnomethodology stemming from Schutz—which, as Richard Bernstein noted a decade later, gave rise to a "restructuring of social
theory."[2] The appropriation of hermeneutics and linguistic analysis convinced me then that critical social theory had to break free
from the conceptual apparatus of the philosophy of consciousness
flowing from Kant and Hegel.[3] The methodological (in the narrower sense) fruits of my efforts consisted chiefly in uncovering the
dimension in which the symbolically prestructured object domain of
social science could be approached through interpreting meaning.[4]
This reconstruction of the buried hermeneutic dimension—whose
rediscovery within analytic philosophy was to await the Popper-
Kuhn debates[5]—had to be combined with an argument against
hermeneutics' claim to universality.[6]

This review was written for a particular occasion. One reason for

These remarks are taken from the author's preface to the fifth edition of "On the Logic of the
Social Sciences," which appeared in 1982 as part of a larger collection with the same title: *Zur
Logik der Sozialwissenschaften* (Frankfurt: Suhrkamp Verlag), pp. 89–330.

its cursory character is that I am not a specialist in this area. More-over, the logic of research has always interested me only in connec-tion with questions of social theory. To be sure, I was convinced for a time that the project of a critical social theory had to prove itself, in the first instance, from a methodological and epistemological standpoint. This was reflected in the fact that I held out the pros-pect of "grounding the social sciences in a theory of language" in the preface to the 1970 edition of this work. This is a prospect I no longer entertain. The theory of communicative action that I have since put forward[7] is not a continuation of methodology by other means. It breaks with the primacy of epistemology and treats the presupposition of action oriented to mutual understanding *indepen-dently* of the transcendental preconditions of knowledge. This turn from the theory of knowledge to the theory of communication makes it possible to give substantive answers to questions that, from a metatheoretical vantage point, could only be elucidated as ques-tions and clarified in respect to their presuppositions.

Munich
August 1982

On the Logic of the Social Sciences

I
The Dualism of the Natural
and Cultural Sciences

The once lively discussion initiated by Neo-Kantianism concerning the methodological distinctions between natural-scientific and
social-scientific inquiry has been forgotten; the problems that gave
rise to it no longer seem to be of contemporary relevance. Scientistic
consciousness obscures fundamental and persistent differences in
the methodological approaches of the sciences. The positivistic self-
understanding prevalent among scientists has adopted the thesis
of the unity of sciences; from the positivist perspective, the dualism
of science, which was considered to be grounded in the logic of
scientific inquiry, shrinks to a distinction between levels of development. At the same time, the strategy based on the program of a
unified science has led to indisputable successes. The nomological
sciences, whose aim it is to formulate and verify hypotheses concerning the laws governing empirical regularities, have extended
themselves far beyond the sphere of the theoretical natural sciences,
into psychology and economics, sociology and political science. On
the other hand, the historical-hermeneutic sciences, which appropriate and analyze meaningful cultural entities handed down by
tradition, continue uninterrupted along the paths they have been
following since the nineteenth century. There is no serious indication that their methods can be integrated into the model of the strict
empirical sciences. Every university catalogue provides evidence of
this actual division between the sciences; it is unimportant only in
the textbooks of the positivists.

This continuing dualism, which we take for granted in the *practice*
of science, is no longer discussed in terms of the *logic* of science. Instead of being addressed at the level of the philosophy of science, it

simply finds expression in the coexistence of two distinct frames of reference. Depending upon the type of science with which it is concerned, the philosophy of science takes the form either of a general methodology of the empirical sciences or of a general hermeneutics of the cultural and historical sciences. At this time the work of K. R. Popper[1] and H. G. Gadamer can be taken as representative of state-of-the-art formulations of this specifically restricted self-reflection of the sciences. Neither analytic philosophy of science nor philosophical hermeneutics takes any notice of the other; only seldom do their discussions step outside the boundaries of their respective realms, which are both terminologically and substantively distinct.[2] The analytic school dismisses the hermeneutic disciplines as prescientific, while the hermeneutic school considers the nomological sciences as characterized by a limited preunderstanding.

The mutually uncomprehending coexistence of analytical philosophy of science and philosophical hermeneutics troubles the rigid self-consciousness of neither of the two parties. Occasional attempts to bridge the gap have remained no more than good intentions.[3] There would be no reason to touch on the well-buried issue of the dualism of science if it did not in one area continually produce symptoms that demand analytic resolution: in the social sciences, heterogeneous aims and approaches conflict and intermingle with one another. To be sure, the current state of the various social-scientific disciplines indicates a lack of even development; for this reason it is easy to ascribe unclarified methodological issues and unresolved controversies to a confusion that can be remedied through logical clarification and a program of unified science. Hence the positivists do not hesitate to start from scratch. According to their postulates, a general and, in principle, unified *empirical-analytic behavioral science*, not different in structure from the theoretical natural sciences, can be produced from the purified corpus of the traditional social sciences.[4] Steps in this direction have been taken in psychology and social psychology. Economics, with the exception of econometrics, is organized on the model of a *normative-analytic science* that presupposes hypothetical maxims of action. Sociological research is carried out primarily within the *structural-functional framework* of a theory of action that can neither be reduced to observable behavior nor reconstructed on the model of purposive-rational action.

Finally, much research in sociology and political science is historically oriented, without any intentional link to general theories.

As I shall demonstrate, all three of these theoretical approaches can lay claim to a relative legitimacy. Contrary to what positivism assumes, they are not based on faulty or unclear methodological presuppositions. Nor can the more complex of these approaches be reduced, without damage, to the platform of a general science of behavior. Only at first glance does the confusion seem capable of being eliminated through clear-cut distinctions. Rather, the competing approaches that have been developed within the social sciences are negatively interrelated, in that they all stem from the fact that the apparatus of general theories cannot be applied to society in the same way as to objectified natural processes. Whereas the natural and the cultural or hermeneutic sciences are capable of living in a mutually indifferent, albeit more hostile than peaceful, coexistence, the social sciences must bear the tension of divergent approaches under one roof, for in them the very practice of research compels reflection on the relationship between analytic and hermeneutic methodologies.

1 A Historical Reconstruction

1.1 Rickert was the first to try to grasp the dualism of the natural and the cultural sciences in a methodologically rigorous way. He restricted the claims of Kant's critique of reason to the realm of the nomological sciences in order to make a place for the cultural sciences, which Dilthey had raised to epistemological status.[5] Rickert's efforts remain within the framework of transcendental philosophy. Whereas phenomena are constituted as "nature" under general laws through the categories of the understanding, "culture" is formed through the relation of facts to a system of values. Cultural phenomena owe their unique historical significance to this individualizing value-relationship. Rickert perceived the logical impossibility of the strictly idiographic science that Windelband proposed.[6]

He acknowledged as a fact the unique achievement of the sciences based on understanding (*verstehende Wissenschaften*): they grasp the unique, that is, unrepeatable meaning of historical events in expressions that are at the same time inevitably general and thus oriented toward what can be repeated. But he could not provide a satisfactory explanation for this fact.

Rickert presupposes—and here he is covertly in accordance with *Lebensphilosophie*—the irrationality of a reality that is integrally present only in nonlinguistic experience: it disintegrates into alternative viewpoints under the transcendentally mediated grasp of the mind engaged in knowledge. These complementary aspects, in terms of which reality must be grasped in the form either of lawful continuity or of heterogeneous particularity, remain separate and distinct. In choosing an appropriate theoretical system we are presented with mutually exclusive alternatives in which the statements of one system cannot be transformed into statements of the other. Only the term "heterogeneous continuum" represents the unity of a reality that, from the transcendental perspective, has been divided; no synthesis produced by the finite understanding corresponds to this purely extrapolated unity. But how can the same reality that is grasped as nature under general laws be individualized through value-relational categories, if these categories themselves must have the logical status of universals? Rickert postulates that values do not have the same logical status as class concepts. He asserts that cultural phenomena are not subsumed by the values that constitute them in the same way that elements are subsumed in a class.[7] But this claim cannot be made good within the framework in which it is posed, that of transcendental logic. Rickert can only sketch the concept of a historical totality, because he distrusts the dialectical tools that would allow him to grasp it. A logic of the cultural sciences that proceeds on the basis of a transcendental critique of consciousness cannot avoid the dialectic of the particular and the general that Hegel identified. This leads beyond Hegel to the concept of the cultural phenomenon as that which is historically individuated, that which demands to be identified precisely as something non-identical.[8]

The philosophy of value (*Wertphilosophie*) itself arises from the same ambivalence of an uncompleted transition from Kant to Hegel. Rickert begins by constructing the concept of culture on the basis of transcendental idealism. Like the category of nature, the category of culture, as representing a totality of phenomena under a system of prevailing values, has transcendental significance; it says nothing about objects themselves but rather determines the conditions of the possible apprehension of objects.

To this construction corresponds the optimistic assumption that a system of values can be deduced a priori from practical reason.[9] But Rickert soon had to abandon this idea.[10] The actual profusion of so-called values could be deciphered only in the real context of cultures in which the value-oriented action of historical subjects had been objectivated—even if the validity of those values was independent of these origins. If this is to be conceded, then the Neo-Kantian concept of culture succumbs to the transcendental-empirical ambiguity that found its dialectical development in Hegel's concept of objective spirit, but that Neo-Kantians had to reject. The cultural sciences encounter their object in preconstituted form. The cultural meanings of empirically functioning values systems are derived from value-oriented action. For this reason, the transcendentally mediated accomplishments of subjects whose actions are oriented to values are at once both incorporated into and preserved in the empirical form of historically sedimented and transmitted values.

With history, a dimension is brought into the object domain of science in which an element of transcendental consciousness is objectivated through the action of historical subjects; that is, a meaning is objectivated that in each case can claim validity only in terms of a transcendental network of values. Rickert tries to do justice to the objectivity of these historically real contexts of meaning with the concept of transcendental "ought."[11] But this concept only exemplifies the contradictions that the firm distinctions between facts and values, empirical being and transcendental validity, nature and culture, seek in vain to resolve. Because Rickert will not abandon the distinctions made by transcendental philosophy, they crumble in his hands despite his intentions. Through the breach of the transcendental "ought" a restoration rushes in that, in opposing Rickert, openly acknowledges in the philosophy of value something that lay hidden in Rickert's philosophy: an insipid ontology of ideal being (Max Scheler and Nicolai Hartmann).

Today the logic of science is no longer based on the Kantian critique of reason; it starts from the current state of self-reflection of the nomological and hermeneutic sciences. Analytic philosophy of science is content with rules for the logical construction and choice of general theories. It establishes a dualism between facts and propositions and refrains from understanding this dualism from a transcendental perspective.[12] Philosophical hermeneutics no longer defines itself in relation to a Kantian concept of nature and general law. It relinquishes the intention of constructing a world of cultural phenomena and is content with explicating traditional meaning. Nevertheless, I believe that a resumption of Rickert's attempt to reflect on the dualism of the sciences, even on a non-Kantian basis, would once again set in motion the movement from Kant to Hegel that was so interestingly modified and then abandoned by Rickert. Today such a movement can no longer begin with a critique of consciousness; it must begin with a transcendental critique of language. Neo-Kantianism itself—not that of the Heidelberg school but that of the Marburg school—reached this point with Cassirer's philosophy of symbolic forms.

1.2 Cassirer avoids the ambiguous category of value, which was supposed to capture the empirical significance of historically realized meanings without relinquishing the transcendental significance of a validity independent of its origins. Instead, he analyzes the logical structure of symbolic forms. In his own fashion Cassirer makes the same shift that positivist linguistic analysis makes, from the logic of judgments to the grammar of sentences. But he does not restrict himself to the formal relationships within the symbol systems used in everyday language or by the empirical sciences; the level of symbols interests him as a medium of transcendental production. Cassirer has read Humboldt from the perspective of a Kant enlightened, rather than rejected, by Hamann. The phenomenal object is no longer constituted directly through the categories of intuition and understanding, but rather through a transcendental achievement that can be grasped within the sphere of sense perception through the creation of systematically ordered symbols that give objectivity to sense impressions. The understanding alone cannot accomplish the synthesis of phenomena; symbols are required to make traces of what is not given apparent in what is given. The inner world presents itself to the mind to the extent to which the mind creates forms that are capable of representing a reality that is not accessible through intuition. Reality manifests itself as something represented. Representation is the basic function of transcendental consciousness; its achievements can be deciphered indirectly from the grammatical relationships of symbolic forms. The philosophy of symbolic forms, which supersedes the critique of pure reason, aims at a logical analysis of language from a transcendental point of view.

Clearly, the language of symbolic forms is richer than the symbol systems constructed for the use of the empirical sciences. In addition to science, it encompasses myth, religion, and art. Like Rickert, Cassirer tries to extend the critique of strictly scientific knowledge to a universal critique of all cultural phenomena:

Every authentic function of the human spirit has this decisive characteristic in common with cognition: It does not merely copy but rather embodies an original, formative power. It does not express passively the mere fact that something is present but contains an independent energy of the human spirit through which the simple presence of the phenomenon assumes a definite "meaning," a particular ideational content. This is as true of myth as of religion. All live in particular image-worlds, which do not merely reflect the empirically given, but which rather produce it in accordance with an independent principle. Each of these functions creates its own symbolic forms which, if not similar to the intellectual symbols, enjoy equal rank as products of the human spirit. None of these forms can simply be reduced to, or derived from, the others; each of them designates a particular approach, in which and through which it constitutes its own aspect of "reality." [13]

Each of the various symbolic systems poses a claim to truth from its own perspective. Science forfeits its privileged claim to truth; philosophy reserves it for itself, in reflexively limited form. "True" knowledge is now possible only with respect to the transcendental conditions of symbolic representation, no longer with respect to what is represented. According to Cassirer, it is only through the image-worlds that are articulated in symbolic forms that

we see what call "reality," and in them alone we possess it: for the highest objective truth that is accessible to the spirit is ultimately the form of its own activity. In the totality of its own achievements, in the knowledge of the specific rule by which each of them is determined . . . , the human spirit now perceives itself and reality. True, the question of what, apart from these spiritual functions, constitutes absolute reality . . . , remains unanswered, except that more and more we learn to recognize it as a fallacy in formulation, an intellectual phantasm. [14]

Cassirer believed that with this self-reflection of representational reason he had opened the way to a new philosophy of the cultural sciences.

Cassirer makes a clear separation between the levels on which the natural and the cultural sciences operate. Rickert had accorded both the same status, that of empirical science. Now the cultural sciences have achieved the status of metatheory. The nomological sciences produce statements about reality within formally defined symbolic systems. In this respect they stand on the same level as myth, art, and religion, which also present a reality selectively comprehended within specific frames of reference. The cultural sciences, in contrast, concern themselves with formal relationships among symbolic forms. They provide no information about reality, but rather make statements about information that is pregiven. Their task is not empirical analysis of segments of reality that can be represented but rather logical analysis of the forms in which they are represented.

By this means the difficulties of Rickert's theory are avoided. The problem of the mediation of an individual particular with a non-classificatory universal does not arise as long as what is required is to analyze given symbolic relations from a formal point of view. Although the grammar of any specific symbolic language will prove to be an irreducible totality, Cassirer is convinced that the diverse grammars of art and myth, religion and science operate with the same categories. Cassirer then explains the transcendental universality of these categories, which synthesize unity in multiplicity, in terms of symbolic representation.

Nor is the place of cultural phenomena a problem. Although as physical signs, symbols extend into the sphere of sense perception, they are not to be equated with the empirical phenomena with which the natural sciences are concerned. Rather, they are the transcendental precondition of the world appearing to subjects in the first place. Thus the science of cultural forms operates in formal-analytic rather than causal-analytic terms. It directs itself to the structural organization of works rather than to factual connections between events. It shares the reflective viewpoint of transcendental logic, even though a moment of historical tradition, and thus empirical givenness, adheres to symbolic forms. But for Cassirer this moment is not, as it was for Rickert, an unanalyzed residue, because Cassirer, in the manner of Hegel, no longer separates reason from its objectivations or transcendental consciousness from its symbol expressions, which can be conceived both transcendentally and empirically. In this way, however, Cassirer elevates the cultural *sciences* to a level on which they can no longer be distinguished from a *philosophy* of symbolic forms. He divests them of their character as science.

Cassirer pays a high price for this interpretation of the dualism of science within the framework of a construction of representational reason. The statements of the nomological sciences can no longer assert their specific claim to empirical validity, because the scientific languages in which they are formulated are, in principle, on the same level as myth and fable. The validity of scientific statements could be legitimated only if Cassirer relinquished the idea of the equal primacy of symbol systems in favor of a developmental history of transcendental consciousness. But the dimension of history cannot be accommodated within the philosophy of symbolic forms. The cultural sciences share this deficiency. They are the exponents of a general grammar of symbolic forms. But the historical process in which these forms are constituted, the contexts of tradition in which culture is transmitted and appropriated, the very dimension, that is, in which culture exerts its effects, remains closed to the cultural sciences. They proceed ahistorically. They are structural sciences under the gaze of which history evaporates. They retain only a morphology of forms immanent in cultural works, on the model of Wölfflin's principles. Thus the historical sciences, whose methodological status Rickert was attempting to clarify, elude Cassirer's grasp.[15]

In 1942 Cassirer once again began to work on the logic of the cultural sciences,[16] focusing on the phenomenology and psychology of the perception of expressions, which was supposed to extend the original unity of apperception to a new dimension that is logically prior to the operations of the understanding.[17] While this approach may have significance for the question of the constitution of the natural lifeworld (thereby for the first time placing Husserl's return to Kant in its true light), it does not provide a meaningful basis for the logic of science. Cassirer wants to derive the various types of science from specific sources of experience: it is in the polarity between the perception of things and the perception of expressions that the opposition that is explicitly developed in the methodological frameworks of the natural and cultural sciences is supposed to reside.[18] But this view would accord with the philosophy of symbolic forms only if specific conceptual and perceptual structures were derived from the employment of specific symbolic systems.

Both of Neo-Kantianism's attempts to account for the dualism of the sciences were fruitless. The problem vanished from philosophical consciousness almost as completely as it did from the methodological self-understanding of the empirical sciences—with one exception. Max Weber began where Rickert stopped and assimilated his methodological principles for the social sciences so effectively that the discussion of Weber's methodology of the social sciences is still going on today.[19] In terms of the history of philosophy this constitutes an anachronism. But it is also a symptom of the fact that, positivist logic of science to the contrary, the problem that Cassirer and Rickert addressed has not yet been resolved in the practice of the social sciences.

1.3 Max Weber was not interested in the relationship between the natural and cultural sciences from an epistemological point of view, as were Rickert and Cassirer. He was not troubled by the implications that the recently arisen *Geisteswissenschaften* might have had for the extension of the critique of pure reason to historical reason. From the philosophical investigations that, since Dilthey, had been concerned with this question, he took only what he needed to clarify his own research practice. He conceptualized the new social sciences as cultural sciences with a systematic intent. Clearly they combine methodological principles that philosophers had found in opposing types of sciences: the social sciences have the task of bringing the heterogeneous methods, aims, and presuppositions of the natural and cultural sciences into balance. Above all, Weber analyzed the combination of explanation (*Erklären*) and understanding (*Verstehen*). The connection between explanation and understanding involves quite different rules, however, depending on whether we are concerned with methods, with aims, or with presuppositions. Weber's intricate philosophy of science becomes easier to understand when one distinguishes among these cases.

The definition of sociology that Weber gives in the first paragraphs of *Economy and Society* applies to *method*: "Sociology is a science concerning itself with the interpretive understanding of social action and thereby with a causal explanation of its course and consequences."[20] We may consider this sentence as an answer to the question, How are general theories of social action possible? General theories allow us to derive assumptions about empirical regularities in the form of hypotheses that serve the purpose of explanation. At the same time, and in contrádistinction to natural processes, regularities of social action have the property of being understandable. Social action belongs to the class of intentional actions, which we grasp by reconstructing their meaning. Social facts can be understood in terms of motivations. Optimal intelligibility of social behavior under given conditions is not, of course, of itself proof of the hypothesis that a lawlike connection does in fact exist. Such a hypothesis must also prove true independently of the plausibility of an interpretation in terms of motivation. Thus the logical relationship of understanding and explanation can be reduced to the general relationship between hypothesis and empirical confirmation. Through understanding, I may interpolate a rationally pursued goal as sufficient motivation for an observed behavior. But only when the resulting assumption of a behavioral regularity occurring under given circumstances has been empirically substantiated can we say that our understanding of motivation has led to an explanation of a social action.

This logical connection also makes clear why Weber accorded methodological primacy to purposive-rational action. As a rule, the interpretively interpolated goal, the assumed intention, will lead to an empirically convincing explanation only if the goal provides a factually sufficient motive for the action. This is the case when the action is guided by the intention to achieve a result to be realized through means chosen in a purposive-rational manner, thus in the type of purposive-rational action that is oriented to the choice of adequate means to achieve an end grasped with subjective clarity. Theories that admit only this type of action proceed, like pure economics, normative-analytically. They can lead to substantive empirical hypotheses only within the very narrow limits in which social processes actually correspond to the methodological principle of purposive-rationality. Thus the discussion leads inevitably to the question how it is possible to form systematic assumptions about actions that are understandable but irrational in relation to ends. Only theories of this kind would combine understanding and explanation within an empirical-analytic framework.

Weber himself believed that, in an interpretive sociology, behavior that was not purposive-rational could be investigated only as a "deviation" from a model of purposive-rational behavior constructed for the sake of comparison. In view of these difficulties, the question emerged whether the social sciences should consider the intentionality of action at all. The problematic of understanding, insofar as it relates to methodology, would be resolved if the assumptions concerning lawlike regularities were restricted to connections among descriptive behavioral variables, whether or not these assumptions could be rendered perspicuous through the interpretation of motivation as well. Weber, too, reckoned with the possibility that "future research might discover non-interpretable uniformities underlying what has appeared to be specifically meaningful action." [21] It would adequately explain social action without fulfilling the requirement of adequate meaningfulness. But Weber excluded such laws from the domain of the social sciences on principle. Otherwise the social sciences would have the status of *natural* sciences of social action, whereas, since they are oriented toward intentional action, they can only be nomological sciences of *mind and culture*.

In his essays on the philosophy of science, Weber often remarks that sociology must both understand social facts in their cultural significance and explain them as culturally determined. Here the relationship between explanation and understanding applies to the *aims* of the social sciences. Weber's statements are ambivalent, for two opposing intentions are involved.

On the one hand, Weber always emphasizes the empirical-analytic task of using proven lawlike hypotheses to explain social action and make conditional predictions. From this point of view, the social sciences, like all nomological sciences, yield information that can be translated into technical recommendations for the rational choice of means. They supply "knowledge of the technique by which one masters life—external things as well as human action—through calculation." [22] Technically exploitable knowledge of this kind is based on knowledge of empirical uniformities; such knowledge is the basis for causal explanations that make possible technical control over objective processes by means of conditional predictions. A social-scientific knowledge guided by this interest would have to develop and apply its instruments with the sole purpose of discovering reliable general rules of social behavior. Insofar as the subject at hand demands it, such an analysis can be mediated by an understanding of the meaning of social action. Nonetheless, the intention of understanding subjective meaning can do no more than open the way to the social facts. These are known only when the analysis proceeds beyond propaedeutic understanding and grasps their lawlike connection in causal terms. In the controversy over value judgments Weber adopted this position, which gives a methodologically subordinate status to the hermeneutic intention of understanding meaning. But he also had another scientific aim in view.

For Weber, as a pupil of Rickert, a cultural science cannot exhaust its interest in the study of empirical regularities. Thus, in other contexts in Weber's work, the derivation and verification of lawlike hypotheses from which technical recommendations can be made is considered a preparatory work that does not, as such, lead to "the knowledge which we are seeking." The overarching interest by which this work is guided is defined hermeneutically: "Analyzing and ordering a particular, historically given and individual grouping of those factors and their concrete and uniquely significant interaction, and, especially, making the basis and nature of this significance understandable, is the next task, one to be solved through the use of that preparatory work, certainly, but completely new and autonomous in relation to it.²³

In this schema for the progress of social-scientific knowledge, causal-analytic and interpretive methods alternate. But in each case the knowledge terminates in the explication of a meaning that has practical significance for life, thus in "making something understandable." With this goal in mind, it is the procedure of explanation rather than that of the interpretive understanding of meaning that is relegated to a subordinate methodological status.

Weber did not expressly link these two conflicting intentions. He was the more easily deceived about their ambivalent character in that he had not sufficiently clarified the categories of meaning (*Sinn*) and significance (*Bedeutung*) in their respective usages. Weber did not distinguish consistently enough between the understanding of motivation, which reconstructs the subjectively intended meaning (*Sinn*) of a social action, and the hermeneutic understanding of meaning that appropriates the significance (*Bedeutung*) objectivated in works or events.

The understanding of motivation can be contained within the

framework of an empirical-analytic science as a methodological step leading to a knowledge of laws that is not hermeneutically intelligible, that is, that has no relation to meaning. Two conflicting cognitive intentions arise in the social sciences only because there the knowing subjects are intuitively linked with their object domain. The social lifeworld is just as much an intentional structure as is social-scientific knowledge itself. Indeed, it is precisely this relationship that was invoked by transcendental philosophy's interpretation of the cultural sciences. Nomological knowledge of social processes can enter hermeneutically into the explication of the self-understanding of knowing subjects and their social reference groups, just as it can be translated into conditional predictions and used in the control of the administered domains of society. The controversial relationship between the methodological framework of research and the pragmatic function of applying the results of research can be clarified only when the knowledge-orienting interests invested in the methodological approaches have been made conscious. Only then will there be a precise answer to the question of when the social sciences in their internal structure are pursuing the intention of planning and administering, and when they are pursuing the intention of self-understanding and enlightenment. Weber neither clarifies nor completely suppresses his ambivalence of aims. In any case, he did not, as did his positivist successors, exempt the social sciences from the repeatedly announced task of interpreting the cultural significance of social relations as a basis for making the contemporary social situation understandable.[24]

The problematic relationship of explanation and understanding concerns not only the methods and aims of the social sciences but also their epistemological *presuppositions*. Are the social sciences, like all cultural sciences, bound in the methodological delimitation of their object domain to an implicit preunderstanding of their subject matter? Weber adopts the category of value-relation introduced by Rickert and uses it in its strict transcendental-logical sense. Value-relation applies primarily not to the selection of scientific problems but to the constitution of possible objects of the experience that is relevant to inquiry in the cultural sciences. The cultural scientist does not communicate with these objects with the naked eye, so to speak. Rather, he inevitably places them in the value-relations in which his own cultural situation is set. Thus he has to mediate the methodologically determinant value-relations with those that are already realized in the preconstituted object. Rickert had failed to recognize this mediation as a hermeneutic problem.[25] Weber analyzes it partially and then counters it with the postulate of value freedom.

In the natural sciences, the theoretical framework of an investigation is subjected to control by the outcome of the investigation itself. Either it proves heuristically fruitful or it contributes nothing to the derivation of usable hypotheses. In contrast, the value-relations that determine method are transcendent to research in the cultural sciences; they cannot be corrected by the outcome of an investigation. When the light shed by value-ideas on important problems shifts, the cultural sciences likewise prepare to shift their standpoint and their conceptual apparatus and "follow those stars that alone can give their work meaning and direction."[26] In the social sciences, theories are dependent upon general interpretations that can be neither confirmed nor refuted by criteria immanent to the empirical sciences. Value-relations are methodologically unavoidable, but they are not objectively binding. Social sciences are thus obligated to declare the dependence of their basic theoretical assumptions on normative presuppositions of this sort. Hence the postulate of value freedom.

In contrast to this position, the current view is that theory formation is subject to the same rules in all the nomological sciences. Value freedom is assured through the logical separation of descriptive and normative statements; only the initial selection of problems is dependent on values.[27] In this narrower formulation, the postulate of value freedom attains the status of a political value; according to it, the only theories that are admissible as scientific are those whose basic assumptions are free of any historical preunderstanding that would require hermeneutic clarification. Such theories could thus be introduced by convention. Weber's formulation of the issue is excluded by definition. For he denied that underlying theoretical suppositions with no relationship to values, thus without ties to historical contexts, are possible at all in the social sciences. Not only the selection of problems but also the choice of the theoretical framework within which they will be analyzed is, according to Weber, determined by historically prevailing value-relations.

Once one has become convinced, as Weber was, of the methodologically significant interdependence of social-scientific inquiry and the objective context to which it is directed and in which it itself stands, a further question necessarily arises. Could these value-relations, which are methodologically determining, themselves be open to social-scientific analysis as a real context operating on the transcendental level? Could the empirical content of the fundamental decisions shaping the choice of a theoretical principle itself be elucidated in the context of social processes? It seems to me that it is precisely in Weber's theory of science that one can demonstrate the connection between methodology and a sociological analysis of the present.[28] Weber himself, however, like the Neo-Kantians in general, was enough of a positivist to forbid himself this type of reflection.

2 Sociology and History: The Contemporary Discussion

2.1 Does our review of these inquiries into methodological dualism merely provide a historical retrospect, or does it point to an ongoing problematic? The dominant conception today is that the social sciences have escaped from the hermeneutic limitations of the *Geisteswissenschaften* and attained an unproblematic relationship to history in which general theories of social action are on a different plane than the historical context of tradition. Sociology, with which we are primarily concerned here, is indifferent to history. It processes its data without regard to any specific context; the historical standing of the data is thus neutralized from the outset. For sociology, all history is made present, but not in the sense of a reflective appropriation of an irreversible and unrepeatable process. Rather, history is projected onto a screen of universal simultaneity and is thus robbed of its authentic spirit. It is the historical-hermeneutic sciences themselves that created the preconditions for this development.

The historical sciences participate in the dialectic of historical enlightenment, which precisely by extending historical consciousness weakens historical traditions: the historical sciences liberate emancipated subjects from the quasi-natural power of traditions that control behavior. By relativizing national history in a global context and objectifying the totality of history as a plurality of civilizations, they create a new distance from historical tradition. In this sense historicism marks the dissolution of the unity of history (*Geschichte*) and narrative (*Historie*) and thus the abolition of the historical processes that we experience as living tradition. Joachim Ritter relates this function of the historical sciences to the rise of industrial society:

The development of the sciences of history and of the historical, spiritual world of mankind belongs to the real process in which modern society in Europe, and now everywhere in the world, constitutes itself through emancipation from its pregiven historical worlds of tradition. Wherever, in the process of modernization, this becomes the human world, it necessarily brings the historically given into flux. Thus the true ahistoricity of society becomes visible; human beings as such can be made into subjects of the law and the state only by removing them from their existence as something embedded in history and ancestry.[29]

Ritter reached this insight through an interpretation of Hegel's political philosophy.[30] In the framework of abstract law, civil society appears as a system of needs based exclusively on the natural will to self-preservation and the satisfaction of natural needs. The theory of nature that civil society develops to explain itself is an accurate reflection of the ahistorical nature of modern society, which brings with it the danger of total socialization of the subject. This society guarantees freedom only in abstract form, as a society reduced to a natural basis; only in this reduced form does it leave open to a subjectivity divided from itself "the right to its particularity and its freedom, and thus the possibility of its preservation."[31] We are concerned here not with Ritter's liberal interpretation of Hegel[32] but rather with the dialectic of ahistoricity to which it leads.

Industrial society frees itself from historical traditions and orients itself to technical control of natural substrata. In equal measure, however, it frees subjects from the organized compulsions of the natural substratum and gives them access to a sphere of subjective freedom beyond society. We can maintain this freedom, however, only if we continually transcend society as a whole by preserving the traditions that have in the meantime become objectified and arbitrary. Thus we guard against the danger of total socialization in which society as matter dominates the efforts of mind to assert itself as subjectivity. In this regard the historical sciences become an "organ of spiritual compensation." What they have destroyed as tradition, they make accessible as quotation.[33]

Helmut Schelsky's conception of a theory of the sciences allies itself with Ritter's position, but with a shift of emphasis.[34] He no longer seriously expects the historical sciences to transcend the realm of social and technical compulsion as a whole through the preservation of defunct traditions. Their task is now limited to extending, by example, the scope of possible scenarios for action beyond the horizon of the immediate present. In other respects they have relinquished the role of orienting action to the natural and social sciences. Thus the present boundary marking the dualism of the sciences runs between the historical *Geisteswissenschaften* on the one hand and the natural and social sciences on the other. The sciences of action purport to generate techniques for the regulation of social action in the same way that the natural sciences generate techniques for the domination of nature. Both the natural and the social sciences are among the foremost forces of production in a technical and scientific civilization developed on a global scale upon the freshly cleared foundation of a neutralized history. Thus, like all the other disiplines that produce technologically exploitable knowledge, the social sciences belong to the post-historical period; even in a methodological sense they have been relieved of the complications that formerly seemed to arise from the linkage of their theories with a historically embedded situational understanding. The historical consciousness of the *Geisteswissenschaften* has absorbed the objectivated contents of world history and deprived it of the force of an objectively compelling context. World history as operative history has been brought to a stop:

In that the past, which in the form of tradition directly prescribed courses of action to individuals and collectivities, has been distanced through the historical sciences to an object domain that can be researched scientifically and critically, modern man has won vis-à-vis the past the freedom of an open future that allows him for the first time to transform the natural and social environment in accordance with scientific insights. The "historylessness" of modern societies, which finds its expression in natural and social technologies, is thus created only through the scientization of the past.[35]

In this ahistorical civilization, the nomological sciences, the methodology of which excludes a connection to history, take over the "direction of action and knowledge": "Modern society obeys the laws of the reconstruction of the world through natural and social sciences that have become technologies. The stability and autonomy of modern industrial and scientific civilization remove the effective possibility of a personality guided by ideas, as they remove the necessity to understand political and social activity in historical terms."[36]

The work of Ritter and Schelsky reflects the historical context in which the sciences operate today. Yet if their thesis of the unreality of history were accurate, the validity of their own reflections would be placed in doubt. The analyses of Ritter and Schelsky belong to that class of investigations that can transform the self-understanding of those to whom they are addressed and that are intended to orient their action. But they are capable of influencing practical consciousness not because they belong to nomological science and provide technologically exploitable information but rather because they themselves belong to the neglected category of historical reflection. But this puts Ritter's thesis and the philosophy of science that Schelsky bases on it into question: instead of comprehending the positivistic self-understanding of the period, they only express it.[37] Once the quasi-natural validity of action-orienting value-systems had been broken, historicism contributes to a situation in which behavior-steering traditions determine, or could determine, the self-understanding of modern societies, and could do so not naively but with the clarity of a historically enlightened consciousness. But the idea that historicism has been able to make an objectivated world history of ideal simultaneity into a cosmos of facts reflects only its own positivistic creed. In fact, the hermeneutic sciences belong, as they always have, to the context of tradition that they elucidate. We have to admit that their objectivistic self-understanding is not without consequences: it sterilizes knowledge, removing it from the reflective appropriation of working traditions, and ensures that history as such is relegated to the archives. Though effective historical continuity may be suppressed in this way, however, it is not suspended. Given such a scientifically legitimated suppression of history, the objective illusion may arise that with the help of the nomological sciences life-praxis can be relegated exclusively to the functional sphere of instrumental action. Systems of research that produce technologically exploitable knowledge have in fact become forces of production in industrial society. But precisely because they produce only technologies, they are incapable of orienting action. Social action is in the first place a cooperative activity mediated by tradition and taking place within ordinary-language communication that seeks answers to practical questions. Praxis could be equivalent to instrumental action only if social life were reduced to existence in systems of social labor and self-preservation through force. The positivistic self-understanding of the nomological sciences does in fact promote the suppression of action through technology. If practical questions, which involve the adoption of standards, are withdrawn from rational discussion, and if only technologically exploitable knowledge is considered to be reliable, then only the instrumentalist values of effeciency participate in what is left of rationality.[38]

With the current development of the forces of production, the relations between technological progress and the social lifeworld can no longer take place as they did earlier, in a quasi-natural manner. Every new thrust of technological capability that intrudes in an unregulated manner into the old forms of life-praxis intensifies the conflict between the results of a strained rationality and traditions that have been overriden. This may appear to be an emancipation of scientific and technological civilization from history as such. But the objective power of this appearance, which is further strengthened by the positivistic self-understanding of all the sciences, only conceals the complex of interests that unreflectively determines the direction of technological progress. The idea that objective technological forces have become autonomous is an ideological one. Thus the problem arises how the practical application of technological knowledge in the context of a historical situation can be rationally determined, how technological knowledge can be legitimately transformed into practical consciousness. The reflection required, which extends to the issue of the incorporation of technological means into the social lifeworld, must do two things at once. It must *analyze* the objective conditions of the situation, including the available and potential technologies and the existing institutions and operative interests. It must also *interpret* these conditions within the framework of the traditionally determined self-understanding of social groups. Thus I see a connection between the problem of a rationally compelling translation of technological knowledge into practical consciousness and that of the methodological preconditions for the possibility of a social science that integrates analytic and hermeneutic procedures.

What the philosophy of history has anticipated since the eighteenth century has been a reality since the middle of this century: a unified world in which humanity is drawn into a single unified context of interaction. In this respect, history has constituted itself *as* world history. Its basis is an industrial society that will soon span the entire world. Traditional consciousness, with its quasi-natural unity of history and narrative, which used to be determining for civilizations, has been replaced by a historical consciousness. The systems of industrial development and nuclear armament compete in an altered historical context. But these changes in historical reference systems can likewise be comprehended only historically. As long as we are not willing to abandon reflection or be deprived of it in favor of a mutilated rationality, we cannot pass over the dimension of mankind's historical development with impunity. Because history is the totality in terms of which we must comprehend even a civilization that has seemingly emerged from history, we have also transcended a system when we have conceptualized it historically. Schelsky,who denies history as totality, finally has to take refuge in a transcendental theory of society in order to fulfill the cognitive intention he pursues.[39]

To be sure, it is a strange kind of transcendentalism that combines an epistemological intention with a practical one. It has the task of clarifying at the same time both the conditions of a possible sociology and the boundaries of the social as such.[40] This new logic of the social sciences can also be formulated as a substantive problem, namely that of man's "freedom from society."[41] The importance of this proposal is indisputable. Sociology, which believes itself to be completely detached from its historical context, falls victim to the immanence of what exists. Thus Schelsky, whose work reflects this situation, yet who does not want to become the "surveyor and mechanic of the social," can transcend the existing society only by relativizing society as such. As a sociologist, he pursues this aim by means of a transcendental delimitation of sociology. He does not foresee that once having attained this level of reflection he will no longer be able to take up any empirically substantive problems—unless, of course, he allows himself to become involved in that dialectic of the historical implications of methodological decisions that he wants to avoid.

It may be that these difficulties forced Schelsky to revise his proposal. In a later study,[42] he removes the theme of "man's freedom from society" from the sphere of transcendental social theory, indeed, from scientific analysis and philosopical reflection altogether. Schelsky now characterizes this problematic in existentialist terms, as one of practiced inwardness:

If "culture" (*Bildung*) is a spiritual and ethical sovereignty in the face of the compulsions of the world and of practical life, . . . then at present it can no longer be acquired primarily and immediately through science. To the contrary: the fact that practical life has itself become a matter of science means that the claim that one is educated now involves the task of distancing oneself from science, rising above it, just as the cultivation (*Bildung*) of the humanists and idealists was once elevated above practical life. Today the formation (*Bildung*) of the person consists in intelllectually overcoming science, particulary in its technical-constructive aspects. We cannot, however, forgo science: in that science has become the substance of the world and of practical life itself, science represents the substance of the very life that it is a question of "cultivating." Only the passage through practical life, through the sciences, will allow mankind to reach the point at which the question of self-formation can be posed in new terms. But the question can no longer be answered within the dimension of science, neither in the form of philosophy nor in the form of a scientific synthesis, because science as the construction of the world has gone beyond all scientific thought.[43]

I believe that Schelsky's diagnosis of the dangers of scientific objectivism is correct. Institutionalized natural- and social-scientific research contributes to the progress of mankind's technical-scientific self-objectivation, which Schelsky calls "the new self-estrangement."[44] But because he believes the positivist notion that the historical *Geisteswissenschaften* have eliminated history and the nomological *Geisteswissenschaften* have eliminated mind, he no longer credits the sciences with the power of self-reflection that would be necessary to confront this estrangement in its own dimension. Even if it does not anticipate its own futility, this appeal to self-formative processes that transcend philosophy and science can be maintained only by the hope, not subject to discussion, for a new religiosity. Schelsky is led to this position because he too unqualifiedly grants sociology the status it claims as a natural science of the social and does not see that sociology cannot remove itself from the dimension of history any more than can the society on which it is based.

2.2 Schelsky does not deny the dualism of science; he accepts it without question. He unreservedly classifies the social sciences with the nomological sciences. Thus he purges them of the ambiguity of a nomological *Geisteswissenschaft*. Schelsky does not, however, establish this thesis in the course of a methodological explication. Rather, he analyzes the functions of the sciences in the social context of technological-scientific civilization. To the ahistoricity of industrial society corresponds the dehistorization of the sciences of action that are integrated into it. Positivism proceeds in a more radical fashion. It rejects the dualism of science as such. It denies that sociology has a connection with history that would extend to the dimension of methodology. There is simply no genuine access to history at all. Hermeneutics is prescientific, and even the historically oriented sciences follow the unitary logic of a unified science that relates systems of abstract statements to empirical data. Methodology cannot make a structural distinction between nature and history in the mass of phenomena with which it is concerned.[45]

Ernst Topitsch attacks the assertion of methodological dualism directly; he critiques the distinction between nature and history as an ideological one.[46] He derives the ecstatic-cathartic belief in a soul from the prehistoric intellectual world of shamanism, in which the soul was seen as an entity separable from the body. Through Plato, this originally magical conception of a soul elevated to the region of the divine and actively superior to the world entered philosophy. It is even present in Kant's concept of the "intelligible ego."[47] Kant combined this tradition with the patristic-Christian tradition of the two kingdoms in the theoretical approach of his transcendental philosophy, which envisioned a thorough separation between the phenomenal realm of nature, operating under causal laws, and the noumenal realm of freedom, operating under moral laws. These moral-metaphysical ideas return in Neo-Kantian form in the opposition between nature and culture and find their methodological expression in the dualism of the natural sciences and the *Geisteswissenschaften*.

Topitsch leaves no doubt that he considers this opposition to be just as ideological as the shaman's belief in the soul. I cannot go into his derivation of Kant's systematic approach here,[48] but it can be shown that in principle a derivation of this type, in terms of a critique of ideology, cannot support the conclusion that Topitsch draws from it. It would be convincing only given a specific concept of ideology in terms of which all statements that do not satisfy the conditions of scientific reliability established by positivism are considered meaningless. But we would thereby implicitly presuppose precisely what is to be proved: that a specific methodological conception that is not in accordance with that of positivism is false. The attempt to establish a criterion of meaninglessness for that concept of ideology would, of course, be no less hopeless than the fruitless attempt to establish an empirical criterion of meaning. But if we cannot simply derive a standard of evaluation from a positivistic concept of ideology accepted as given, then we cannot exclude the possibility that a methodological distinction could very well reflect a moment of truth in the philosophical, religious, or mythical traditions to which it can be historically traced.

Topitsch also overlooks the fact that Rickert and Cassirer developed their methodology in opposition to the Kantian dualism of natural science and moral philosophy. It is precisely Kant's distinction between the empirical and the transcendental realms, a distinction that placed nature and spirit in irreconcilable opposition, that was put into question when the new historical-hermeneutic sciences analyzed spirit (*Geist*) as a fact. The methodology of the *Geisteswissenschaften* takes into account the fact that transcendental consciousness assumes empirical form, be it in historically realized values or in symbolic forms. Rickert tends to emphasize the objectivated meanings in terms of which intentional action is oriented, while Cassirer emphasizes the medium of representation through which acting subjects conceive their world. In their own way, both men understand that the phenomena of the historical world are related to the phenomena of nature as metafacts are related to facts. In cultural phenomena, that is, the transcendental achievement through which nature is comprehended scientifically has taken on the form of an empiricallly accessible "second nature." To use a different terminology: natural-scientific theories present themselves in the form of statements about matters of fact, whereas the matters of fact that the *Geisteswissenschaften* analyze already incorporate the complex relationship between statements and matters of fact. To first- and second-order facts correspond first- and second-level experiences: observation and understanding, whereby understanding already includes the perception of representational signs. Even the logical analysis of language is directed to given data in the form of signs. Because in the formal sciences we either posit or produce these signs, we usually fail to notice that they too are given through experience. We become more conscious of this moment of experience when, as in the *Geisteswissenschaften*, the symbolic relationships we grasp through understanding hold between unsystematic and unformalized expressions, that is, between handed-down meanings.

There is no systematic connection between the metaphysical opposition of nature and spirit on the one hand, and the distinction between nomological and hermeneutic sciences on the other. Thus George Herbert Mead arrived at the same insights as Cassirer in an evolutionist context. He demonstrated how social action can take shape only under conditions of linguistic communication.[49] The specific interaction through which mankind reproduces its life is tied to the transcendental role of language. Mead disregards the opposition of spirit and nature; he recognizes only the objective context of the natural history of the species. But because human behavior is always transcendentally mediated by a social lifeworld, it has a special place within the class of all observable events, to which there corresponds a special method of scientific analysis. This argument was decisive for the principle of subjective interpretation on which Parsons, following Weber, based the theoretical framework of a theory of action.

At this level of discussion, a critique of conceptions of the soul in terms of ideology can accomplish nothing. Theses disputing the methodological unity of the cultural and natural sciences cannot be convincingly challenged in this way. Those who reject the dualism of science must demonstrate that the historical-hermeneutical sciences can be completely subsumed under the general methodology of the empirical sciences.

2.3 Karl Popper conceptualized the unity of the nomological and historical sciences in terms of the different functions of scientific theories. Theories permit us to derive hypotheses concerning laws; these in turn serve the purposes of explanation and prediction.

These two activities have a symmetrical relationship to one another. Under given initial conditions, one can, with the help of a law, deduce a result. Given the final conditions, one can infer the antecedent initial conditions on the basis of a law. We call these events 'cause' and 'effect' because their relationship is governed by natural laws. Only knowledge of laws allows us the specific prediction of observable events or their causal explanation. The theoretical sciences have an interest in selecting theories, thus in confirming nomological knowledge; they test assumptions concerning laws by means of specific predictions. Historical sciences, on the other hand, have an interest in explaining specific events. They presuppose more or less trivial laws; in this respect, they use theories: "This view of history makes it clear why so many students of history and its method insist that it is the particular event that interests them, and not any so-called historical laws. For from our point of view, there can be no historical laws. Generalization belongs simply to a different line of interest, sharply to be distinguished from that interest in specific events." [50]

Carl Hempel gives a more precise account of this idea:

The explanation of the occurrence of an event of some specific kind E at a certain place and time consists, as it is usually expressed, in indicating the causes or determining factors of E. Now the assertion that a set of events—say, of the kinds C_1, ..., C_n—have caused the event to be explained amounts to the statement that, according to certain general laws, a set of events of the kinds mentioned is regularly accompanied by an event of kind E. Thus, the scientific explanation of the event in question consists of

1. a set of statements asserting the occurrence of certain events C_1, ..., C_n at certain times and places.

2. a set of universal hypotheses, such that

   (a) the statements of both groups are reasonably well confirmed by empirical evidence,

   (b) from the two groups of statements the sentence asserting the occurrence of event E can be logically deduced.

In a physical explanation, group 1 would describe the initial and boundary conditions for the occurrence of the final event; generally, we shall say group 1 states the determining conditions for the event to be explained, while group 2 contains the general laws on which the explanation is based; they imply the statement that whenever events of the kind described in the first group occur, an event of the kind to be explained will take place. [51]

In agreement with Hempel, Ernest Nagel points out that historical explanations do not imply assumptions about universal laws. The premise used to deduce the cause normally assumes the form of a statistical generalization of the kind that states that under given conditions a specific behavior can be expected with a greater or lesser probability. Thus the historian must be content with probabilistic explanations:

The point just made in terms of an example can be stated more generally. Let A_1 be a specific action performed by an individual x on some occasion t in order to achieve some objective O. Historians do not attempt to explain the performance of the act A_1 in all its concrete details, but only the performance by x of a type of action A whose specific forms are A_1, A_2, ..., A_n. Let us suppose further that x could have achieved the objective O had he performed on occasion t any one of the actions in the subset A_1, A_2, ..., A_k of the class of specific forms of A. Accordingly, even if a historian were to succeed in giving a deductive explanation for the fact that x performed the type of action A on occasion t, he would not thereby have succeeded in explaining deductively that x performed the specific action A_1 on that occasion. In consequence, and at best, the historian's explanation shows only that, under the assumptions stated, x's performance of A_1 on occasion t is probable.[52]

Furthermore, the historian is hardly ever in a position to explain an event on the basis of sufficient conditions, that is, to give a full explanation of it. As a rule, he is limited to indicating a series of necessary conditions. He is left to judge when it makes sense to end the search for further "causes." He is methodologically compelled to make a decision within an arena that is in principle one of uncertainty. Insofar as he has not made this decision unintelligently, he relies on the authority of his "historical judgment"; within a positivist frame of reference, justifications of this kind are not susceptible of further analysis. The historian's judgment also comes into play when complex events, or aggregates, which cannot as such be subsumed under a law, are analyzed:

Historians cannot deal with such an event as a single whole, but must first analyze it into a number of constituent "parts" or "aspects." The analysis is frequently undertaken in order to exhibit certain "global' characteristics of the inclusive event as the outcome of the particular combination of components which the analysis seeks to specify. The primary objective of the historian's task, however, is to show why those components were actually present; and he can achieve this aim only in the light of (usually tacit) general assumptions concerning some of the conditions under which those components presumably occur. In point of fact, even the analysis of a collective event is controlled in large measure by such general assumptions. First of all, the delimitation of the event itself—the selection of some of its features rather than others to describe it and thereby also to contrast it with earlier states of affairs out of which it presumably developed, and the adoption of some particular time or circumstance for fixing its supposed beginnings—depends in part on the historian's general conception of the "basic" variables in terms of which the event is to be understood. Secondly, the components a historian distinguishes in an event when he seeks to account in a piecemeal fashion for its occurrence are usually those whose "most important" determining conditions are specified by the generalizations he normally assumes about those components, so that these determinants are frequently the ones he tries to discover in some actual configuration of happenings that took place antecedently or concurrently with the collective event he is investigating. In short, generalizations of some sort appear as essentially in the premises of explanations for aggregative occurrences as they do in explanations of individual actions.[53]

Nagel seems to overlook the fact that the selective points of view in terms of which the historian distinguishes the aspects of an event (and specific classes of variables for each aspect) precede probabilistic assumptions about the connection of a specific variable with a selected characteristic and thus cannot be confirmed directly. Those viewpoints belong to the "general interpretations" that Popper admits as the temporary, and in principle unconfirmable, framework theories used in the work of the historian. Such quasi-theories establish general interpretive viewpoints; they seem to correspond to the value-relations in terms of which, according to Rickert, a specific object domain may be delimited.[54] However this activity is interpreted, even within the positivist perspective, the historian retains a latitude for decision that can be intelligently occupied only by historical judgment. The logical achievements of this judgment escape the grasp of a methodology that encloses scientific analysis within the boundaries of logical explanation through general laws. They can be fully comprehended only within the framework of a philosophical hermeneutics.[55]

Despite the reservations incorporated into their model, Popper, Hempel and Nagel adhere firmly to the notion that the work of the historian, insofar as it is governed by standards of research other than criteria of literary presentation, terminates in causal explanation of events and circumstances, with subsumption under general laws assumed to be the schema of explanation. William Dray, who was influenced by Collingwood as well as by philosophers of the analytic school, challenges the applicability of the "covering law model" to historical inquiry.[56] He tries to show that historical explanations do not usually satisfy the condition of subsumption under general laws and that, for reasons of principle, they do not need to fulfill them.

Dray illustrates his thesis with the rather unfortunately chosen example, "Louis XIV died unpopular because he had pursued policies which were detrimental to the national interests of France." The logician insists on formulating explicitly the law to which the historian implicitly refers in his explanation: "Rulers who pursue policies directed against the interest of their subjects become unpopular." When the historian rejects this suggestion with the argument that it holds only for specific policies under specific conditions, the logician incorporates specifications into the law, as for instance, "Rulers who involve their countries in wars, persecute religious minorities, and maintain a parasitic court become unpopular." The logician will attempt to accommodate every further objection by the historian in this manner. He will incorporate every new specification of Louis XIV's policies and the situation in contemporary France, even in Europe, into the "law" as specific conditions. What conclusions does Dray draw from this hypothetical dialogue between the logician and the historian?

Covering law theorists will no doubt say that what the dialectic elicits is a set of sufficient conditions falling under a covering law; for at every stage, the logician's revision answers the historian's objection that what the law sets out need not be universally true. But opponents of the model may very well insist that the series of more and more precise laws which the historian's objections force upon the logician is an indefinite one. And I think it is true that, in an important sense of "need," the historian, having given his explanation, need not accept any particular candidate the logician formulates. It is always logically possible for the explanation to be just out of reach every time the logician's pincers snap shut. To this extent, the logician's argument from meaning still remains inconclusive; for the conjunction of an explanatory statement and the denial of any law that might be suggested, is never self-contradictory, or even strictly unintelligible. To put it another way: no matter how complicated the expression with which we complete a statement of the form, 'E because ...,' it is part of the "logic"of such "because" statements that additions to the explanatory clause are never ruled out by our acceptance of the original statement.[57]

The historian would be satisfied only with a formulation that would no longer have the logical status of a law: "Every ruler who follows Louis XIV's policies under exactly the same conditions as he did would lose his popularity." This statement includes a proper name and thus does not have the status of a statement of a law. It can be seen as an expression of the absurd maxim that all possible initial conditions of an incompletely formulated law should be incorporated successively into the statement of the law itself as "qualifications."

Evidently the historical explanation of Louis XIV's loss of popularity can be considered as a deductive explanation only if it refers to a sociological law about the loss of popularity of incumbents in positions of authority in any system whatsoever, or even to a social-psychological law at a still higher level of generalization. Even if there were such laws, it would be doubtful whether the historian's task should consist in formulating characteristics of Louis XIV's policies, his system of rule, and the French population of that time as initial conditions for one or more of these laws. Rather, the actual historical work would already have to be completed before one could make a connection between the historical knowledge and nomological knowledge.

Popper gives the investigation of a murder as an example of historical explanation. Insofar as it is a question of reconstructing the observable steps in the event, logic is adequate for the explanation. The immediate somatic cause of death, indirect causes like the use of a deadly weapon, or the causal nexus of events that determined the behavior of the murderer at the time of his deed—all these can be defined as initial conditions for the natural laws invoked in the explanation. But as soon as the event is viewed as the consequence of an intentional act, the motive of the perpetrator must be explained so that we can "understand" the murder. Perhaps the action can be classified as a symptom of a disease that has been well researched in its physiological aspects and the corresponding oeganic illness can be identified in the perpetrator. Then the explanation would fall within empirical medicine's domain of competence. Perhaps one can find sufficiently reliable indices of purpose-rational behavior so that the murder can be understood as action under pure maxims. The authors of detective stories operate in this way: the motives are "obvious" and are not, as such, at issue. But usually the motive cannot be explained through reference to causal laws or pure maxims. It is here that the work of the historian begins. First he investigates the life-history of the perpetrator. The circumstances in which he was raised reflect the more complex conditions of his surroundings, including both the immediate and the larger environment, and ultimately even traditions that may reach very far back in time. One may succeed in reconstructing the murder of President Kennedy and identifying the perpetrator in a relatively short time; but journalists will first write reports and historians will later write books about Oswald's motives. Such studies extend far beyond the biographical framework of the individual life-history. During the course of these studies many explanations will be brought together; as in the example of Louis XIV's loss of popularity, general statements will be implicit in them. But each of these general statements can claim only tentative validity, because each always presupposes qualifications that can only be indicated through examples and for the rest must be left to a complex preunderstanding of overall situations that could be explicated, or complex references to overall situations that have been explicated elsewhere. Thus historical explanations themselves are shown to be only steps in a sequence of possible explanations that is in principle infinite.

Dray gives two viewpoints in terms of which such "explanations" can be elucidated. A historical explanation produces a connection between an event and conditions necessary for the occurrence of this event. These conditions are not the conditions that would be sufficient for the prediction of the event; and as necessary conditions they are valid only within the framework of a given overall situation. The logical connection between explanandum and explanans, between what is to be explained and what explains it, can claim empirical validity only in relationship to an unanalyzed system of conditions. The explanation would have no meaning if this system of conditions could not by grasped in some form, even if only a global one. The historian makes his first decision when he defines the system of conditions within which he will look for necessary conditions. He selects the overall economic, strategic, cultural context within which the event is to be explained. He possesses a complex knowledge of the overall context, derived from a global preunderstanding or from previous explications. Historical explanation directs itself to events that are conceived as deviations from an overall situation: wars and revolutions are exemplary events that attract historical interest. Similarly, the stability of an overall situation, that is, the nonoccurrence of an anticipated event, demands a historical explanation. When an event y is explained historically in terms of an event x, then it is asserted that in a given overall situation x is a necessary, even if not a sufficient, condition for the occurrence of y. In such an "explanation," the historian is saying that [in the absence of x]

... in that particular situation, if everything else remained the same, the y which in fact occurred would not have done so; or, at any rate, that it would have been different in important respects. The law, "Only if x then y," might be quite false, without the historian's conclusion having to be withdrawn. There may, for instance, be a number of things which Louis XIV might have done to make himself unpopular besides pursuing the policies he actually did. But the question whether the effect could have been brought about in other ways is not directly relevant to the historian's judgment that, in the particular situation under examination, the cause was necessary.[58]

Strictly speaking, the historical explanation always requires the addition of a qualification: "It would read, not other things being equal, but, the sitation being what it was—indicating that other mentioned and unmentioned features of the particular situation have been taken into account in arriving at the causal conclusion."[59]

Certainly the historian's claim always to have an overall situation in view would scarcely be plausible if it implied an analytic comprehension of a system of conditions related to observable events. Such a claim becomes plausible only with reference to the hermeneutic interpretation of a context of meaning, for the latter already presumes at the outset a global preunderstanding of the whole. Dray does not address this problem, but the second viewpoint in terms of which he discusses historical explanation refers to it.

The historian is concerned with a context of events that are mediated by the intentions of acting subjects. The historian therefore fastens onto the subjectively intended meanings and traditional significations. In these, the self-understanding of the social lifeworld and of individual life-histories is articulated. Historical explanations relate an observable event, not directly to another observable event, but to a context of intentional action. They name not a cause but rather a rational basis for the event. The explanation does not say why, in factual terms, an event occurred, but rather how it was possible for a subject to act this way and not otherwise. In this sense Dray distinguishes between "how questions" and "why questions." The one class of questions requires dispositional explanations; the other, causal explanations. Explanation by subsumption under general laws would, in principle, relate to historical events only insofar as their intentional content was ignored Those who, like Popper, do not wish to subject historical events to a logic of natural relations, but nevertheless want to explain them through subsumption under laws, must make a clear distinction between explanations based on empirical regularities and explanations that refer to maxims of action:

It is quite true that "reasons for acting" as well as "conditions for predicting" have a kind of generality or universality. If y is a good reason for A to do x, then y would be a good reason for anyone sufficiently like A to do x under sufficiently similar circumstances. But this universality of reasons is unlike the generality of an empirically validated law in a way which makes it especially hazardous to say that by giving a rational explanation, a historian commits himself to the truth of a corresponding law. For if a negative instance is found for a general empirical law, the law itself must be modified or rejected, since it states that people behave in a certain way under certain circumstances. But if a negative instance is found for the sort of general statement which might be extracted out of a rational explanation, the latter would not necessarily be falsified. For that statement would express a judgment of the form: "When in a situation of type $C_1 \ldots C_n$ the thing to do is x." The "implicit law" in such explanation is better called a principle of action than a generalization.[60]

Dray's reflections lead him to distinguish between explanations that follow a logic of natural relations and those that follow a logic of action. Recently A. C. Danto[61] has given a new twist to this point of view, a twist that brings analytic philosophy to the edge of hermeneutics. To deductive explanation, Danto opposes the form of narrative explanation. We explain an event in narrative form when we show how a subject was involved in a story (*Geschichte*).[62] Thus we can explain Louis XIV's loss of popularity by telling the story of how, under the influence of a series of events, the French populace's attitude toward the king changed from an initial condition of great respect to a final condition of predominating indifference or antipathy. In this story individual names will occur, for every story is concerned with changes in the situation of a subject or a group of subjects. The unity of the story is established through the identity of a horizon of expectations belonging to these subjects; for the narrative reports only on the influence of events that occur in a social life-world and attain meaning for acting subjects, thus altering social conditions. In the use of the designation "the French people under the regime of Louis XIV" there is an implicit reference to the whole system of values that concretely determines the meaning of the king's behavior for the people and thus the conditions of the king's popularity. In every new event adduced to make the loss of popularity plausible, the historian's narrative bases itself implicitly or explicitly on assumptions about socially binding behavioral expectations and institutionalized values. The names of the individual subjects in the narrative are instructions to the audience, as it were, to explicate further the meaning of the contexts named. In terms of that context the historical event can be made understandable to any desired degree of precision.

Such narrative explanations can also be translated into deductive ones. The explanandum must in that case be described in terms of general expressions. The new description of the historical event must already correspond to the universal expressions of the explanans. This reformulation has surprising consequences. It becomes apparent that the values or expectations that are stated in the form of general laws stand in a very loose relationship to the individual instances through which they are "fulfilled":

...any such law is almost certain to have non-homogeneous and open classes of instances ... it is particulary difficult to specify the entire membership of the class. Perhaps it is impossible to do so, for there is always the possibility that human inventiveness will contrive a novel instance which we can recognize afterwards as belonging to the class but which we could not have anticipated even though, in a general way, we might have predicted the general description this instance falls under. In a comparable way, even knowing that a man has a disposition to do kind things, and knowing that a given occasion is one on which he can be expected to do something kind, it is not always a simple matter to say what precise kind thing he will do. To be kind is to be creative in benignity, to be considerate, to surprise people by a singular appropriateness of one's gestures. To ascribe such a disposition to a person is then to allow room for creativity, kindness not being a ritual affair, and there being no precisely enumerable set of things which exhausts the manner in which the disposition functions. . . . We can recognize them afterwards as proper instances without being able to predict them.[63]

When specific general propositions about behavioral regularities are detached from the context of a linguistically articulated horizon of expectations or a value system, these universal laws are not related to their initial conditions in the same way that a class is related to its elements. For behavioral reactions are always mediated by interpretations through which the acting subjects understand the "influencing" events in terms of their horizon of expectations, in other words, within the grammatical framework of their everyday language. In the universal expressions of laws formulated in general terms, the individual or concrete generality of everyday language and the value system articulated in it is suppressed. In the unity of a story, which always tells of changes in the situation of a world held together by an ego-identity, however, this concrete generality is maintained. Because the "influence" of events on an acting subject is dependent on a specific interpretation, the behavioral reaction is also mediated by a concrete understanding of the meaning of given situations. This involves an application of rules that is guided by a complex preunderstanding and that brings the general and the particular into a dialectical relationship. Thus laws defined in terms of abstract generality prove to be only rules that allow for "creative opportunities"—"for the class of events they cover is open, in the sense that we can in principle always imagine an instance covered by them, which need not in any obvious way resemble past instances."[64] Danto himself draws no conclusions from these insights. With certain reservations, he considers the transformation of narrative into deductive explanations possible, without seeing that these very reservations invalidate the covering law model.[65]

The historian will not be able to limit himself in his explanations to a logic of action that incorporates the hermeneutic understanding of meaning, for the historical context is not exhausted by the mutual intentions of human beings.

Motivated actions are embedded in a quasi-natural context that is mediated by subjectively intended meaning, but not created by it. For this reason the historian cannot limit himself to the "inner side of events," as Collingwood's idealist proposal would have it; he must also analyze the causal context in which intentions are entangled. With this we have raised an issue that neither the positivists nor their critics have satisfactorily posed, not to mention resolved.

2.4 The division of labor between the nomological and the historical sciences is not as simple, nor their methodological unity as unproblematic, as it would seem to positivism. If the work of the historian were limited to the explanation of individual events through their subsumption under laws, it would have a reciprocal relationship with that of the sociologist, who uses predicted events to test assumptions about laws. In fact, however, the historian has to rely on step-by-step explication of contexts of meaning. The relationship of the two disciplines is not adequately described by the model in terms of which the historical sciences are dependent on nomological knowledge provided by the social sciences. The question even arises whether, on the contrary, the selection of fundamental assumptions for sociological theories does not depend of necessity on a historical preunderstanding of complex contexts.

In recent decades, initially in the United States, the ground has been laid for a cooperation between the disciplines of historical science and sociology. The model created by Popper, Hempel, and Nagel has been definitive for the self-understanding of both sides. Among American historians the reception of social-scientific problems and methods came early, under the influence of analytic philosophy of science. The volume *Theory and Practice in Historical Studies*[66] put out by the Committee on Historiography attests to this. One does not find a serious initiative on the part of the sociologists until the mid-1950s. One result of these efforts is the volume *Sociology and History*,[67] which shows how even the return of a dehistoricized sociology to history is guided by a positivisic self-understanding. These programmatic statements, of course, do not show the actual conduct of research as inspired by the discussion about the relationship of history and sociology.

In the practice of historiography, the initial result of these discussions has been greater carefulness with respect to logic. This has been true both for certain viewpoints and theoretical assumptions that have to be made explicit and for conditional generalizations that can claim validity only within a specific realm.[68] Further, where they have borrowed categories from sociology and used the tools of role-analysis,[69] historians have felt encouraged to make statements at a relatively high level of generality. Finally, statistical procedures have also gained acceptance in historiography. They may open up new areas of data that were formerly given scant or only imprecise attention (statistical data on election behavior, income distribution, occupational stratification, etc.) or they may be used in research techniques that permit a quantitatively reliable evaluation of data (for instance, content analysis of literary documents).[70] In terms of the logic of science, a historiography sociologized in this way does not differ from traditional history.

The passage from sociologizing historiography to sociological historiography, that is, to historically directed sociological research, is a fluid one. In general, sociologists gather their data in accordance with more abstract points of view and work with them at a higher level of generalization than do traditional historians. Their interpretation takes account of variables of social structure (as, for example, demographic composition, social stratification, distribution of leadership positions, means of production, and communications networks).[71] The sociologist is also on the alert for key historical events that give a decisive turn to some long-term development. A system of reference oriented to structural connections affords a better analytic grasp of the points of departure for directional processes, that is, for the cumulative intensification of emergent historical tendencies.[72]

Many studies that appear to be systematic sociology are in actuality pieces of systematized history. Social analyses that have as their aim a global analysis of the present fall into this category: for example, the studies by Fromm, Marcuse, Mills, and Riesman of structural changes in social systems and personality structures in the advanced industrial societies of the West; the studies by Aron and Perroux of the interaction between the two great systems of industrial development; and finally, the studies by Dahrendorf, Marshall, Schumpeter, and Strachey of the development of capitalism and democracy in Western Europe. Hypotheses proposed in the context of such systematically ambitious sociological history and used as a basis for the interpretation of complex developments require new research approaches, namely, longitudinal studies and the cross-cultural comparisons developed in anthropological research.[73]

Most sociological studies that deal with contemporary subject matter and do not require longitudinal sections or comparisions are also, strictly speaking, answers to historical questions. Whether it is a question of social stratification and mobility, of family structure and social character, of scientific productivity and the organization of labor; whether the ideology of a class is being investigated during a specific historical period or in specific geographical areas in the present, it is always a question of analyses of an individual case. The assumptions used in the explanation of the case are often formulated as universal propositions, despite the fact that they implicitly include a reference to specific conditions within a complex overall situation and thus can claim only the validity of historical generalizations.

We find something substantially different only in the case of systematic attempts to use historical material to verify general theories or indivdual lawlike hypotheses. One leaves the standpoint of sociological historiography only when historical data are used to test theoretical assumptions in the same way that one uses experimental readings. The construction of historical types is an initial step toward a more rigorous identification of characteristic indicators in areas that are culturally or temporally remote. Max Weber's studies of religious sects exemplify an intention that today guides research that is more specialized and more theoretically ambitious.[74] In the more rigorous studies, however, one sees that the theoretical assumptions diminish in empirical content to the degree to which it is possible to find initial historical conditions to be used as test cases. Attempts to develop general theories of social change have fared equally badly. In their logical structure, such theories would not differ from other sociological theories. Whereas historical data *can* be adduced for verification of sociological theories in general, theories of social change *necessarily* refer to historically observable regularities.[75] Thus, there results the methodological difficulty that for central lawlike assumptions only a few cases can be found in the known course of history to serve as tests for verification. This is shown by attempts to formulate a theory of revolution, which must of necessity contain assumptions about the conditions of stability in social systems.[76]

Some authors hold the view that attempts to develop general theories of social action do not fail accidentally but rather encounter limits of principle. It seems to be the case that theories whose content is historical always proceed on the basis of a system of reference whose elements can be interpreted only in terms of a preunderstanding of a specific historical situation. The categorial framework within which we formulate assumptions about sociological laws corresponds as a rule to the logical form of general theories: the fundamental assumptions contain no individual names and are not limited to a specific time period; nevertheless, the substantive interpretation of fundamental predicates may be dependent upon a specific context of meaning that has to be hermeneutically explicated with reference to a specific historical situation. Bendix unwittingly provides an example of this when he uses concept pairs to establish a historically substantive theoretical framework. These concepts are supposed to exhaust the ambiguity of human relationships:

The basic concepts of sociological theory should be applicable to all societies. With the aid of such concepts, we should be able to formulate propositions which are true of men by virtue of the fact that they have been members of social groups everywhere and at all times. In order to achieve such comprehensiveness, these concepts should, at their appropriate level of abstraction, encompass the full range of human experience in society rather than single out some dominant feature of that experience and thereby leave some residue aside.[77]

Pairs of concepts familiar from from older theories are supposed to satisfy this condition: status and contract, *Gemeinschaft* and *Gesellschaft*, mechanical and organic solidarity, informal and formal groups, primary and secondary relationships, culture and civilization, traditional and bureaucratic authority, rural and urban community, sacred and secular associations, military and industrial society, status and class, and so forth. But C. Wright Mills is correct in saying of a list of such categories that they are "historically rooted conceptions" that did not arise accidentally in the analysis of the unique historical transition of European society from feudalism to modern capitalist society. They are particularly suited for grasping specific tendencies in this historical development: urbanization, bureaucratization, industrialization, and so forth: "Even those who believe they do not work historically generally reveal, by their use of such terms, some notion of historical trends."[78]

In the same way, categories such as role and reference group are dependent on the self-understanding of advanced industrial society. None of these categories loses its situation-specific content through formalization. This becomes evident precisely when a theoretical framework constructed of historically substantive concepts is to be used for the analysis of historically distant and culturally alien contexts; in the altered context, the tool becomes peculiarly blunt. This experience leads one to suspect that in sociology there is an unexpressed relationship between the categorial framework of general theories and a guiding preunderstanding of the overall contemporary situation. The further such theories are removed from the realm of application in the analysis of contemporary matters, the less useful are their hypotheses in the explanation of more distant objects, because without the implicit agreement produced by the reference to analysis of the present they contribute less to an interpretation; they "signify" or "elucidate" less.

Among sociologists themselves three positions on the relationship between sociology and history can currently be distinguished. The first is the positivist one. According to this position, two categories of inquiry must be distinguished: on the one hand, theoretically oriented research in the strict sense, which serves to validate lawlike assumptions; on the other hand, studies that are oriented to historical problematics without express historical reference, that is, studies that grasp individual context with the aid of generalizations. Malewski, who advances this thesis of the two sociologies,[79] would consider all investigations of the second category to be social and cultural history, while he would simply incorporate sociological theories in the strict sense into the corpus of the behavioral sciences. This proposal serves more than a terminological intention; it expresses a systematic conviction. As examples of theoretically oriented sociology, Malewski mentions only social-psychological studies that, like those of Festinger, Hopkins, and Homans, belong to the class of experimental small-group research. Apparently general theories of social behavior are possible only on a level of abstraction at which the primary experiences of the social lifeworld can be resolved into relationships of abstract variables. Theories whose basic predicates are still so closely tied to a concretely identifiable context of experience that their assumptions can be verified through reference to historical evidence do not fulfill those conditions of a reconstruction of reality; theoretical knowledge in the strict sense cannot be achieved at this level at all.

The second position, which is the predominant one in contemporary sociology, proceeds, however, directly from this assumption. In addition to contributions to a sociological historiography, the real task of sociology, according to this position, consists in constructing general theories of social action, not of behavior as such. The theories constructed are thus at a level of abstraction that allows social events to be explained in the dimension of historical processes. This position challenges positivism's claim that theoretical knowledge in the strict sense can be achieved only through the transformation of contexts of action into variables of observable behavior, thus through the reduction of sociology to social-psychological behavioral research.

Finally, the third position retains the classical approach of the older sociology, which was developmentally oriented. It is in agreement with the second position in the view that sociology cannot let itself be robbed of its unique object domain; but it shares with the first position the conviction that substantive historical theories only appear to take the form of general theories, but are limited in their claim to validity to specific temporal and cultural contexts. Mills is an emphatic advocate of this viewpoint: "All sociology worthy of the name is 'historical sociology'."[80] Sociology is the systematic attempt to reconstruct the present out of the past; it is an attempt at an analysis of the present as history.[81] Thus the theoretical framework is related to the structural complex of developmental tendencies in terms of which the determining conflicts are problems that are objectively posed, that is, prescientifically experienced as relevant, and that a historically oriented sociology analyzes in order to prepare for their practical solution. At one time, the class conflict in bourgeois society represented the problematic situation that was the point of departure for the construction of theories; now it is the conflict between systems of industrial development. From a developmental perspective the constellation of the conditions of such conflicts becomes apparent. Thus the regularities that express the functional relationship of institutions always refer to a specific historical society:

There is, I believe, no 'law' stated by any social scientist that is transhistorical, that must not be understood as having to do with the specific structure of some period. Other 'laws' turn out to be empty abstractions or quite confused tautologies. The only meaning of 'social laws' or even of 'social regularities' is such *principia media* as we may discover, or if you wish, construct, for a social structure within an historically specific era. We do not know any universal principles of historical change; the mechanisms of change we do know vary with the social structure we are examining. For historical change *is* change of social structure, of the relations among their component parts. Just as there is a variety of social structures, there is a variety of principles of historical change.[82]

What Mills, following Karl Mannheim, calls "principia media" is another expression for the concrete generality of social totality. So much that is specific to an individual epoch inevitably enters into the elementary specifications of a theoretical framework that all theoretical statements made within this framework are valid only for the social-structural context of a specific social system. Mills did not go further into the logic of a historically oriented sociological inquiry that aims at an analysis of the present with practical intent. The few references he makes can hardly stand up to Popper's critique of the so-called historicism of the older social theories.[83] We shall return to this discussion after we have clarified the methodology of general theories of social action.[84]

II

On the Methodology of General Theories of Social Action

This review of the methodological inquiries of Rickert, Cassirer, and Weber has recalled arguments that, from within the framework of a Kantian critique of knowledge, assert a dualism of the sciences and thus also reserve for the social sciences a special status vis-à-vis the natural sciences—that of nomological *Geisteswissenschaften*. Our discussion of the relationship between sociology and history could not support the positivistic counterthesis of the logical unity of theoretical and historical sciences. The question remained open whether social inquiry is in the last analysis reducible to a systematized historical research or whether sociology as a rigorous science can purge itself of historical contamination to the point where, methodologically speaking, the natural sciences and the sciences of action have the same status. We shall now attempt to clarify the question how general theories of social action are possible. Can they be formulated independently of historical knowledge, or do their fundamental assumptions always include a situation-specific understanding of meaning that can be explicated only hermeneutically?

The rudiments of theories concerning empirical uniformities of social action are to be found in all social-scientific disciplines: in economics, in sociology and cultural anthropology, and in social psychology. Insofar as it is not narrowly concerned with history or oriented to intellectual history, political science uses the theoretical approaches of related disciplines. In each case, to be sure, these disciplines construct general theories within a specific framework: either they are theories of pure choice, or they are formulated within the framework of the theory of action, or they form part of a general science of behavior. Comparing these three theoretical perspectives will allow us to explore three problems. First there is the question whether theories whose assumptions are aimed at an explanation of intentional action must proceed on the basis of maxims of action, or whether we may relinquish this normative approach in favor of an analysis of contexts of action. This leads to the further question whether an empirical-analytic procedure necessarily requires the reduction of intentional action to stimulus-response behavior. If, however, as will be demonstrated, nonreductive theories of social action must forgo the elementaristic structure of behavioral-scientific theories in favor of functionalism, we must consider the question under what conditions social-scientific systems research can go beyond prescriptive knowledge and contribute to the empirical analysis of social contexts. This last question again raises the issue of the boundaries of general theories of social action.

Paul Lazarsfeld once complained that methodologists do not aid social scientists in the solution of their practical methodological problems.[1] He attributes this to the fact that the social sciences have not yet succeeded in developing theory in the strict sense: "What we have at our disposal are research techniques and a number of generalizations at a relatively low level of abstraction." For this reason, he says, the programmatic aspects of scientific logic pass over practitioners' heads. This reflection, I believe, contains false assumptions. Methodology is concerned with norms of the research process, which claim to be simultaneously logically binding as far as factual context is concerned and factually binding where the researcher is concerned. Regardless of whether methodology reflects on a research practice that is already in use, as in the case if physics, or whether, as in the case of sociology, its recommendations precede the research practice, methodology sets out a program to guide the advance of science. Thus it is not meaningless to discuss methodological requirements, even if they have not yet been fulfilled by research practice: they influence the way the sciences articulate their self-understanding. In part, methodological viewpoints set standards for research, and in part they anticipate its general objectives. Taken together, these two functions establish the system of reference within which reality is systematically explored. By reflecting on the conditions of possible research, the logic of science fulfills, whether intentionally or not, the function of providing a preliminary interpretation of reality. The expectation, however, that methodology itself should take on the attitude of the sciences and fulfill the function of an auxiliary science of research strategies and technologies reflects a positivistic bias. Insofar as methodology accepts this bias as its own, it acknowledges the criterion of Lazarsfeld's critique and is proceeding in an instrumental fashion. I would like to discuss methodological questions from an opposing point of view, that of reflection.

3 Normative-Analytic and Empirical-Analytic Approaches to Social Science

3.1 The methodological controversy carried on in classical economics by Schmoller and Menger created distorted battle lines. It originated in conflicting conceptions of the role of general theories in the social sciences. Whereas the "theoreticians" insisted that economics could derive assumptions concerning functional relationships between quantifiable flows of goods and money in the form of axiomatic-deductive systems of statements, and thus could be established as mathematical economic theory, the "historians" understood the economic process as a real social life-process that would have to be grasped descriptively in terms of the institutions of economic activity. Whereas, according to the "historians," mathematical economic theory could only construct models without empirical content, a sociological economics proceeding on the basis of historical understanding could grasp actual economic processes. The historical school's counterargument establishes a suggestive link between two theses. The first holds that economics is concerned not with the functions of quantities of goods but rather with the interdependence of economic actions. The second seems to follow from the first: since intentional action can be grasped only by means of understanding, there can be no rigorous, mathematically formulated economic theories. "Understanding" seemed to be equivalent to the historical comprehension of concrete meaning. As early as the 1930s, Ewald Schams (in *Schmollers Jahrbuch*, volume 58) tried to dissolve the conjunction of these two assertions by pointing out that it is precisely mathematical economic theory that, disregarding all historical specificities, fulfills the conditions of a *verstehende* economics. Continuing this train of thought, Jürgen von Kempski shows that "mathematical economic theory does precisely what *verstehende* economics, which is intended as a theory of economic actions, would have to do."[2] The mathematical expressions that refer directly to relationships between prices and quantities of goods are an indirect representation of functions of the decisions of acting subjects. For the economic theory in which they occur is a system of statements that rests on fundamental assumptions about rational economic action. It presupposes that economic subjects act in accordance with maxims; usually this takes the form of maximization strategies. Formalized economic theories make intentional action systematically comprehensible by grasping relationships among measurable quantities as functions of actions in accordance with maxims. This intelligibility is related to the structure of a rational choice among alternative uses of means on the basis of specifiable preferences. Thus it refers to strategic action. This is the only form of intentional action that can be grasped in a theoretically rigorous way within a normative-analytic framework. Indeed, a general theory of social action seems to be possible only if it proceeds on the basis of fundamental assumptions about intelligible action of this specific type.

Purposive-rational action can intend the use of appropriate instruments; the behavior is then guided by technical rules. But the choice of strategies can also be a purposive-rational one. Here, the behavior is guided by pure maxims that determine decisions among alternative uses of means; in the ideal case, the purposive-rationality of the means, that is, the appropriateness of the instruments, can be disregarded. Thus economic theory proceeds as though the strategic action of economic subjects who choose from among alternative courses of action regarding supply and demand had no technological aspects. For this reason, von Kempski emphasizes that theories of strategic action use basic concepts concerning actions taken in accordance with maxims in defined situations: "We take action to be the transformation of situations. This transformation of a situation follows a maxim, and in the ideal (that is, theoretically relevant) case, it does so in such a way that the end-situation is given by the initial situation plus the maxim of the acting subject. If the initial situation involves several persons, then the end situation can be thought of as determined by the maxims of all participants.... I would like to point out that a mental element is included in the action, namely, what I call maxims."[3]

Von Kempski is convinced that all social sciences, including jurisprudence and ethics,[4] can be construed as theories of strategic action on the model of mathematical economics. In contradistinction to natural-scientific theories, they base their predictive statements on hypothetical normative rules of action rather than on empirical uniformities. They constitute nomological *Geisteswissenschaften* in the sense that, rather than explaining phenomena on the basis of natural laws, they derive actions of choice from laws of freedom. It is not fortuitous that von Kempski works within the Kantian tradition. To the natural laws of the phenomenal realm, Kant opposed the maxims of action in the realm of freedom. It is from this same perspective that von Kempski draws his distinction between the natural and the social sciences:

The crucial distinction between theoretical social science and physics consists in the fact that the human behavior studied by the social sciences is always presupposed to be governed by certain maxims to which men may hold, or may not hold. Social-scientific models always presuppose the validity of certain maxims. For this reason, social-scientific studies based on theoretical models are fundamental investigations of possible action, whereas theoretical physics is always concerned with actual nature, and the determination that nature behaves differently than the theory would lead one to expect is fatal for physical theories. Thus a general theory of action is problematic in a completely different way than is a general theory in physics, for a general theory of action, which would have to cover the possible models, inevitably involves man's freedom with respect to the maxims of his action.[5]

Von Kempski's discussion of the status of general theories of action is ambiguous. On the one hand, they are supposed to serve to explain factual contexts of action; on the other hand, they are not in a position to allow conditional predictions of observable behavior.[6] Von Kempski leaves no doubt that the nomological *Geisteswissenschaften* analyze possibilities of action, that is, provide information about how actions would have to take place in a given situation under a given maxim to fulfill the conditions of strategic purposive-rationality. And yet they seem to provide information not only for practical but also for descriptive purposes, for actual courses of action can be elucidated with respect to the field of possible action. Here von Kempski is following Weber's proposal that modes of behavior that are irrational with respect to ends should be conceived as deviations from the ideal type. Similarly, the distinction introduced by Felix Kaufmann between theoretical laws that are based on idealizing assumptions and protected by corresponding stipulations from empirical refutation, on the one hand, and empirical laws that under normal test conditions are capable of refutation through experience, on the other hand, makes sense only when theories of strategic action are used in some way for empirical analysis, and thus contribute to descriptive knowledge.[7] This conception has a certain plausibility only in the context of Kantian presuppositions. Just as the achievements of transcendental consciousness are not a matter of indifference to empirical consciousness, so the laws of practical reason through which, as a free person, I determine my actions are not a matter of indifference with respect to the consequences of these actions in the phenomenal world. For this reason, regularities among empirical actions cannot be analyzed without reference to the fact that acting subjects are intelligible beings, that is, must always act under the presumption of legitimation through reason: they act under the force of an imputed freedom. Such considerations, however, remain arbitrary unless they are systematically tied to methodological assumptions.

The weaknesses of social-scientific normativism are obvious. The basic assumptions refer to idealized action under pure maxims; no empirically substantive lawlike hypotheses can be derived from them. Either it is a question of analytic statements recast in deductive form or the conditions under which the hypotheses derived could be definitively falsified are excluded under *ceteris paribus* stipulations. Despite their reference to reality, the laws stated by pure economics have little, if any, information content.[8] To the extent that theories of rational choice lay claim to empirical-analytic knowledge, they are open to the charge of Platonism (*Modellplatonismus*). Hans Albert has summarized these arguments:[9] The central point is the confusion of logical presuppositions with empirical conditions. The maxims of action introduced are treated not as verifiable hypotheses but as assumptions about actions by economic subjects that are in principle possible. The theorist limits himself to formal deductions of implications in the unfounded expectation that he will nevertheless arrive at propositions with empirical content. Albert's critique is directed primarily against tautological procedures and the immunizing role of qualifying or "alibi" formulas.

This critique of normative-analytic methods argues that general theories of rational action are achieved at too great a cost when they sacrifice empirically verifiable and descriptively meaningful information. Apparently von Kempski's justification of mathematical economics as a *verstehende* economics disregards one requirement that was also contained in Schmoller's critique of the model-building of pure economics, namely, that the factual context of the institutionalized actions of economic subjects be taken into consideration. This requirement is not met by the reconstruction of economic processes on the basis of the hypothetical normative context of idealized actions. Against the recent normativism of pure economics, Albert adduces the old viewpoint that an economic theory must make assumptions about the actions of subjects in their social roles. The relationships of exchange that economics grasps in systematic terms are interactions of persons in social groups:

The central idea of economic thought is, in a very fundamental sense, a sociological idea, namely, that the production and distribution of goods in a system, supported by juridical sanctions, of commercial relationships among the persons and groups in a society, is regulated quasi-automatically in a manner relevant to the satisfaction of needs. Thus it is a matter of analysis of specific effects of events in a sector of society organized in market form. In this analysis, the attempt is made to explain all relevant events in terms of decisions made by economic subjects in accordance with certain maxims.... The explanation deals primarily with such factors as motivational structures, attitudes, and value-orientations, as well as the social context of the modes of behavior in question, even external to the field of commercial relationships.... The significance of these factors does not seem to be limited to special areas of society. For the most part, however, such factors are not incorporated into the models of the pure theoreticians. Rather, they postulate reaction functions that are clearly either completely or at least to a great degree independent of the dispositional characteristics of persons as well as independent of all noncommercial components of their social milieu.[10]

The system of exchange relationships is so little isolated from society as a whole that the social behavior of economic subjects cannot be comprehended independently of the institutional context, that is, the extraeconomic motivational patterns: "Immunization against the influence of so-called extra-economic factors leads to immunization against experience as such."[11]

On the basis of similar considerations, Grunberg early reached the conclusion that the unconvincing constructions of economic theory would have to be reestablished on the foundation of an empirical-analytic behavioral science.[12] As a theoretical empirical science, economics can arrive at empirically substantive hypotheses only in the form of an economic sociology. It would also need to explain sociological uniformities in terms of laws of social-psychological small-group research. In fact, Grunberg does not exclude the possibility that a further reduction to propositions concerning physiological, chemical, and physical uniformities may prove necessary.[13]

3.2 Even if we ignore such extreme variations and limit ourselves to the demands of a modest reductionism, the conception of economics as a special form of sociology is unsatisfying. On the one hand, the arguments against social-scientific normativism cannot be disputed, but on the other hand, the incorporation of economics into orthodox behavioral science does not really correspond to the intention of economic theory. The latter clearly aims to provide a type of information different from anything that sociology or social psychology can provide. Strictly speaking, the critique of economic models on the basis of their lack of empirical substance is aimed at a false self-understanding, not at the practice of economic research. The critique becomes superfluous as soon as theories of rational economic action relinquish the false claim that they provide information about empirical uniformities. Von Kempski's interpretation of pure economics with the aid of a schema of actions under pure maxims can already be seen as an attempt to interpret economic theory in terms of the logic of decisions. But he ignores the question whether one can equate normative-analytic and empirical-analytic sciences of social action. Sciences whose theories incorporate basic assumptions concerning idealized action proceed normative-analytically. These assumptions about action under pure maxims do not have the character of conditional, thus empirically verifiable, hypotheses; their validity is hypothetically unconditional, and thus they establish the meaning of the possible validity of normative-analytic knowledge. Such knowledge contains no information about empirical uniformities—technologically exploitable knowledge of the first order, but only information about a purposive-rational choice among strategies that presuppose the use of first-order technological knowledge. We can consider such information second-order technological knowledge.

Gäfgen has presented an analysis of the logic of the economic significance of rational action that, following the mathematical game theory developed by von Neumann and Morgenstern, systematically incorporates economic theory into a general theory of strategic action.[14] Decision theory is not concerned with adaptive behavior. To be sure, it is possible to understand any behavior in terms of adaptation to a given situation. But to do so is to exclude the analytic point of view from which behavior is evaluated as strategic action, namely, in terms of whether the movement of adaptation leads to an optimal condition of satisfaction for the acting subject. Adaptive behavior can, however, be included in the data base of the decision calculus as an external condition, along with the techniques available. This calculus is concerned only with strategic action that leads from one situation, consisting of the acting subject and his relevant environment, to a new situation, through application of a defined maxim of decision and a system of values. The value system contains rules of preference that indicate how the foreseeable consequences of alternative decisions are to be evaluated by the acting subject. The decision maxim indicates what choice between different strategies will be made on the basis of an evaluation of the consequences. For every kind of evaluation there is a corresponding maxim. The rationality of the action to which decision theory gives normative status is the rationality of a choice between alternative paths to the realization of ends. It is formal because it does not refer to the technological appropriateness of the means. And it is subjective, because it is measured only in terms of the system of maxims and rules for evaluation that are binding for the acting subject himself.

The abandonment of a psychological foundation for acts of economic choice, as suggested by Pareto, was the most important precondition for an interpretation of economic theory in terms of the logic of decisions. This interpretation has the advantage of relativizing the classical assumptions of maximization as limiting cases on a spectrum of possible maxims of choice. In addition, one can now calculate choices of action in situations where the economic subjects do not possess complete information, and thus have only a portion of the variables under control. The general theory of rational choice or strategic action covers all situations of choice in which a given quantity of resources permits a specific number of alternative uses of available means, whereby each of these alternatives sets specific degrees of fulfillment for various goals.[15] Economic theory can be regarded as a special decision theory relating to situations of economic choice. It calculates the market-relevant behavior of individual and collective households, of commercial enterprises, and of trade associations.[16]

The interpretation of pure economics in terms of a logic of decisions sacrifices the empirical-analytic claim of general theories of strategic economic action. Gäfgen reassesses the empirical-descriptive use of decision models and comes to the negative conclusion that "decision theory can make weak empirical statements about individual economic behavior, but even these weak statements could possess only limited empirical validity."[17] Decision theory provides no first-order technologically exploitable knowledge. Nevertheless, economic theory, like all theories of strategic action, can be used for prescriptive purposes. In such cases it serves as a normative aid in decision-making and provides second-order technologically exploitable knowledge. The information it provides does not require empirical verification, since it can not be "true" or "false" in the sense of empirical accuracy. Rather, it has the status of conditional imperatives (statements of command, prohibition, and permission), which may be deductively "valid" or "invalid." Even if one must for this reason forgo a descriptive use of theory, "one can still use the model to recommend to specific actors an action in accordance with the model: by claiming for the maxims of action presupposed in the model ethical (social) validity as norms of correct action, one can derive 'ought' statements rather than 'is' statements from them."[18] Gäfgen conceives economic theory as a formalized practical system that provides an axiomatic-deductive foundation for economic policy formulation.[19] Just as lawlike empirical-analytic knowledge can be translated into technological recommendations and used for the production of technologies, so normative-analytic statements take the form of strategic recommendations that, given specific technologies, values, and goals, determine the choice of possible strategies.

Decision theory is a general theory of social action; it concerns itself, however, with an extreme variant of action—with the action and interaction of subjects acting in a purposive-rational manner. For this reason, it is useless for empirical analysis. Does it follow from this that to be usable for empirical analysis, theories of social action must disregard the intentionality of action and limit themselves to stimulus-response behavior? From the positivist perspective, a theoretical empirical science of social action is possible only on the condition that lawlike relationships apply exclusively to variables of observable behavior. It must abstract from the subjectively intended meaning to which the acting subjects are oriented. In this way a generalizing behavioral science would take account of the historical school's critique of pure theory's lack of empirical substance, but it would do so at the price of a requirement that the interpretive theory of strategic action tried to meet, namely, at the price of gaining access to social facts through understanding.[20]

But is social-scientific reductionism an adequate methodological basis for the descriptively useful theories of social action that cannot be constructed on the basis of social-scientific normativism?

4 Intentional Action and Stimulus-Response Behavior

4.1 At the present time there are two theoretical points of departure for a rigorous empirical-scientific analysis of social processes: a general behavioral science, which permeates ethology and social psychology, and a theory of action, which is dominant in cultural anthropology and sociology. The behavioristic approach restricts the choice of fundamental theoretical assumptions in such a way that lawlike hypotheses refer to a relationship between stimuli and behavioral reactions, whereas the action approach establishes a categorial framework within which statements about intentional action are made. Learning theory (Skinner, Miller, Dollard), hypotheses concerning cognitive dissonance (Festinger), and theories of small-group behavior (Lippit) document the first successful attempts to construct general theories of a behavioral-scientific type. The theory of action, on the other hand, is a categorial framework (Parsons, Merton, Shils, et al.) that serves for general orientation in social research and, to this point, has led to empirical generalizations but not to actual theories, even middle-range ones.[21]

The approach in terms of a theory of action was formulated by Max Weber. He conceived social action as behavior that is subjectively meaningful, that is, oriented to a subjectively intended meaning, and thus also motivated. It can be appropriately understood only with reference to the goals and values to which the acting subject is oriented. The methodological rule that results from this was established by W. I. Thomas as the principle of subjective interpretation of social facts: only the meaning intended by the acting subject provides adequate access to behavior performed in a situation that he himself has interpreted. Social action is not independent of a socially binding definition of the situation. For this reason, observable social action must be grasped from the perspective of the acting subject himself, a perspective that is removed from direct observation; that is, it must be "understood."[22] The principle of subjective interpretation, or, better, of *verstehende* interpretation, concerns access to social facts, the gathering of data. Understanding symbols takes the place of the controlled observation, for the subjectively intended meaning is given only is symbolic contexts. Thus that principle defines the experiential basis of the sciences of action. Experience here is not tied to private sensory perception, the intersubjectivity of which is guaranteed only through monitoring the results of instrumental action (usually in an experiment), but to linguistic communication: "On the level of understanding, scientific research is basically a process of meaningful communication, even when it is a one-sided process, as for example, when the objects are dead. In principle, it is always desirable for the object to be available for interviews; written statements from him or reports about him are always appropriate only as second choices— thus it would be extremely desirable to have the opportunity to interview Brutus about Caesar's death."[23]

If we do not wish to abandon intentional action as data in the social sciences, the system of experience in which these data are accessible is linguistic communication, not communication-free observation.

There is, however, a limiting case of intentional action, namely, strategic action, in which the subjectively intended meaning does not need to be appropriated from cultural tradition, clarified and understood in communication as a concrete meaning, thus "experienced." The meaning in terms of which strategic action is oriented can always be unambiguously specified as a rule for the maximization or optimization of measurable or at least comparatively specifiable quantities. Here lack of ambiguity is guaranteed by the form of the statement, which gives a maxim of purposive-rational action, and through the universality of the interpretation, which constitutes the semantic content of the goal being sought. For strategic action always has as its goal categories of wealth or power that can be operationalized in different ways in accordance with the criteria of the institutional framework. Wealth can be measured in terms of prices or goods, that is, in terms of potentials for the satisfaction of needs; power can be measured in terms of votes or weapons, that is, in terms of potentials for the legitimation of domination or for physical annihilation. The semantic content of the predicates used to formulate maxims of action, that is, the meaning of wealth and power, clearly expresses experiences that are deeply rooted in the anthropological sense, and thus universally distributed, so that these expressions do not need to be explicated in each individual case through communication with the acting subjects themselves or with the traditions in terms of which their actions become understandable. The limiting case of strategic action has the advantage that the subjectively intended meaning can be determined monologically; it is "unambiguously" understandable, accessible without hermeneutic effort. In this area, the experiential basis of understanding has become almost completely detached from the context of ordinary-language communication, so that we appear to ascertain it "introspectively"; in fact, however, the "unambiguous" meaning of strategic action is an "understandable meaning" only because it can be brought into communication at any time and can, by way of symbolic interpretation, be interpolated into the actor's observable behavior by a partner.

Strategic action is only a limiting case of social action, which is normally oriented to a meaning that can be communicated. This meaning is concrete; it stems from the contents of a cultural tradition and, to the extent that it motivates social action, it enters into the definition of socially binding norms. Durkheim understood social norms as moral rules (which Freud explained in terms of their function of censoring instincts). G. H. Mead, on the other hand, understands social norms as social roles. In both cases, the orienting meaning takes the form of an obligatory group expectation of situation-specific ways of behaving. Social action is an adherence to norms. Norms that determine action are collective behavioral expectations. These expectations are a facet of cultural tradition that is relevant to institutionalized action. Cultural tradition is a symbolic context that defines the worldview of a social group, articulated in ordinary-language form, and therewith the framework of possible communications within the group. Thus social action exists only with reference to the system of traditional cultural patterns in which the self-understanding of social groups is articulated. The methodology of the sciences of action cannot avoid the problem of understanding meaning, of hermeneutically appropriating cultural tradition.

For this reason, positivism prefers a theoretical approach that makes the principle of the subjective interpretation of social actions superfluous. If social norms can be understood as behavioral expectations, why should these expectations not be expressible in terms of variables of observable behavior? In this way, at the level of the experience of social contents a framework of linguistic communication would not be necessary; observation, rather than a problematic understanding of meaning, would then suffice.

4.2 In an essay that has become famous, Abel analyzes the understanding of motivation.[24] He proceeds from a trivial observation: On an April day, as it becomes cool, a neighbor gets up from his desk, goes to a shed and splits wood, makes a fire in his fireplace, and returns to his work. Obviously—so we "understand" his behavior—the neighbor built a fire because he was cold. Two events are directly accessible to observation: the drop in temperature, and the building of a fire in the fireplace. We make the external connection between these events—which is at first established only within the coordinate system of time and space—understandable through the interpolation of a maxim of behavior. We begin by translating the first event (the initial condition) into a subjective stimulus and the second event (the resulting action) into a response to this stimulus: the "inner condition" of being cold is linked with the drop in temperature; the condition of getting warm, with the fire in the fireplace. Then the application of a maxim of behavior (as for instance, a cold person seeks warmth) suffices to interpret the two observed events as parts of a situation that is actively changed in pursuit of a subjective goal, and to "understand" the nexus of the observed event, the action itself:

By specifying the steps which are implicit in the interpretation of our case, we have brought out two particulars which are characteristic of the art of

Verstehen. One is the "internalizing" of observed factors in a given situation; the other is the application of a behaviour maxim which makes the connection between these factors relevant. Thus we "understand" a given human action if we can apply to it a generalization based upon personal experience. We can apply such a rule of behaviour if we are able to "internalize" the facts of the situation.[25]

Abel conceives *Verstehen* as the interpolation of a maxim of behavior. These maxims are unproblematically given. They have the form of universal statements, but they are in no way empirically verified laws. They claim to be self-evident on the basis of self-observation. We simply know that one seeks warmth when one is cold, that one defends oneself when one is attacked, that one inclines to caution when one is afraid, that one hates one's enemies, avoids injury, seeks advantage, and so forth. The act of understanding seems only to make use of such trivial rules but not to be directly concerned with them.

Less trivial rules, however, cannot be simply presupposed as self-evident. This is demonstrated by the second example that Abel discusses. The connection between the success of the harvest and the frequency of marriage in a rural community over a period of time is made understandable through the assumption that loss of income arouses anxiety, and anxiety dampens readiness to take on new obligations. In this case the maxim of behavior is not at all unproblematic. Marriage does not need to be evaluated primarily as being an economic burden; having one's own family as an intimate group promising security could just as well seem desirable, precisely in situations of insecurity. How farmers behave within their family circles during times of poor harvest clearly depends on traditional notions of value and institutionalized roles. But such cultural patterns and social norms have to be grasped descriptively. They do not belong to the class of behavioral rules that appear to be introspectively certain but rather require a controlled appropriation through hermeneutic understanding of meaning.

In such cases, where the act of understanding is directed to meanings objectivated in symbolic contexts, Max Weber spoke of value-interpretation. Only when the symbolic content of prevailing norms has been disclosed through an understanding of meaning can the understanding of motives grasp an observed behavior as subjectively meaningful action in relation to those norms.

The distinction between the hermeneutic understanding of meaning and the understanding of motivation makes it clear that the operation of *Verstehen* is not limited to the application of a maxim to behavior in a given situation. Rather, this application presupposes the explication of subjectively intended meaning in terms of cultural tradition. Hermeneutic understanding of traditional meanings is independent of whether these meanings have also been incorporated into the definition of social norms and thus into the intentions of acting subjects. If that is the case, we can also interpret the action itself as meaningfully motivated in relation to the action-orienting meaning. If Abel had chosen examples of actions from foreign cultures or distant epochs, he would hardly have escaped noticing that the interpreter must determine the relevant nontrivial maxims of behavior before he can apply them to meaningfully motivated action. The maxims of behavior are not given through something like introspection; rather, they are objects of experience at the level of the understanding of symbols, just as physical events are objects of experience at the level of direct observation.

Abel's restriction of his choice of examples is not accidental. He restricts his analysis to modes of behavior that can be conceived as the adaptation of an organism in need to its environment and that can thus be ordered within a stimulus-response schema. Without discussion, he conceives the initial conditions as a stimulus, the manifest behavior as an adaptive response, and the final state as the result of stimulus-response behavior. The translation of events into psychic conditions interpolates only a subjective apprehension of the tension triggered by the stimulus and the release of tension attained through adaptation. This so-called internalization of the initial conditions and the final state permits the application of a maxim of behavior in such a way that the event observed as adaptive behavior can also be understood as purposive-rational action: "The generalizations which we call 'behaviour maxims' link two feeling-states together in a uniform sequence and imply a functional dependence between them. In the cases cited it can be seen that the functional dependence consists of the fact that the feeling-state we ascribe to a given human action is directed by the feeling-state we presume is evoked by an impinging situation or event. Anxiety directs caution; a feeling of cold, the seeking of warmth;

a feeling of insecurity, a desire for something that will provide reassurance."[26]

The triviality of the behavior maxims is due to the fact that Abel considers only adaptive behavior that can also be interpreted as instrumental action. In these cases, the subjectively intended meaning is determined in accordance with need-dispositions that can be stimulated and that, in conjunction with technical rules, establish specific modes of satisfaction. In this way Abel reduces *Verstehen* to an operation used in interpreting adaptive behavior either as a purposive-rational organization of means (the neighbor fetches wood and lights the fire to warm himself) or as a purposive-rational choice of strategies (the farmers try to avoid additional obligations so that the anxieties aroused by loss of income will not increase). But such a reduction clearly lacks the understanding of motivation directed toward social action, for purposive-rational modes of behavior are only limit cases of communicative action. Similarly, the behavior maxims for purposive-rational adaptation to given situations are only limit cases of norms that determine action. The latter can be understood as behavioral expectations of social groups that are by no means simply given in self-evident form but rather whose meaning in turn requires explication through *Verstehen* before they can form the basis for an understanding of motivation.

The intention behind Abel's analysis is a critical clarification of what *Verstehen* actually accomplishes. He assumes that the methodologies of the *Geisteswissenschaften* are attempting to justify the substitution of *Verstehen* for the explanation of actions. This thesis is not tenable, for the understanding of motivation is not a procedure for verifying the empirical accuracy of assumptions, although it may lead to hypotheses. Any maxim whatsoever that can be interpolated into behavior in given circumstances satisfies the desideratum of intelligibility in the same way. No choice between competing interpretations can be achieved through *Verstehen* itself. The interpretations remain arbitrary until they are subjected to a test in the usual manner. Weber pointed this out unequivocally: "The disclosure of the meaning of an action in a given situation . . . is merely a hypothesis taken on for the purpose of interpretation, which in principle always requires empirical verification, however certain it may seem in thousands of cases."[27] Abel goes one step further; since, fundamentally, he understands social action in terms of adaptive behavior, the interpretation of intentions is external to the observed behavior. The understanding of motivation is a supplementary rather than a necessary methodological step that, aside from the satisfaction we derive from incorporating objective events into the horizon of our personal experiences, has at most heuristic significance. When we render an observed event intelligible through interpolation of a maxim of behavior, we are making conjectures that can be translated into verifiable hypotheses: the understanding of motivation provides an impetus to the hypothesis-creating imagination.[28] This cognitive-psychological point, however, should not be confused with a methodological one.

This argument is correct, but it is irrelevant as long as *Verstehen* is claimed not for the purpose of causal explanation but only for access to social fact. Within the framework of the theory of action, explication of role behavior through understanding meaning serves only to obtain data. Of themselves, the various roles of the farmer and the institution of marriage in a rural community explain nothing; they serve only to describe interactions. Assumptions about the empirical relationships of roles require the usual verification procedures. Only a critique that challenged the very need for subjective access to social facts would call into question the methodological principle of *Verstehen*. Interpretive sociology, which uses the categorial framework of the theory of action, claims *Verstehen* for analytic purposes only insofar as hypotheses must be formulated in terms of the covariance of quantities that can be understood—but the operation of *Verstehen* is irrelevant to the logical form of the analysis of the lawlike regularities of social action.

The behaviorist argument in the narrower sense is directed against the subjective comprehension of social action. In ethology, the study of animal behavior, objective methods have proved successful. Goal-directed, adaptive behavior can be grasped and analyzed without reference to intentions. Nagel emphasizes that the theoretical approach of the behavioral sciences does not exclude "consciousness" or inner states. But when mental states or psychic events have an adjectival or adverbial relationship to physical conditions or events, the manifest behavior offers a sufficient basis for assumptions about social behavior as a whole. Intentional action does not need to be denied, but it is sufficient to investigate the observable behavior in which it is manifested. Nagel accepts the burden of proving that subjectively meaningful action does not necessarily need to be understood in terms of categories of self-understanding, that is, in relation to the subjective meaning of action-orienting rules or motivational patterns. He puts forth the counterthesis that, on the contrary, culturally transmitted meanings or value-orientations can be clearly defined only in variables of observable behavior:

The point I wish to make is that in imputing a certain schema of values to a community, one is imputing to its members certain attitudes. But an attitude is not something that can be established by introspection, whether in the case of our own person or of others. An attitude is a dispositional or latent trait; and it is comparable in its theoretical status with viscosity or electrical resistance in physics, even if, unlike the latter, it can be usefully defined for sociopsychological purposes only in statistical terms. In any event, the concept is cognitively valuable only insofar as it effects a systematic organization of manifest data obtained from overt human responses to a variety of conditions, and only in so far as it makes possible the formulation of regularities in such responses.[29]

In opposition to the thesis of action theory that socially binding behavioral expectations have to be explicated in terms of cultural contexts of meaning, Nagel asserts the necessity of expressing behavioral norms in the terminology of behavior itself: the intentional content of the social norms that determine social behavior can be clearly defined only in relation to behavioral variables.

4.3 The transformation of statements concerning subjectively intended meaning into statements about objective behavior does, however, encounter logical difficulties. Every direct attempt to translate intentional statements into the expressions of a strictly empiricist language is doomed to failure.

An empiricist language is extensional; in it, two predicates are synonymous when they define classes with the same extension. In this framework, a class of metal states is synonymous with the class of behavioral variables that regularly accompany those states. Further, empiricist languages fulfill the condition of truth-functionality. Propositions may appear within more complex propositions only as a condition of the truth of the latter; that is to say, the truth values of global statements are determined by those of their arguments. Clearly, however, intentional statements cannot be construed in such a way that their truth value follows from their logical form alone. In intentional statements the dependent portion of the sentence (that is, the content that is intended, willed, hoped, feared, uttered, disputed, questioned, or defended) is not a condition of the truth of the statement as a whole: the truth-value of the intended content remains to be determined. If A R p is a proposition S in which R comprises the class of all intentional expressions, then p does not appear as an argument-value in a truth function for S.[30] I shall not go into the extensive discussion of the status of so-called belief sentences here.

The difficulties encountered in translating intentional statements into empiricist language demonstrate unmistakably that, as regards the logic of science, statements about facts cannot be equated with statements about statements. The metaphysical assumption that intentional content and subjectively intended meaning can be reduced to mental states and psychic events that stand in clear reciprocal correlation with the corporeal world is not tenable. What Neo-Kantianism represented as a problem regarding the epistemological status of values or symbolic forms (the empirical externalization of the transcendental achievements of consciousness) forces recent positivism to a methodological application of type theory: the contents to which intentional statements refer are not at the level of facts but at the level of statements about facts. Empirical theories of communicative action, which refer to an object domain that is already linguistically constituted, must therefore be understood to be metalinguistic theories. But this consequence was not drawn until linguistically oriented philosophy drew it, on the basis of the self-reflection of positivism introduced by Wittgenstein.

To avoid this consequence, recent behaviorism has modified the strict demands of the older behaviorism.[31] Whereas formerly a direct translation of intentional contents into statements about physical events was to permit the complete neglect of so-called introspective experiences, now the dimension of language itself, which creates difficulties for the reduction, is drawn into the object domain: "Professed behaviorists today generally accept introspective reports by experimental subjects, not as statements about private psychic states of the subjects, but as observable verbal responses the subjects make under given conditions; and accordingly, introspective reports are included among the objective data upon which psychological generalizations are to be founded."[32]

Linguistic communication is conceived as verbal behavior that stands in empirically verifiable causal relationships to other modes of the organism's behavior; the use of linguistic symbols is part of adaptive behavior. The program of behavioral science thus presupposes a behaviorist theory of language. Building on the earlier work of pragmatists (Peirce, Dewey, Mead) and positivists (Carnap), Charles Morris provided the framework for this kind of general theory of the use of signs and symbols.[33] Morris understands linguistic communication in terms of the functional relationship between symbols and the behavior that is guided by symbols. He derives this symbolically guided behavior from the sign-controlled behavior that can be observed in animals. Thus from a certain level of organic development on, verbal behavior belongs to the sphere of adaptive behavior and can itself be studied from a strictly behavioral-scientific perspective. In the process whereby organisms adapt to their environment, signs have a behavior-guiding function. When in a given situation an event A regularly evokes an adaptive behavior in the same way as event B, we say that A is a sign for B. The organism that reacts to the sign is the interpreter. Decisive for the interpretation are the need-dispositions that cause the organism to react to signs, and the behavioral schemata in accordance with which the reactions proceed. Every object that is a suitable goal for the reactions that have been caused belongs to the class of events designated by the sign. All the empirical conditions that suffice for the prediction of a designated event make up in their totality the meaning of the sign.[34] Signs that control behavior are thus substitutes for natural stimuli that trigger the adaptive activity of an organism in a given situation. Morris calls natural signs "signals." When the interpreter himself produces signs that take the place of natural signs, we speak of "gestures." Such gestures have meaning in the semantic sense only when in communication they have the same meaning for the organisms producing them as for the interpreter. G. H. Mead calls these gestures with identical meaning "symbols"; they have a representational meaning in Cassirer's sense. A language consists of signs that all the partners in the linguistic community can produce, interpret in the same way regardless of situational context, and combine in accordance with rules. But then linguistic communication is equivalent to the reciprocal use of systematically ordered symbols that have consistent meanings for a given group. The semantic content is determined by observable modes of behavior that are symbolically regulated. All responses can be described as adaptive behavior. Verbal behavior can thus be studied as adaptive behavior and expressed in terms of variables of this behavior.

There does, however, arise a difficulty in the definition of symbols with identical meanings. Identity of meaning cannot be reduced to intersubjective agreement within a group. Within the framework of linguistic behaviorism, symbols have the same semantic content if and only if any member of the linguistic community responds to them with the same mode of behavior. The condition that on the level of linguistic communication all partners in the dialogue connect the same meaning to the signs they produce is fulfilled when they respond to these signs in the same way under given conditions. Morris uses the model of the individual adaptive process of the individual organism. He derives all communicative events from these elements. For this reason, he has no plausible way of distinguishing between coordinated monological responses to a symbol and linguistically mediated interaction:

It is sufficient that organisms perform response-sequences of the same behavior family, as would be the case of two dogs each seeking food without cooperating in the process. Even if two dogs were competing for food, our analysis would permit the genesis of signs of food producible by either organism and giving rise to similar interpretants regardless of which organisms made the sign in question. And even if the organism had to cooperate to secure food, it is not a social goal which is essential but similar response-sequences (and so similar individual goals). Response-sequences of the same behavior-family are necessary to secure similar sign-vehicles and similar interpretants, but such response-sequences are possible without there being cooperative social acts.[35]

This argument challenges G. H. Mead's theory of language, which assumed that the identity of meaning of symbols that was presupposed in linguistic communication is fulfilled not through the uniformity of responses as such but only by the reciprocal anticipation of the same behavioral response: "The critical importance of language in the development of human experience lies in the fact that the stimulus is one that can react upon the speaking individual as it reacts upon the other.''[36] A symbol has the same meaning content for two individuals when the speaker can anticipate the response of the other just as the other can anticipate his anticipation: The identity of meanings is constituted not by uniform responses as determined by the observer, but by the expectation of a response on which the speech partners themselves are in agreement, that is, by the intersubjectivity of expectations about behavior. Mead derives linguistic communication from role-interaction, where, however, role-action includes intentionality. To understand the meaning of a symbol means to be able to take on the role of a partner, to anticipate his behavioral response. Conversely, symbolically regulated behavior is precisely not sign-controlled adaptive behavior in Morris's sense but rather intentional action—behavior guided by the other's anticipation. It takes the other's role as its own. Interaction in roles is correlated with the intersubjectively intended meaning of an expectation of responses that is *shared* by the actors. The meaning content of symbols is defined by the behavioral *expectations* and not by the *modes* of behavior themselves. For this reason, the use of symbols cannot be reduced to mere behavior. Morris, on the other hand, wants to derive verbal behavior from stimulated behavior, and intentional action from verbal behavior. In his view, linguistic communication makes reciprocal action in accordance with anticipated roles possible; but interaction in roles is not the precondition of linguistic communication:

At times [Mead] talks as if role-taking were a precondition of the significant symbol and at times as if it were made possible by such symbols. The ambiguity is at least partially resolved, if we recognize two senses of role-taking; the sense in which a person simply as a fact responds to a sound he makes as others respond, and the sense in which a person identifies the response he makes to this sound as the kind of response another person makes. Role-taking in the first sense is involved in language signs, but adds no new factor to our previous account; role-taking in the second (and more usual sense) would seem to require complex signs (and perhaps even language), since it requires the signification of another person and the attribution to that person of a disposition to respond similar to that of the interpreter himself. The distinction is important, since there is no evidence that taking the role of the other in the latter sense is required to explain the genesis of the language sign.[37]

Morris's distinction does not do away with the logical difficulties of reducing language to behavior but rather makes them clear. Like

Mead, he establishes as a criterion for linguistic communication that the meanings symbolized must remain constant in changing contexts and must be identical for any member of the linguistic community. This criterion is derived from the intuitive knowledge of those who have taken part in such communications. As speakers, we experience the intersubjective validity of norms, which consists in the fact that we can all follow them. The community of intentions or obligations is the basis on which we communicate; the identity of a meaning is measured by intersubjective agreement in a symbolically expressed expectation of behavioral responses. Now this subjective grasp of the identity of meanings is to be replaced by an objective one. The intersubjectivity of roles, which can be maintained for the actors only through successful interaction, is now replaced by the identity of observed modes of behavior. If the meaning of a sign can be adequately established via the criteria of the modes of behavior stimulated by the sign, then a symbol, to which different organisms react in the same way, fulfills this condition of identical meaning for these interpreters. Strictly speaking, this definition establishes an interpretation only for the observer who, because he is able to speak, knows in advance what identity of meaning is. He can identify modes of behavior as being similar in terms of a criterion, or, if sufficiently similar, as identical, because he himself can maintain an identical perspective; that is, he can follow an intersubjectively valid rule. A preunderstanding that cannot be confirmed on the level of the interpreted behavior enters into the interpretation of the observer. In a discussion with Strawson, who took Morris's position, Winch develops this argument in the following way:

Strawson argues that we can quite well imagine, as a logical possibility, a desert-islander who has never been brought up in a human society devising a language for his own use. We can also, he says, imagine the introduction of an observer (B) of the user of this language who

observes a correlation between the use of words and sentences and the speaker's actions and environment.... Observer B is thus able to form hypotheses about the meanings (the regular use) of the words of his subject's language. He might in time come to be able to speak it; then the practice of each serves as a check on the practice of the other. But shall we say that, before this fortunate result was achieved (before the use of the language becomes a shared "form of life"), the words of the language had no meaning, no use?[38]

To Strawson it seems self-evidently absurd to say such a thing. The persuasiveness of his position lies in the fact that he appears to have succeeded in giving a coherent description of a situation which, on Wittgenstein's principles, ought to be indescribable because inconceivable. But this is only appearance; in fact, Strawson has begged the whole question. His description is vitiated at the outset as a contribution to the problem under discussion by containing terms the applicability of which is precisely what is in question: terms like "language," "use," "words," "sentences," "meaning"—and all without benefit of quotation marks. To say that observer B may form hypotheses about the meanings (the regular use) of the words in his subject's language is senseless unless one can speak of what his subject is doing in terms of the concepts of meaning, language, use, etc. From the fact that we can observe him going through certain motions and making certain sounds—which, were they to be performed by somebody else in another context, that of a human society, it would be quite legitimate to describe in those terms, it by no means follows that his activities are legitimately so describable. And the fact that B might correlate his subject's practice with his own does not establish Strawson's point.[39]

Once again this difficulty results from the reflexive relationship of theoretical level and object level, which was to have been eliminated through the reduction of language to stimulated behavior. Only one path leads out of this logical difficulty: the inclusion of the methodological rules in the empirical investigation itself. Communication among researchers can be conceived as verbal behavior, and the application of theories to reality can be included in the object domain of the analysis of behavior. That would be a naturalistic application of the behavioral-scientific theory of language back onto the communication of the behavioral scientists themselves. In this way, the behaviorist approach would become dependent on an empirically decidable question. If we accept this proposal, the value of the behavioral-scientific model would no longer be measured in terms of the criteria of a research strategy but would rather be submitted to a test: the model is meaningful if it succeeds in grasping the genesis of language in causal-analytic terms such that any form of verbal behavior, including the verbal behavior of the behaviorist researchers themselves, can be predicted with sufficient reliability.

4.4 B. F. Skinner attempted this with a learning theory of language. His theory claims to indicate the conditions under which rules for the application of linguistic signs are acquired.[40]

In a thorough critique of Skinner, Chomsky has shown that the process of language learning cannot be adequately grasped within the framework of learning theory. He shows that the concepts of stimulus and response, reward and punishment, reinforcement and extinction—concepts established in behavioral research—lose their operational clarity when applied to verbal behavior and are in fact only vague translations of the traditional expressions of mentalistic linguistic analysis. Skinner does not take into consideration the synthetic achievement of the rules that organize the elements of language. It is precisely the failure of the attempt to reduce language to behavior that makes the particular role of grammatical rules evident. They are not directly manifested in observable verbal behavior, and they cannot be derived from the sequence of behavioral responses to external stimuli or from corresponding combinations of signs. The grammar that we have mastered enables us to distinguish correctly constructed sentences from incorrect sentences, to generate or understand new sentences in given situations, and to produce and comprehend the ambiguity of reflexive, metaphorical, or ironic expressions, that is, the ambiguities of language use. These creative achievements of language can be analyzed with reference to an apparatus of internalized grammatical rules but cannot be derived from cumulative experiences in trial-and-error form:

We constantly read and hear new sequences of words, recognize them as sentences, and understand them. It is easy to show that the new events that we accept and understand as sentences are not related to those with which we are familiar by any simple notion of formal (or semantic or statistical) similarity or identity of grammatical frame. Talk of generalization in this case is entirely pointless and empty. It appears that we recognize a new item as a sentence not because it matches some familiar item in any simple way, but because it is generated by the grammar that each individual has somehow and in some form internalized.[41]

Chomsky conceives of grammar in terms of synthetic, or, in his terms, generative achievements. As an internalized system, grammar makes possible the selection of rules for the use of symbols and for new combinations of symbols that are compatible with a suitable sentence. In this generative perspective, grammar appears as the very essence of transcendental achievements. It is itself the product of a learning process, for children have to grow into the language system of their environment. But once it has been internalized, grammar sets the conditions for possible learning processes. It provides the person who has mastered it with possible forms of the interpretation of reality, thus with schemata for understanding the world, or with learning models. The learning of language takes place on a transcendental level that is different from the level of the learning process (behavior, attitudes) that has already been linguistically conditioned. Observation of children's rapid acquisition of extraordinarily complicated language structures leads Chomsky to postulate that we are organically equipped with a system of "language as such." He assumes "that the structure of the grammar internalized by the learner may be, to a presently quite unexpected degree, a reflection of the general character of his experience. It seems not unlikely that the organism brings, as its contribution to the acquisition of a particular language, a highly restrictive characterization of a class of generative systems from which the grammar of its language is selected on the basis of the presented linguistic data." [42] Be that as it may, in any case an analysis of the behavior of people who speak, understand language, and learn language that does not take into account the grammatical rules that are grasped independently thereof has no prospect of success: "It seems natural to suppose that the study of actual linguistic performance can be seriously pursued only to the extent that we have a good understanding of the generative grammars that are acquired by the learner and put to use by the speaker or hearer." [43]

Here Chomsky rejects linguistic behaviorism, pointing out that "the common characterization of language as a set of verbal habits or as a complex of present dispositions to verbal behavior, in which speakers of the same language have perforce come to resemble one another (Quine) is totally inadequate. Knowledge of one's language is not reflected directly in linguistic habits and dispositions, and it is clear that speakers of the same language or dialect may differ enormously in dispositions to verbal response, depending on personality, beliefs, and countless other extra-linguistic factors. [44]

Linguistic communication cannot be adequately understood on the level of stimulus-response behavior alone. It is the grammatical pattern that establishes the framework for the learning processes from which linguistic behaviorism tries to derive the grammatical pattern. At the same time, the system of rules, which plays a quasi-transcendental role, is not a constant of nature. In the processes through which it mediates the internalization of rules and thus the socialization of individuals, it is itself subject to social change.

The attempt to reduce language to behavior remains problematic. In principle, communicative action cannot be completely expressed in terms of adaptive behavior. Bennett reaches the same conclusion through a sort of thought experiment. He starts with the signal behavior of a bee dance and introduces new assumptions one by one in order to bring an idealized bee behavior nearer to the model of linguistic communication.[45] At the end of this fable of the bees the author has provided his creatures with language. Actions governed by norms have taken the place of regular behavioral responses controlled by signs and stimuli. Bennett introduces behavior contrary to norms as the criterion of linguistic communication. Only when the bees in his fable can break the rules that symbolically govern their behavior, and can thus act in accordance with maxims or expectations, does the expression "bee language" have a precise meaning. The steps in the fable, which are precisely constructed, show that the bees cannot reach this stage without the presentation overstepping the vocabulary of observable behavior. In contradistinction to behavior controlled by signs, action governed by norms presupposes rules the validity of which is guaranteed not by a natural law but rather intersubjectively through acknowledgment by the participating interpreters. Thus action taken by an interpreter in accordance with prevailing norms cannot be derived from an isolated connection between behavior, signal, and environment. Norms always rest on mutual recognition and thus presuppose an identity of meaning for the universe of all who participate, continuously over a period of time. Meanings that are constant in the sense of having intersubjective and temporally continuous validity can be constituted only as language.

MacIntyre also follows this line of argument in his critique of the conceptions of Marx and Pareto on the one hand and Weber on the other. They all seem to presuppose a causal relationship in social action between subjective convictions and manifest behaviors.[46] They claim that there is an empirical connection between the ideas and the behavior of acting subjects, regardless of whether the ideas or the modes of behavior are thought of as the dependent variable. Beliefs and ideas influence social life, and social life influences beliefs and ideas. MacIntyre challenges the idea that the distinction between these classes of variables is meaningful for social action. It is true that intentional contents can be studied independently of the actions they serve to orient. They have an existence in symbolic contexts that is independent of actions. The converse, however, is not true. Actions cannot be understood without reference to the intentions that guide them; that is, independently of something like ideas, they cannot be studied at all. An empirical connection cannot exist between actions and intentions, because they are not independently identifiable quantities. Rather, they relate to one another in the same way that signs and meanings relate to one another in words. Actions express intentions in the same way; or better, they represent them in the same way that linguistic symbols represent their meanings. Just as signs cannot be understood without the symbolized content, actions cannot be understood without their intentional content, unless they are no longer identified *as* signs or *as* actions. But if intentions appear independently of actions only in linguistic expressions, the relationship between idea and behavior merely reproduces the connection between a symbolized meaning and an observable behavior we assume can be interpreted as action. This connection is a logical, not an empirical one. To determine whether specific ideas "go" with specific ways of behaving, we carry out operations that correspond more closely to hermeneutic than to empirical-analytic procedures. We test whether the hypothetically assumed intention that allows an observed behavior to be interpreted as action can be formulated in propositions that accord with the expressed or reported ideas. In this sense we test the "consistency" of behavior and ideas: "It is because actions express beliefs, because actions are a vehicle for our beliefs that they can be described as consistent or inconsistent with beliefs expressed in avowals. Actions, as much as utterances, belong to the realm of statements, concepts and beliefs; and the relation of belief to action is not external and contingent, but internal and conceptual."[47]

If action is linked with intentions in such a way that it can be derived from the propositions that bring these intentions to expression, then conversely the thesis is also true that a subject can carry out only those actions whose intentions he can in principle describe. The limits of action are determined by the range of possible descriptions. This in turn is established by the structures of language in which the self-understanding and worldview of a social group is articulated. Thus the boundaries of action are drawn by the boundaries of language.

All relevant investigations—the logical discussion of intentional statements, the empirical analysis of linguistic behavior, the linguistic analysis of language-learning, and the methodological investigation of the relationship of ideas and modes of behavior—agree on one conclusion: the reduction of intentional actions to stimulated behavior is not possible. But the fact of successful behavioral-scientific analyses in the area of social action contradicts this. This contradiction can be cleared up, provided that we do not confuse the strategy of the behavioral sciences with their declared self-understanding.

The program of behavioral science requires that animal and human behavior be analyzed according to the same methodological rules as natural events in physics, namely, without reference to meaning that is supposedly accessible only through introspection. In fact, however, the restriction of the procedure to observable behavior does not satisfy this postulate. For an anticipation of intentional relationships has slipped into the theoretical approach unnoticed. Behavior itself is defined as intelligible behavior; it only appears to be "objective." Behavior is always interpreted from the perspective of a situation we interpolate from our own experience. The class of observable events we call "modes of behavior" is distinguished from the class of other events through a reference system that makes an intelligible connection explicit. The latter establishes a functionalist relation among the initial state of an organism, its environment (with conditions of existence and stimuli), and the end state of the organism: they are linked by an observable behavioral response. Functionalistically this connection is made from the perspective of a need-satisfaction that is inaccessible to direct observation. This means that we have always already understood how to satisfy a need; we would never understand the need through observation alone. This interpretation is not simply added from the realm of one's own experience; it furnishes the preliminary criterion for delimiting the class of events that can be understood as behavior; it also permits theoretical assumptions about the constant meaning of classes of events for a given organism. Thus biological behavioral research deals with stimuli that "mean" enemy, prey, nesting, or sex. Learning theory deals, independent of instinctual tendencies, with two classes of stimuli that the organism can clearly distinguish as reward or punishment. Thus in both cases behavior is functioning within an intentional context.[48] The hypotheses of behavioral science cannot refer to events that are completely free of intentional content.

On the level of animal behavior, on the other hand, the moment of intentionality has not yet become detached from the modes of behavior and incorporated into symbolic contexts. Only the autonomy of intentional contents in language makes action possible. A more or less rigid system of instincts that defines meanings specific to a species from behind, so to speak, and attaches them to selected environmental conditions, is only freed from one-to-one correlations with the environment at the cultural level. Only then can the system of instincts be subjected in turn to new definitions, through a linguistic system with variable meanings. Whereas meanings that are signaled depend on need dispositions and merely indicate preselected objects of drives, symbolic meanings that have become autonomous in linguistic systems have acquired the power to interpret needs retroactively. Action theory bases itself on this in assuming that the course of an action must be understood through the interpretation of the acting subject himself. The motive for the action shifts from the level of a system of drives to that of linguistic communication. Behavioral research, in contrast, maintains an attitude even toward social action in which, again, linguistic symbols are understood as signals, motivations through symbolized meaning are understood as drive motivations, and intentional actions are understood as stimulated modes of behavior. This is achieved not through the complete suspension of meaning and its understanding but rather through a radical limitation of the horizon opened by language to a few elements. In this way the reduced components remain fundamentally tied to the horizon of linguistic communication. When we call the abstraction of need satisfaction and deprivation "reward and punishment," we are referring to a system of prevailing norms; and no matter how elementary the drives we distinguish qualitatively from one another by referring to "enemies," "prey," and "sex" may seem to us, we shall never arrive at such a thing as drives that have not been linguistically interpreted.

The indissoluble but unadmitted connection of the behaviorist perspective with a preunderstanding, articulated in ordinary language, of experiences in our social lifeworld makes the possibility of behavioral-scientific theories of human behavior plausible. Although language cannot be reduced to behavior, under the presupposition of a preunderstanding, bound to linguistic communication, of the secret intentionality of behavior, we can analyze intentional action from the perspective of behavioral research. Because the behavioral sciences systematically disregard what is specific to collective cultural life, the information they produce has meaning only within specifiable limits. If we do not wish to pay this price to reduce action to behavior, we shall have to have recourse to general theories of intentional action, and they will have to gain access to social facts through the understanding of meaning.

5 Three Forms of Functionalism

5.1 The behaviorist approach has the advantage that it encounters no fundamental complications in the construction of theories. If we have accepted the basic assumptions of behavior theory, we can proceed as we do in the natural sciences: as in the natural sciences, we are concerned with deriving and confirming assumptions about empirical uniformities; we are not concerned with structural distinctions between object domains. When, in contrast, the object domain is designated as a class of social facts, which, as intentional actions, can be understood only through interpretation based on the understanding of meaning, theory formation is affected. How are general theories of social action possible at all?

If we understood social action as action under prevailing norms, theories of action must refer to contexts of norms that permit us to predict the course of interactions. Since norms are given in symbolic form, it seems obvious to derive systems of action from the conditions of linguistic communication. Where the boundaries of language define the boundaries of action, the structures of language determine the channels of possible interaction. Thus a systematic extension of the understanding of meaning, which in any case provides access to social facts, will suffice for the analysis of the contexts of communicative action. We can make use of the methods of linguistic analysis or linguistic hermeneutics. Linguistics concerns itself with the grammatical rules for communication within a given society, and hermeneutics concerns itself beyond this with the traditions that are appropriated culturally within the linguistic framework of a society.[49]

These procedures, however, are too far-reaching for an interpretive sociology—following this path, sociology would be dissolved into intellectual history or comparative linguistics. We may ask, in fact, whether linguistic analysis and linguistic hermeneutics actually cover the domain of social action. There is certainly always an element of cultural tradition in the definition of prevailing norms, and the communicative context that regulates interactions is certainly established through the rules of a binding grammar. But these systems of traditional and systematically ordered symbols only provide the material, of which part is used for the institutionalization of action. In the terminology of Max Weber, which is widespread in current sociology because of Weber's influence in America, we can say that in a certain way sociology presupposes the value-interpretation of the hermeneutic sciences, but is itself concerned with cultural tradition and value-systems only insofar as they have attained normative power in the orienting of action. Sociology is concerned only with institutionalized values. We can now formulate our question in a more specific form: How are general theories of action in accordance with institutionalized values (or prevailing norms) possible?

General theories of this kind must proceed from basic assumptions that cover neither only the empirical context of observable events nor only the logical context of symbolized meaning. For, on the one hand, prevailing norms are institutionalized contexts of meaning that cannot be adequately expressed in variables of observable behavior; and, on the other hand, they do not have the form of pure maxims of strategic action from which possible decisions can be deduced. The required theories must permit assumptions about the empirical context of prevailing norms. In one sense this context extends beyond the subjectively intended meaning of those who act in accordance with norms; but as a real connection among norms it shares with them the element of meaningfulness. The connection is not intended by the acting subjects, but at the same time it is intentional. We can also say that the meaning institutionalized in rules and roles is manifest, whereas the meaning of the objective context of these roles remains latent. Lawlike assumptions appropriate for the explanation of communicative action refer to covariances of grammatical rules, social roles, and empirical conditions that are in turn latently meaningful. This is a consequence of the intelligibility of social facts.

The meaning intended in action and objectivated both in language and in actions is transferred from social facts to the relationships among facts; there is no empirical uniformity in the domain of social action that is not intelligible, even though not intended. But if the covariances asserted in the lawlike hypotheses are to be meaningful in this intelligibility, they must themselves be conceived as parts of an intentional context. From the perspective of normal empirical-scientific theory with an elementaristic structure, the various lawlike hypotheses have an exclusively logical relationship with one another that in no way expresses a real connection between the covariances asserted in the individual laws. For this reason, the additional assumption of an objective context within which empirical uniformities appear as meaningful is required; it is introduced in the form of a functionalist assumption. One proceeds on the assumption that general theories of social action refer to systems in which elements fulfill specifiable functions for a defined state or for a continuous change of state of the system. The functionalist assumption presumes that a systematic connection exists in reality, not only for purposes of analysis. It permits the usual functional connection between individual variables, formulated in statements of laws, to be further interpreted as meaningful with reference to the overall functional context of system maintenance.

The philosophy of history has made us familiar with proposals for such objective-intentional contexts. They are ascribed to the intention of a collective subject that achieves its goal over the heads of acting individuals. The plan can be understood teleologically, in which case it is based on the *artisan model* of instrumental action through which an end is reached through appropriate means. The plan can also be conceived dialectically, in which case it is based on the *dramaturgic model* of communicative action, in which an author makes an experience transparent through the role-playing of actors. Whereas the state of a completed production process can be identified through observation, the experience of a dramatic event can be explicated only in speech. In the first case the intention is concerned with the work that is finished; in the second, with the word that resolves. Both intentions are appropriate for interpretations in terms of the philosophy of history, but not for an empirical-scientific functionalism that has to avoid any world-historical subject.

Another model is borrowed from biology: the reproduction of every individual organism seems to warrant the assumption of purposiveness without purposeful activity, and thus of an objective-intentional context. According to this model, systems can be understood as organized unities that, under changing circumstances, maintain themselves in a specific state through self-regulation. The adaptive behavior of self-regulating systems can also be interpreted as instrumental action, but the assumption of an acting subject is superfluous. The intention of self-preservation is objective, as it were, not only for the elements within the system but also "in itself"; for it does not need to be justified by being ascribed to a collective subject that acts behind the backs of individuals and groups.

The social sciences have taken over this functionalist approach from biology. This gives the appearance of being unproblematic because in the realm of social action there is a structure that corresponds to that of the organism—the organization. Social organizations can be planned and directed, but afterward they reproduce themselves in the manner of self-regulating systems. Just as strategic games provide the model for the theoretical framework of decision theory, so social organizations provide the model for the theoretical framework of systems research. Nature, however, provides no prototype for social games as it does for the social arrangements of the organism. After initial steps in the older German sociology and in Durkheim, the English cultural anthropologists (Malinowski, Radcliffe-Brown) were the next to adopt a functionalist framework for empirical analyses.[50] The biological model is in evidence:

If we consider any recurrent part of the life-process (of an organism), such as respiration, digestion, etc., its function is the part it plays in, the contribution it makes to, the life of the organism as a whole. As the terms are here being used a cell or an organ has an activity and that activity has a function. It is true that we commonly speak of the secretion of gastric fluid as a "function" of the stomach. As the words are here used we should say that this is an "activity" of the stomach, the "function" of which is to change the proteins of food into a form in which these are absorbed and distributed by the blood to the tissues. We may note that the function of a recurrent physiological process is thus a correspondence between it and the needs (i.e., necessary conditions of existence) of the organism. . . .

To turn from organic life to social life, if we examine such a community as an African or Australian tribe we can recognize the existence of a social structure. Individual human beings, the essential units in this instance, are connected by a definite set of social relations into an integrated whole. The continuity of the social structure, like that of an organic structure, is not destroyed by changes in the units. Individuals may leave the society, by death or otherwise; others may enter it. The continuity of structure is maintained by the process of social life, which consists of the activities and interactions of the individual human beings and of the organized groups into which they are united: The social life of the community is here defined as the functioning of the social structure. The function of any recurrent activity, such as the punishment of a crime, or a funeral ceremony, is the part it plays in the social life as a whole and therefore the contribution it makes to the maintenance of the structural continuity.[51]

Primitive societies, with which cultural anthropology is primarily concerned, have the advantage of being units that are relatively easy to delimit and relatively static. Merton and above all Parsons have gone on to elaborate the functionalist framework for social-scientific theories as such.[52] This development follows an internal logic, for as soon as we conceive social action to be intentional, general theories with elementaristic structures become unusable.[53] Only when social norms that institutionalize cultural patterns or values are understood as structures within self-regulating systems can social processes be analyzed on the basis of assumptions about the understandable empirical context of organized behavioral expectations. The functions that they then have in maintaining or changing a defined state of the system are an expression of the latently meaningful empirical context of the manifestly, that is, subjectively, meaningful actions of individuals and groups. Without a functionalist framework, assumptions about the empirical context of social norms would be possible only under the condition that the norms be expressed exclusively in variables of observable behavior, and thus that social action be reduced to behavior and stripped of its intentional content. This would contradict our presupposition.

Parsons conceives social systems as the functionalist context of institutions. In them, cultural values, which enter the system from above, as it were, are made binding for social action. The normative validity of the roles and rules defined on the basis of the stock of cultural traditions is secured through their adequate integration with drive energies, which, along with personality traits, enter the system "from below." The institutions mediate action-orienting values with interpreted need-dispositions (value orientations with motivational forces or potency). Institutions are composed of roles and norms that are binding for groups and individuals. Institutions stand in a functional relationship when they can be delimited as a system (with controlling values and internal conditions) from the external conditions of the environment.

In recent studies Parsons has been using the language of cybernetics.[54] Control values define the equilibrium state in which the system maintains itself. Internal conditions define the drive potential that the system must process. External conditions define the environment to which a system, if does not control them, must adapt. It is assumed that every system tends toward the maintenance or achievement of a desired state. Every state of a system can be described with the help of values that can be independently varied in four dimensions. These are measures of the fulfillment of four basic functions on which the maintenance of the system depends: the degree to which given goals have been achieved, the flexibility of adaptation to external conditions, the degree of integration, and the stability of existing institutional patterns: "The four exigencies to which a system of action is subject are those of 'goal attainment,' 'adaptation,' 'integration,' and 'pattern maintenance.' These are dimensions of a space in the sense that a state of the system or of its units' relations to each other may be described, relative to satisfactory points of reference, as 'farther along' or less far along on each of these dimensions; a change of state may be described in terms of increases or decreases in the values of each of these variables."[55]

Institutions stand in a functional relationship when a change in their elements can be measured in terms of how they influence a state of the system determined by control values. The steering mechanisms through which the system maintains its equilibrium work on the model of cybernetic governors: even when they possess a lesser amount of energy, universal media, such as gold in economic systems, regulate systems with essentially greater amounts of energy. Parsons attempts to conceive media such as power and public opinion as regulative languages, like money. They regulate activities within institutions, and changes in the relations of institutions to one another, in such a way that the control values of the system are adhered to.

These few remarks will have to suffice for the characterization of the functionalist approach in social-scientific systems research. Parsons himself has elaborated this approach for processes of the macroeconomic cycle and political will-formation.[56] Clearly, like living organisms, domains of social organization can be understood and analyzed as self-regulating systems. If the logic of systems research is the same in both cases, and if the similarity between organization and organism from the functionalist perspective is not a false one, then Parsons has demonstrated the conditions of the possibility of general theories of social action. But this is disputed by the positivists, with good reason.[57]

5.2 Hempel and Nagel have analyzed the logical form of functionalist explanation. In every case, two preconditions must be met: the empirically reliable delimitation of a system and the identification of a specific state of the system, under the assumption that the system tends to stay in this state of equilibrium even under altered external conditions. The task of a functionalist analysis consists in grasping the connections among variables that influence the equilibrium state of the system in order to establish how these covarying quantities are related to other variables, both inside and outside the system. If the state of equilibrium is characterized by a process P, then the function that an element or a relationship among elements A has for the maintenance of the state of equilibrium may be expressed as follows: "Every system S with organization C in environment E engages in process P; if S with organization C and in environment E does not have A, then S does not engage in P; hence, S with organization C must have A"[58]

The functionalist explanation makes possible statements about the *consequences* that a part of the system has for the maintenance of a specific state of the system; this teleological statement can also be employed in a nonteleological form. In that case it gives the sufficient *conditions* for the designated state of equilibrium of a system. Both statements are arrived at through deduction and are equivalent; both establish the same empirically verifiable causal relationship between identifiable quantities. To this extent, the logic of functionalist explanation does not differ from that of causal explanation.

Despite this equivalence, the functionalist approach is not interchangeable with the traditional one. For not all physical systems are organized in such a way that they adhere to specific control values in changing external environments. It is especially the organization of living beings that lends itself to analysis in terms of such self-regulating mechanisms. The functionalist viewpoint corresponds to a specific class of objects that are organized on the model of purposiveness without purposeful activity:

On the hypothesis that a teleological explanation can always be translated, with respect to what it explicitly asserts, into an equivalent nonteleological one, let us now make more explicit in what way two such explanations nevertheless do differ. The difference appears to be as follows: Teleological explanations focus attention on the culminations and products of specific processes, and in particular upon the contributions of various parts of a system to the maintenance of its global properties or modes of behaviour. They view the operations of things from the perspective of certain selected "wholes" or integrated systems to which the things belong; and they are therefore concerned with characteristics of the parts of such wholes, only insofar as those traits of the parts are relevant to the various complex features or activities assumed to be distinctive of those wholes. Nonteleological explanations, on the other hand, direct attention primarily to the conditions under which specified processes are initiated or persist, and to the factors upon which the continued manifestations of certain inclusive traits of a system are contingent. They seek to exhibit the integrated behaviours of complex systems as the resultants of more elementary factors, frequently identified as constituent parts of those systems; and they are therefore concerned with traits of complex wholes almost exclusively to the extent that these traits are dependent on assumed characteristics of the elementary factors. In brief, the difference between teleological and nonteleological explanations, as has already been suggested, is one of emphasis and perspective in formulation.[59]

What is crucial here for the positivist expounding the logical unity of the sciences is that the causal connections among the variables in a self-regulating system, as well as those between the system and its environment, can be analyzed without reference to a meaning or goal that is anchored in reality itself. Teleology is a matter of formulation, not a formulation of the matter. Hempel too understands functionalism from this perspective, as a useful research strategy that proves its value heuristically through the fruitfulness of its hypothesis construction. But the moment of intelligibility in self-regulating systems, which we can interpret as purposeful in terms of the model of instrumental action, remains external to the functionalist method.[60] This is certainly true of biological research. Nagel and Hempel, however, overlook the fact that the functionalist approach recommends itself for social-scientific analyses precisely because of the moment of intelligibility. We have shown that the meaningful structuring of facts with which interpretive sociology is concerned permits a general theory of social action only if the relationships among facts are understandable. Under these conditions the functionalist framework has not only an analytic significance; rather, it represents, on the theoretical level, one of the characteristics of its object domain—namely, the intentionality of the interconnections of social systems themselves, which, of course, is not ascribed to a subject.

Since they remain fixated on the model of a behavioral science, positivists are naturally blind to this state of affairs; but their logical clarification of the functionalist mode of proceeding brings to light a point that is critical for the social sciences. In biology, a functionalist explanation can generally satisfy the stated preconditions without difficulty. A biological organism is by nature a delimited system; and the state in which an organism reproduces its life can easily be identified through a series of important life processes (metabolism). In sociology, on the other hand, both preconditions are either difficult to fulfill or cannot be fulfilled at all. In terms of delimiting social systems from their environment, it may be a question of a pragmatic difficulty that can be overcome through skillful definitions; but it seems doubtful to me that systems research in the strict empirical-analytic sense is possible when the system units are not merely introduced but actually constructed by definition.

The other difficulty, the need for an adequately reliable identification of the equilibrium state, is fundamental in nature. The reproduction of social life is not determined through values that can be grasped descriptively, as is that of organic life. Physical survival is a necessary but in no instance sufficient condition for the maintenance of social systems. Nor can one find in social processes important life functions that suffice to define the maintenance of the system in a state of equilibrium, as is the case with organic functions in living creatures. The difficulty is clear: the criterion for historical life and survival is dependent on the interpretations that have validity in a social system; but these interpretations are in turn dependent on the objective conditions of the system and its environment. Parsons makes the mistake of regarding whole social systems as if they were individual social facts. He presumes that the control values that define a system's equilibrium are "given" in the same way as the cultural values that determine social norms: "We can say that the regulating elements have primarily normative and cultural reference."[61] In fact, parameters for the desired state of a social system cannot be determined in the same way as for the parametrically determined state of equilibrium of an organism. Thus the empirical values that can be determined in the dimensions specified for a given system cannot be given an optimal value. Such control values are not "given," although they could be "found" through political will-formation. But this would be possible only under the presumption of a general and public discussion of the assembled members of the society based on information about given conditions for the reproduction of the system. In this way, relative agreement about a value system could be achieved that would include the objective control values that had previously been withheld from the knowledge and will of the citizens. In such a form of communication, previously acknowledged cultural values would not only function as criteria; the cultural values themselves would be submitted to discussion. They would be pragmatically reviewed in conjunction with available techniques and strategies, taking both given and potentially changing circumstances into consideration, and would be purged of their ideological components.

The control values that Parsons introduces for social systems refer not to actual but to possible conditions of functioning. They are dependent on rules of evaluation that would have to be constructed through a hypothetically specifiable procedure of will-formation. Without these standards we do not have a system of reference within which we could measure the values for goal-attainment, integration, adaptation, and pattern maintenance in terms of control values for an equilibrium state. Nagel's critique of social-scientific functionalism seems compelling:

It follows that proposed explanations aiming to exhibit the functions of various items in a social system in either maintaining or altering the system have no substantive content, unless the state that is allegedly maintained or altered is formulated more precisely than has been customary. It also follows that the claims functionalists sometimes advance (whether in the form of "axioms" or of hypotheses to be investigated) concerning the "integral" character or "functional unity" of social systems produced by the "working together" of their parts with a "sufficient degree of harmony" and "internal consistency," or concerning the "vital function" and "indispensable part" every element in a society plays in the "working whole," cannot be properly judged as either sound or dubious or even mistaken. For in the absence of descriptions precise enough to identify unambiguously the states which are supposedly maintained in a social system, those claims cannot be subjected to empirical control, since they are compatible with every conceivable matter of fact and with every outcome of empirical inquiries into actual societies.[62]

Rüschemeyer[63] draws the conclusion from these considerations in the logic of science. He formulates the following conditions for functionalist analysis: first, the social system about which statements are to be made must be empirically delimited; second, the state of the system for which self-maintaining tendencies are assumed must be operationally determined; third, the functional requirements of this state must be identifiable; fourth, it must be possible to specify the alternative processes that correspond to the same requirements. Rüschemeyer does not see, however, that in the social sciences conditions two and three (and condition four, which depends on them) can be fulfilled only through normative prescription. We cannot grasp a state of equilibrium for a delimitable social system descriptively; rather, we may prescribe control values for such a state from a pragmatic point of view. This is how systems research operates in the economic domain. In making the transition from organisms to organizations, which are not "determined" in the same way, we have to abandon functionalism's descriptive claim. But then what Parsons proposes with an empirical-analytic intention becomes a mode of systems research that investigates the functioning of social institutions given pragmatically predetermined system goals. Technical imperatives assume the logical position occupied in theories of strategic action by hypothetical maxims. In both cases, the status of statements—which hold more information, the more empirically derived data are included in the calculation—is the same: like decision theory, systems research produces information that can be employed prescriptively, thus the kind of information that we have called second-order technological knowledge. We would do well to distinguish between the systems research with empirical-analytic intent that is spreading in the biological sciences and a systems research that, in view of its object domain, must proceed normative-analytically, whether or not it is aware of this.

5.3 The logical restriction of functionalist theories of action to the validity of normative-analytic sciences is not satisfying. Discussions of the meaning and limits of functionalism[64] still exhibit the intent, with all due reservations, to find a usable empirical-analytic frame of reference. The older, historically oriented sociology was also systems research with an empirical intent. I suspect that if we abandoned the claim to establish *general* theories of social action, we could achieve a historically substantive functionalist investigation of social systems. This method corresponds not only to a controversial scientific tradition but also to a not very widespread scientific practice (I am thinking here of the work of Mills, Marcuse, Riesman, Schelsky, and Dahrendorf). At this point I would like to discuss two difficulties that point toward a solution through rehistorizing social analysis.

The first difficulty results from the fact that the analysis of role-systems presupposes comprehension of so-called cultural value systems. The action-orienting meaning of cultural norms derives from an accompanying cultural tradition. True, the social sciences are concerned with traditional semantic contents only insofar as they are incorporated in institutions; but the problematic of the understanding of meaning cannot on that account be displaced onto the historical-hermeneutic sciences through a kind of division of labor. For this would not eliminate the hermeneutic problematic but simply reduce it to the level of an unreflected point of departure. If they are to be grasped descriptively as facts, and not construed as pure maxims of behavior, value systems pose the same methodological problem for the social scientist as the meaning of documents does for the historian or the meaning of texts for the philologist. Institutionalized values also form part of the worldview of social groups that is handed down in ordinary language, is more or less articulated, but is always historically concrete. Parsons divests the understanding of handed-down meanings of its problematic through the simplifying assumption of value-universalism. According to that assumption, the meaning-contents objectivated in value systems are not embedded in unique cultures and traditions; rather, they are constructed of fundamental value-components that remain constant in different cultures and epochs while merely appearing in different combinations.[65] This elementaristic assumption, in conjunction with the presumption of the autonomy of the value system of institutionalized science, precludes the question whether theories of action, in the unavoidable dimension of a hermeneutic appropriation of traditional meaning, must not confront the problem that Max Weber always considered under the name of value-interpretation. The reconnection of *Verstehen* to the initial hermeneutic situation is linked with value-interpretation, which has to direct itself to historically objectivated cultural meanings from within the irreducible value relationships of its own situation.

A social science that does not simply turn its back on the emerging hermeneutic problematic cannot avoid admitting that a preunderstanding of historical situations is inevitably incorporated into the fundamental assumptions of its theories. This may make the identification of social systems easier; but it does not accomplish much in terms of the identification of a state of equilibrium. For cultural values not only serve to regulate social systems; they also function as goals within the system, goals that are not reflected in the values themselves. Only if it were possible to distinguish the utopian, the purposive-rational in pragmatic terms, and the ideological contents of value systems, could we specify for a given system the objectively possible conditions of a state of equilibrium. Thus the second difficulty consists in the fact that the categorial framework proposed by Parsons does not permit such distinctions.

In the theoretical framework of action theory, motives for action are harmonized with institutionalized values, thus with the intersubjectively prevailing meaning of normatively binding behavioral expectations. Drive energies that have not been integrated and find no legitimate chance of satisfaction in role-systems cannot be grasped analytically. But we may presume that these repressed needs that have not been reabsorbed by social roles, transformed into motivations, and sanctioned have their interpretations nevertheless. Either these interpretations transcend what exists and represent a group-identity that has not yet been formed, in the form of utopian anticipation, or, transformed into ideologies, they serve to legitimize instances of drive-suppression and projective substitute gratification; in other words, they serve to legitimate positions of authority and to direct socially undesirable drive impulses—that is, those that cannot be used for collective self-preservation—into non-threatening channels. Given such criteria, a state of equilibrium would be determined by whether the authority system of a society realized the utopian contents and dissolved the ideological contents to the degree made objectively possible by the given state of the forces of production and technological progress.[66] In that case, however, society can no longer be conceived exclusively as a system of self-preservation; the objective-intentional context is no longer determined by the purposive-rational adequacy of instrumental action or adaptive behavior, that is, by technical rationality. Rather, the meaning in terms of which the functionality of social processes is measured is now linked to the idea of a communication free from domination. The functionalism of the artisan model gives way, without falling back into philosophy of history, to that of the dramaturgic model.[67]

These two approaches to theories of social action are complementary: the level of adaptive behavior is too low, that of communicative action too high. In the span of historical memory, social action has always been both. This is what we need to understand. The reduction of action to stimulated behavior runs up against the limits of linguistic communication; it is not possible to eradicate intentionality completely. But the projection of behavior onto the level of intentional action proves to be an anticipation that is in need of correction: action cannot be completely inferred from subjectively intended meanings. The empirical context of actions regulated by social norms transcends the manifest meaning of intentions and calls for an objective frame of reference in which the latent meaning of functions can be grasped; for in the final analysis, the actors' orientation is not the same thing as their motives. Traditional meanings or cultural values are institutionalized and thereby gain normatively binding power over social action. Institutionalization takes previously free-floating intentions or behavioral expectations and binds to them a sufficient quantity of energies or needs whose interpretation accords with the content of role-definitions. The institutionalization of values is equivalent to a corresponding channeling of drive energies. If we do not proceed on the basis of unfounded presuppositions of harmony, however, the binding of instinctual energies to rules and roles is always coupled with the repression of interpreted needs that cannot be integrated into the roles offered. The rigidity of institutions, which hinders reflection, can be measured by the relationship of integrated to suppressed needs. When both motivate behavior equally, it becomes evident that we need to understand the institutionalization of values dialectically. By giving intentional behavioral expectations intersubjective validity and thus motivating force, the institutionalization of values transforms repressed needs both into stimuli for unintended modes of behavior and parapraxes and into a potential for dreams that transcend conscious intentions. Thus social action is the combined result of reactive compulsions and meaningful interactions. The ratio of action that is merely elicited by split-off motives to action that is intentionally guided by the communication of meaning determines the degree of freedom of the social action— the degree of flexibility of institutions and the degree of individuation of the individuals. These can be read in the aggregate condition of history at any point. The emancipation of the human race from the compulsion of nature is mirrored in it, as is the reproduction of that compulsion.

Only when split-off motives and deeply internalized rules have been understood in their objective connection with the rational compulsions of collective self-preservation on the one hand and the irrational compulsions of superfluous authorities on the other, when they have been reconciled with subjectively meaningful motives in the minds of the acting subjects themselves, can social action develop as truly communicative action. But a theory that does not incorporate this understanding will make unreflected predeterminations in a matter about which we have no apriori certainty; it will be making methodological decisions about whether we more closely resemble animals or gods. Those who have prematurely concluded that we resemble gods lead their heroes through a back door into the animal realm again. The acting subjects whose intentions have been acknowledged suddenly find themselves and their cultural values yoked in systems that respond only to the fundamental biological values of survival and efficient adaptation.

So much extravagant wisdom must positivism claim before it can place dimensions of what is knowable off limits of itself and to others.

III

On the Problem of
Understanding Meaning in the
Empirical-Analytic Sciences
of Action

The understanding of meaning (*Sinnverstehen*) becomes a methodological problem when the appropriation of traditional meanings is involved: the "meaning" to be explicated has the status of a fact, something encountered empirically. The understanding of symbolic contexts that we produce ourselves is unproblematic. Thus, formalized statements such as mathematical propositions or rigorous theories do not impose tasks of hermeneutic interpretation on us as do traditional texts or documents. For metalinguistic rules of constitution are part of formalized languages, and with their help we can reconstruct given statements, that is, produce them again ourselves. In this respect, analytic thinking is justly contrasted with hermeneutic discussion.[1]

Nor does the problematic of understanding meaning arise in the social sciences as long as they proceed in a normative-analytic manner. Behavioral maxims (or, in systems research, the values of the goal state) are introduced analytically. The theory preestablishes the "meaning" of social action (or of the behavior of the parts of a system). It is defined on the theoretical level and does not need to be grasped and explicated on the level of data. Insofar as the social sciences proceed in an empirical-analytic manner, the understanding of meaning cannot be formalized in this way. If they follow the model of the behavioral sciences, the problem of understanding meaning is simplified by limiting the data to observable events. Behaviorism does not, as we have shown, achieve a complete suspension of meaning and its understanding; but because of its radical restriction of the linguistic horizon to a few elementary and well operationalized meanings (satisfaction of needs, punishment and reward), the preunderstanding that it assumes does not need to be thematized. To the extent that the empirical-analytic sciences of action do not accept behavioristic restrictions on their object domains, their theories have reference to objectively meaningful contexts of subjectively meaningful action. The result is the functionalist approach to theory construction. In that framework the problematic of understanding meaning cannot be eliminated although it can be reduced to the level of an unreflected point of departure. Parsons's thesis of value universalism is an example of that.

Since Dilthey, we have been accustomed to thinking of the distinguishing feature of the *Geisteswissenschaften* as the relationship within them of the epistemological subject to an object domain that itself shares the structures of subjectivity. In the idealist tradition, this particular position of subject and object can be interpreted as spirit encountering itself in its objectivations. Collingwood still adopts this view. Historians and philologists are concerned not with an objective context of events but with the symbolic context of a spirit that expresses itself in them. Reflection on what the hermeneutic sciences do must thus first clarify how the formative process in which spirit objectivates itself is to be understood, and how, complementarily, the act of understanding that translates what has been objectivated back into something inward is to be understood. In this tradition, methodological considerations, in the narrower sense, of the logical structure of theories and the relationship of theories to experience were superseded by epistemological investigations of the transcendental-logical structure of the world of possible subjects and the conditions of the intersubjectivity of understanding. The phenomenology of understanding meaning then took the place of the psychology of understanding expressions that was grounded in *Lebensphilosophie*. This problematic was then linked with linguistic communication and developed, on the one hand, by linguistic philosophy via the indirect route of positivist linguistic analysis and, on the other hand, by philosophical hermeneutics, following Husserl and Heidegger.

These discussions, which are certainly not less articulate or conducted on a lower level than those of analytic philosophy of science, have nevertheless failed to have an impact on recent work in the logic of the social sciences. This is due in part to the idealist presuppositions that, especially in Germany, have been borrowed from the philosophy of reflection [*Reflexionsphilosophie*, i.e., German Idealism—translator] almost as a matter of course. Among these is the model of a spirit that understands itself in its objectivations. In part the reception of these discussions has been inhibited by the fact that the relevant phenomenological, linguistic, and hermeneutic studies have not been conducted in the only dimension that positivism considers appropriate for methodology. Whereas positivism, with the direct attitude characteristic of the sciences, discusses methological rules for the construction and verification of theories as if it were a question of the logical connection between symbols, phenomenological, linguistic, and hermeneutic analyses, with the indirect attitude characteristic of reflection, are directed to the epistemological context in which methodological rules are considered to be rules of synthesis and conceived in terms of the constitution of possible experience.

I would like to discuss the problematic of understanding meaning not so much directly in terms of this transcendental-logical framework, but rather on a methodological level that even positivist prejudices cannot eliminate. Kaplan's recent methodology of the sciences of action,[2] which takes the viewpoints of instrumentalism into consideration, offers a point of departure. This tradition, which goes back to Dewey and Peirce, has the advantage of being closely linked to a logical analysis of inquiry without assuming the positivist restriction of methodology to linguistic analysis. Pragmatism has always conceived methodological rules as norms for the practice of inquiry. The frame of reference for the philosophy of science is therefore the communicative context and the scientific community of researchers, thus a network of interactions and operations based on linguistically secured intersubjectivity. Thus Kaplan makes a distinction from the outset between logic-in-use and reconstructed logic. The task of methodology is to reflect on the rules of research practice in terms of the intentions of that practice rather than, conversely, making research practice fit the abstract principles that are valid for the deductive structure of formalized languages.[3]

Not only does the pragmatist logic of science emphasize the descriptive moment in contrast to the constructive; it also avoids the positivist prejudice concerning the status of the rules that govern research practice. It does not conceive them as grammatical rules from the outset, but rather knows that in another respect they are also equivalent to rules of social action. In other words, it does not preclude a transcendental analysis. Yet in doing so it does not succumb to the prejudice of subjective idealism according to which the rules of synthesis are part of the makeup of an invariant consciousness that transcends experienceable reality. This approach is so liberal that it allows the problematic of the understanding of meaning to become visible. But even within this frame of reference, the full implications of the problematic are not understood. Thus, unfortunately, this thematic complex has retained something of the appearance of a European speciality that belongs to the unassimilated residue of traditional philosophy and can make no serious claim to a place in the corpus of the philosophy of science. But the problematic can be thoroughly expounded on the level of methodology in the strict sense. It is the doorway through which methodology must pass if reflection, which positivism has immobilized, is to be revived.

6 The Phenomenological Approach

6.1 The object domain of the sciences of action consists of symbols and modes of behavior that cannot be conceived *as* actions independently of symbols. Here access to data is constituted not solely through the observation of events but at the same time through the understanding of contexts of meaning. In this sense we can distinguish sensory from communicative experience. Naturally, all sensory experiences are interpreted; to that extent they are not independent of prior communication. And conversely, understanding is not possible without observation of signs. But communicative experience is directed not to matters of fact, as observation is, but rather to preinterpreted matters of fact. It is not merely the perception of facts that is symbolically structured, but rather the facts as such. Unless we artificially privilege one of the two modes of behavior and largely ignore the other one, as the behavioral sciences do, difficulties arise that "are not diminished by assertions of the universal applicability of the scientific method."[4] A broadened experiential basis for the sciences of action allows for the intersubjectivity of experience. In confirming strictly empirical theories, only standardized, not arbitrary, observations are allowed; the conventional rules for operations of measurement suffice as standards. Can the intersubjectivity of communicative experience be sufficiently guaranteed by standards of measurement in the same way?

As the name indicates, communicative experience originates in an interactive context in which at least two subjects are linked within the framework of a linguistically produced intersubjectivity of agreement on meanings that remain constant. In that framework the "observer" is just as much a participant as the "observed." The situation of "participant observation" attests to that just as clearly as does the technique of questioning. The relationship between observing subject and *object* (*Gegenstand*) is certainly extremely complex and is rendered unproblematic only by the assumptions of correspondence made by epistemological realism. The relationship between subject and *partner* (*Gegenspieler*) that replaces it is even more complex. Here experience is mediated by the interaction of the two partners. Its objectivity is threatened from both sides: by the influence of the "observer," whose instruments distort the answers, just as much as by the reactions of the partner, which make the participant observer self-conscious. By describing the threats to objectivity in this way, we have, it is true, already adopted a perspective that is suggested by the familiar preconditions of controlled observation. It seems as though communicative experience can be purged of subjective distortions only by a countervailing suspension of the claims that entangle the observer in the interaction. But the role of a disengaged observer may be a false model for the experiential domain of communication; perhaps the role of the reflective participant is more appropriate. This is the reason why psychoanalysis defines the role of the therapist in dialogue with the patient as that of the reflective participant. Transference and countertransference are mechanisms that cannot be excluded from the experiential basis of clinical work as sources of error but instead are derived from the theory itself as constitutive elements of the experimental design. Transference phenomena come under control by being systematically produced and interpreted. The communicative situation is not made to approximate the seemingly more reliable model of controlled observation through restrictive measures; rather the theory addresses the conditions of intersubjectivity of experience that arise from communication itself.

Kaplan does not conceal these difficulties; he takes them as his starting point: "Most of the problems of observation in behavioral science (and some problems of theorizing too) stem from the shared humanity of the scientist and his subject-matter, or rather from the richer and the more specific commonalities to which the abstraction 'humanity' points."[5]

Kaplan also sees that the fact that the object domain of the social sciences is subjectively prestructured has consequences not only on the level of the data but also on the theoretical level. He makes a careful distinction between "act meaning," the "meaning" to which the acting subject is oriented, and "action meaning," the "meaning" that an action can have for the scientist from a theoretical point of view.[6] To this distinction correspond two categories of explanation: the semantic explanation of the subjectively intended meaning, which grasps social facts descriptively; and the causal, or functional explanation, which represents the connection of social facts in relation to a lawlike hypothesis. The explanation of the action-orienting meaning refers to the level of data; the explanation of subjectively meaingful action refers to the theoretical level. The question arises, however, whether data and theories can be separated in the usual way when the facts themselves are symbolically mediated and preinterpreted. For if theory formation must be linked to the categorial formation of the object domain, theoretical perspectives are no longer external to social facts in the same way that hypotheses are external to the observable events through which they can be falsified. It is unclear whether under these circumstances theoretical explanations do not also take the form of an explication of contexts of meaning, or whether perhaps the semantic interpretations already perform the function reserved for causal explanations:

Many other methodological problems concerning explanations in behavioral science stem from the complex interrelations between the two sorts of interpretation—of acts and actions; it is easy to understand why they are so often confused with one another. In particular, the behavioral scientist often makes use of what might be called the circle of interpretation: act meanings are inferred from actions and are then used in the explanation of the actions, or actions are construed from the acts and then used to explain the acts. Thus Collingwood has said about the historian that "when he knows what happened he already knows why it happened."[7]

We shall see versions of an interpretive sociology that are so taken up with the problem of an accurate description of symbolically mediated modes of behavior that explanation of social action coincides with interpretive explication.

We are faced with the alternative whether the problematic of understanding meaning remains external to the methodology of the sciences of action and in the last analysis has no fundamental bearing on the logic of research, or whether the problematic has such weight that it cannot be incorporated easily into the positivist model of a strict empirical science. If we should have to abandon the generally presumed relationship of theory and reality in the case of the sciences of action, the traditional path of epistemology, which transcends the actual methodological domain, suggests itself. In that case, a discussion of research techniques and data preparation is no more helpful than an explanation of hermeneutic statements in terms of the logic of language. The experiential basis proper to theories of action should rather first be investigated from the transcendental point of view: under what conditions are communicative experiences as such constituted? The starting point for such analyses is no longer the research situation but rather the network of interactions in which the practice of research is embedded. What is at issue here is the transcendental conditions of the intersubjectivity of linguistically mediated systems of action as such, and thus the logical structure of the social lifeworld, which has a twofold status in research. On the one hand it is the object domain of research; in this respect a transcendental analysis yields information about structures of reality that are prior to any empirical analysis. On the other hand, however, the social lifeworld is also the very basis of research; in this respect a transcendental investigation permits a self-reflection of the methods employed. We find three approaches to analyses of this kind in the tradition. The phenomenological approach leads to an investigation of the constitution of everyday life-practice. The linguistic approach concentrates on language games that at the same time transcendentally determine forms of life. Finally, the hermeneutic approach conceives the transcendental linguistic rules of communicative action in terms of an objective context of effective tradition—and in doing so it goes beyond the transcendental-logical frame of reference.

Kaplan, who does not deny the problem of understanding meaning in the social sciences, is nevertheless of the opinion that it does not necessitate such systematic reflection. According to him, the distinction between semantic clarification and causal explanation suffices to purge theory formation of the problem. It can be confined to the level of data and trivialized if we can show that social facts, despite their being mediated by communicative experience, can be grasped operationally in the same way as observable events. For then they would have, methodologically speaking, the same status as other data. Thus the crucial question for the problem is whether and how we can measure social facts.

We can think of measurement as the essence of procedures that allow objects of experience to be symbolically ordered according to a rule. Normally this involves number systems, but counting is only one kind of possible measurement. For measurement to occur, it suffices that we coordinate objects with systematically ordered symbols so that each element of experience corresponds unambiguously and reversibly to a symbol. We should not confuse measuring with the logical act of coordination; rather, measurement includes the technical operations on the basis of which coordination is possible. In measuring we apply a standard that is a matter of convention but may not be arbitrarily chosen.[8] Logically, measurements can never be better than allowed by the operations we use in making them. These operations often presuppose knowledge of empirical regularities; in that case, we are dealing not with elementary but with "derived" measurements. Every scale employed in the social sciences as a measuring instrument rests on theoretical assumptions. It rests on proven lawlike hypotheses and not merely on conventions; of course, the inventor's spontaneity also enters into the construction of such measures.

Methodologically speaking, measurements fulfill two functions. Data that have been measured have the advantage of making possible a reliable simplification of controversies about the accuracy of existence claims; measurement operations that can in principle be repeated guarantee the intersubjectivity of experience. Measurements are also of interest in the construction of categories. Data that have been measured have the advantage of being precisely defined through operations; the measurement standards permit subtle distinctions and thus more precise descriptions than are possible in everyday language, even though the operational definitions themselves remain dependent on ordinary-language explanations.

As long as we define the criteria and the accomplishments of measurement on this abstract level, it is not clear why social facts should not always be accessible to measurement. Nor are symbolically mediated modes of behavior barred by their structure from being transformed into measured data. Kaplan can point to the arsenal of empirical social research, which has been enriched with an abundance of techniques in recent decades, when he asserts "that whether we can measure something depends, not on that thing, but on how we have conceptualized it, on our knowledge of it, above all on the skill and ingenuity which we can bring to bear on the process of measurement which our inquiry can put to use .... To say of something that it is incapable of being measured is like saying of it that it is knowable only up to a point, that our ideas of it must inevitably remain indeterminate."[9]

That social facts are in principle measurable says nothing, however, about how they are subjected to the operations of measurement.

We know that there are no uninterpreted experiences, neither in everyday life nor, especially, within the framework of scientifically organized experience. Standards of measurement are rules in accordance with which everyday experiences that have been interpreted in ordinary language are reorganized and transformed into scientific data. No such interpretation is fully determined by the experienced material itself. It could be the case that we transform sensory experiences into data through measurement differently than we do communicative experiences. Perhaps the modes of transformation are different in the sciences of action than in physics; and perhaps as a consequence the relationship of data and theories is different in the latter than it is in the former.

Paul Lorenzen has outlined the transcendental framework of the object domain of physics in the form of a protophysics, that is, a nonhypothetical theory of time, space, and mass.[10] This theory contains the basic principles of geometry, kinetics, and mechanics; they can be thought of as a system of ideal requirements for operations of measurement. Measurement deals with times, spaces, and masses. Taken together, these three classes of operations make possible what we call physical measurement. They all derive from the measurement of moving bodies. The theory of time, space, and mass, conceived as a protophysics and presupposing nothing but arithmetic, makes explicit our transcendental preunderstanding of the domain of possible physical objects. It contains only derivations of propositions that express the idealized relationship of measurement operations practiced every day. We could also say that protophysics is the elaboration of the grammar of a specific language game that we call "physical measurement."

All physical theories are formulated in such a way that their expressions relate directly or indirectly to this language game. For every test, instructions regarding measurement can be derived from the theory. In the social sciences such a continuum does not exist. For there is no protosociology that would explicate a unified transcendental preunderstanding of its object domain in the manner of protophysics. There is no language game in actual practice that corresponds to the abstract requirement to measure social facts and to which the expressions of sociological theories could refer. Measurement techniques are constructed on a case-by-case basis after the fact. The operationalization of theoretical expressions is external to the theory itself. It requires additional steps of interpretation. Only through this interpretation are communicative experiences transformed into data. There is no counterpart to this in the exact natural sciences. Even in physics, operational concepts define only the conditions of application of theories, the basic theoretical predicates of which do not refer directly to experience and do not exhaust their semantic content in the operational conditions of application; nevertheless, there is a deductive relationship between theoretical and operational expressions. Carnap in particular has analyzed this relationship between the theoretical language and the language of observation in which hypotheses must be formulated.

This continuum from categorial framework to standards of measurement to experiential basis does not exist in the empirical-analytic sciences of action. There, instruments of measurement are selected on an ad hoc basis without knowing whether the assumptions implicit in them have a systematic relationship to the theories to be confirmed. Cicourel has elaborated upon this point:

Our lack of methodological sophistication means that the decision procedures for categorizing social phenomena are buried in implicit commonsense assumptions about the actor, concrete persons, and the observer's own views about everyday life. The procedures seem intuitively "right" or "reasonable" because they are rooted in everyday life. The researcher often begins his classification with only broad dichotomies, which he expects his data to "fit," and then elaborates on these categories if apparently warranted by his "data." Finally, he may employ classification procedures which conform to the progression (from rating and ranking scales to interval or ratio measures) mentioned by Lazarsfeld and Barton. Although some "rules" exist for delineating each level of classification, our present knowledge seldom permits us to link category and thing according to theoretically and substantively justified derivations; instead, the coupling between category and observation is often based upon what are considered to be "obvious" "rules" which any "intelligent" coder or observer can "easily" encode and decode. Each classification level becomes a more refined measurement device for transforming commonsense meanings and implicit theoretical notions into acceptable "evidence." The successive application of classificatory operations produces "data" which assume the form of conventional measurement scales.[11] The lack of a developed social theory forces all researchers in sociology to employ common-sense concepts that reflect common knowledge known to both sociologists and the "average" members of the community or society. By assuming from the outset that the social scientist and his subjects form a common culture which each understands in more or less the same way, the "obvious" meanings of the operationalized questionnaire items on which the indicators are based, will incorporate properties only vaguely defined in social theory but nonetheless taken for granted as relevant to the research project.[12] Cicourel does not shrink from the radical conclusion: "The fact that we cannot demonstrate a precise or warranted correspondence between existing measurement systems and our theoretical and substantive concepts but must establish the link by fiat, means we cannot afford to take research procedures and, therefore, the conclusions based on them for granted."[13]

It may be the case that this unsatisfactory situation reflects not difficulties of principle but rather the unsatisfactory state of theory formation. If this were the case, we would need only to try to develop analytic systems of reference that accord with natural-scientific theories in that numerical characteristics corresponding to existing standards of measurement could be derived from its basic predicates. If we accept Lorenzen's proposal, then the correspondence between categorial framework and experiential basis in physics is secured from the outset through a protophysics, that is, through a theory of time, space, and mass in which rules for elementary operations of measurement appear in the form of axioms; the language game of physical measurement transcendentally determines the domain of possible objects of relevant scientific experience. In the sciences of action there is also an antecedent correspondence between the experiential basis and the analytic framework, but it is produced by completely different language games, independently of possible measurement operations, namely, by ordinary-language interpretations of everyday life-praxis. Sociological concept-formation builds directly on communicative experiences that are prescientifically structured. Operations of measurement must adapt after the fact to a transcendental consensus developed in the cultural self-understanding of social lifeworlds without regard for the practice of measurement, that is, the practice of making things available technologically. For this reason there cannot be a protophysics for the sciences of action. Strictly speaking, what would correspond to it would be an analysis of the rules that transcendentally determine the structure of social lifeworlds. Since these rules certainly do not coincide with the ideal requirements for measurement operations, the problematic relationship between theories and data is not accidental, and in any case it is not dependent on progress in theory itself. The arbitrariness of operationalizations could be limited, however, if we could make conscious the process whereby measurement procedures are adapted, after the fact, to a prescientifically grounded correspondence between sociological concepts and communicative experiences. This is why Cicourel returns to Husserl's phenomenological analysis of the life world, available to him in the interpretation of Alfred Schutz.

6.2 The problem of the measurement of social facts is linked to that of the transformation of communicative experience into data. It is of less importance in those social sciences that are not dependent on the hermeneutic understanding of meaning. Insofar as those sciences proceed in a normative-analytic manner, measured data can be defined unambiguously within the framework of theory. The relevant behavior, which can be either directly observed or indirectly measured via movements that can be ascribed to behavior (such as the flow of goods), is interpreted, in accordance with rules established by theory, as rationally chosen behavior, and thus as an index of decisions. The standards of measurement correspond to prescientifically institutionalized computations (such as criteria of rationalized economics, bureaucratic domination, or weapons technology). The operational determination of preferences in dimensions such as power or wealth is not difficult because the systems of action to be calculated (economic exchange, political contests, warfare) are already established as institutional domains of purposive-rational action. Theories can adopt standards developed in the object domain (prices, votes, or weapons, for example) and put them into idealized form. Such standards can also be used as criteria in delimiting the object domain: modes of behavior that meet the standards are identifiable as relevant objects. Here, then, rules for measurement operations establish a transcendental framework, as in protophysics. The data measured do not stand alone but are rather symbols for decisions within a theoretically determined system.

Nor is measurement problematic within the strict behavioral sciences, but not because, as in decision theory, the data measured are only indices of logical relationships—rather, on the contrary, because the data approximate observed events in physics. The symbolic relationships between events and subjective meaning are restricted in such a way that the residual meanings can be easily standardized. When categories like "reward" and "denial" are incorporated into the theoretical framework, the experimentally produced stimuli that are interpreted as reward or denial by a given organism are certainly not meaningless data. But if we know the normal need for nourishment, we can reliably measure the subjective meaning of "hunger" through deprivation of nourishment over a given time period. In animals, the horizon of meaning has not acquired linguistic autonomy vis-à-vis the interpreting instinct system; it has not yet become historically variable. In experiments with human subjects the linguistic horizon can also be restricted in such a way that we can make attributions with analogous certainty. The measurement of behavior that occurs in response to a stimulus appears to remain unproblematic as long as one is successful in excluding intentional action as something intentional.

But as soon as observed modes of behavior have to be interpreted in relation to expectations, the conditions of action are no longer given independently of the interpretation of the actor himself. Interpretive schemata are interposed between the stimulus and the responding behavior, and they must be uncovered, because they preform the worldview as well as the needs of the actor. This has been well understood in sociology since W. I. Thomas elaborated it once again with clarity: "If men define situations as real, they are real in their consequences." [14]

Action-orienting meaning is accessible only in communicative experience. The attempt to predetermine it through criteria of observable behavior is circular. For we encounter the symbolic content of an action only because on the level of intentional action the immediate correlation of stimulus and response becomes blurred: the same stimuli can evoke different reactions when they are interpreted differently by the actor. At the same time, we must be able to correlate measured data with the action-theoretical concepts that are to deal with this symbolic mediation of behavior. There are no fixed rules for this correlation, because the operations of measurement are not themselves anchored in the theoretical framework. The standards of measurement that we develop for interviews, participant observation, and experiments in order to produce ordered data (behavior and symbols) do not establish anything like a transcendental framework. The rules that determine the domain of possible objects have been constituted in everyday communicative experience, prior to any measurement. We interpret a succession of observable events as social action or as part of an action situation if the events can be identified as meaningful elements of interactive contexts and thus pass the prescientific test of communicative action. For this reason, in the sciences of action there is no theory of measurement that would preexplicate the relevant segment of possible experience as protophysics does for nature. For society, this explication has already been accomplished, prescientifically and informally, without explicit reference being made to operations of measurement. Therefore the relationship between objects that have been identified *as* something in communicative experience, on the one hand, and measured data, on the other hand, must be established after the fact. The relationship is not predefined by the measurement operations themselves. Methodologists have often emphasized this, particularly with respect to scaling procedures:

We might call this measurement by fiat. Ordinarily, it depends on presumed relationships between observations and the concept of interest. Included in this category are the indices and indicants so often used in the social and behavioral sciences. This sort of measurement is likely to occur whenever we have a prescientific or common-sense concept that on a priori grounds seems to be important but which we do not know how to measure directly. Hence, we measure some other variable or weighted average of other variables presumed to be related to it. As examples, we might mention the measurement of socio-economic status, or emotion through use of GSR, or of learning ability through the number of trials or the numbers of errors it takes the subject to reach a particular criterion of learning.[15]

For this reason, Coombs has developed a theory of data. It attempts to restrict the inevitable scope for discretion on the part of the sociologist who cannot derive standards for measurement from his theoretical framework. A number of years ago, he explained the general program of his project:

The method of analysis, then, defines what the information is and may or may not endow this information with certain properties. A "strong" method of analysis endows the data with properties which permit the information in the data to be used, for example, to construct a uni-dimensional scale. Obviously, again, such a scale cannot be inferred to be a characteristic of the behaviour in question if it is a necessary consequence of the method of analysis.—It therefore becomes desirable to study methods of collecting data with respect to the amount and kind of information each method contains about the behaviour in question as distinct from that imposed. Similarly, it becomes desirable to study the various methods of analyzing data in terms of the characteristics of properties each method imposes on the information in the data as a necessary preliminary to extracting it.[16]

Coombs seems to presuppose that we can determine the degree of adequacy of measurements for given object. We can question the data, as it were, about whether they were produced arbitrarily or by an adequate application of standards of measurement.[17] This alternative, however, is not reasonable, for data are simply not produced without a transformation of experience. Physical measurements appear to be less arbitrary than those of empirical social research because the protophysical rules for measurement simultaneously establish the transcendental conditions of possible experience. Because that is not the case with the empirical-analytic sciences of action, their measurement operations are always burdened with subsequent reconstruction. The moment of arbitrariness cannot be eliminated from them. Cicourel understands this:

The present state of sociological method makes difficult the adherence to Coombs' earlier remarks about mapping data into simple or strong measurement systems because the correspondence between measurement scale and observed and interpreted objects or events is imposed without our being able to ask—much less determine—if it is appropriate. Once imposed, the measurement framework "translates" or "transforms" the common-sense responses into "data." The logic of the measurement operations assures the necessary transformation for producing the desired product.[18]

Cicourel deserves credit for not displacing the difficulties that arise in establishing data onto the level of research techniques but rather making us aware of them in their epistemological significance. He sees that (instead of a protophysics, which cannot exist for the sciences of action) we need a theory that explicates the structures of the everyday lifeworld articulated in ordinary language. Without recourse to a preunderstanding of the social lifeworld we cannot know what we are grasping with measurement operations. Hence we have to begin by subjecting the transcendental framework of communicative experience, within which we relate measured data to theoretical concepts, to a process of reflection. If we do not want to continue to grope around blindly, the role of a protophysics of the social must be filled by a theory of culture. Cicourel does not seem to recognize clearly that such a theory of the lifeworld can only have the status of a theory of the transcendental conditions of the constitution of lifeworlds; the "theory of culture" he calls for should not be confused with an empirical science of culture. Given this qualification, Cicourel's program is clear and consistent:

What are the appropriate foundations for measurement in sociology? The literature discussed above implies that with our present state of knowledge rigorous measurement (in the literal sense which obtains with the use of explicit theoretical systems) cannot be obtained in sociology for properties of social process. The precise measurement of social process requires first the study of the problem of meaning in everyday life. Social inquiry begins with reference to the common-sense world of everyday life. The meanings communicated by the use of ordinary day-to-day language categories and the nonlinguistic shared cultural experiences inform every social act and mediate (in a way which can be conceptually designated and empirically observed) the correspondence required for precise measurement. The literal measurement of social acts (which implies that conceptual structures generate numerical properties corresponding to existing or constructable measurement systems) requires the use of linguistic and nonlinguistic meanings that cannot be taken for granted but must be viewed as objects of study. In other words, measurement presupposes a bounded network of shared meanings, i.e., a theory of culture. The physical scientist alone defines his observational field, but in social science the arena of discourse usually begins with the subjects' preselected and preinterpreted cultural meanings. Because the observer and subject share cultural meanings interwoven with the language system they both employ for communication, the shared everyday meanings and the particular language used by the sociologist form a basic element of the measurement of social acts. The "rules" used for assigning significance to objects and events and their properties should be the same, i.e. the language systems should be in some kind of correspondence with each other. But in sociological discourse the "rules" are seldom explicit even though there is a concern for precise definition and operational criteria. The "rules" governing the use of language and the meanings conveyed by linguistic and nonlinguistic utterances and gestures are unclear and remain an almost untouched problem for empirical research. If the "rules" governing the use of language to describe objects and events in everyday life and in sociological discourse are unclear, then the assignment of numerals or numbers to the properties of objects and events according to some relatively congruent set of rules will also reflect a lack of clarity.[19]

The rules to which Cicourel refers are not the grammatical rules of language games; rather, like Alfred Schutz, he has in mind fundamental rules to which communicative action in the world of everyday life conforms: "These 'rules' and properties are invariant to the actual content and types of 'norms' which govern social action in particular situations. The study of these 'rules' and properties provides an experimental foundation for the measurement of meaning structures basic to all sociological events."[20]

Cicourel examines the difficulties of determining data that arise in various domains of sociological research technique as a result of the fact that the object domain is preinterpreted by the actors themselves. He is able to demonstrate that, from content analyses and surveys, to techniques of participant observation and sociographic investigation, and ultimately to the experiment, the researcher cannot completely step out of the role of communicative participant.[21] The things taken for granted in any sociocultural world are the indispensable basis of communicative experience that inconspicuously binds subject and object together. There are invariant properties and constitutive rules for the primary lifeworld that are accepted without question as the conditions of possible communication. It is essential that they be brought to awareness through phenomenological reflection. Thus by grasping the structures of everyday life, Cicourel hopes to make explicit a system of reference that always implicitly predetermines the transformation of communicative experience into measured data.[22]

Cicourel's program can be fully understood only against the background of Alfred Schutz's theoretical work. In the 1920s, Schutz was already occupied with the transcendental structure of the social lifeworld. *Der sinnhafte Aufbau der sozialen Welt* appeared in 1932.[23] In it Schutz makes a systematic attempt to take the fundamental problems of an interpretive sociology, as posed by Max Weber, out of Rickert's frame of reference and bring them within the horizon of a phenomenology of the lifeworld that follows Husserl closely. In retrospect, this closeness to the work of the late Husserl, especially the *Cartesian Meditations*, creates a false impression. At that time, Schutz could draw only on the phenomenology of inner time consciousness, and he extrapolated from it a reconstruction of the world of everyday life that also anticipates the point of view of Husserl's analysis of the lifeworld. Weber's methodological concept of subjective meaning provides a guide for a phenomenological clarification of constructive subjectivity and of access to an intersubjective world of social action: "Only such a clarification of the hitherto obscure nature of the root phenomenon of social being can guarantee a precise grasp of social-scientific methods."[24] Today this emphatic appeal to the phenomenal facts of consciousness sounds somewhat outmoded; but even in the alien Anglo-Saxon context of the works written during the emigration, the old design and even the Husserlian terminology are still easily recognizable. Certainly Schutz learned a great deal from contact with the pragmatic tradition, above all from Dewey, and he involved himself very seriously with Parsons's theory of action, into which the great European sociology has been assimilated; but if one looks closely, the basic outlines of his analysis of the constitution of the lifeworld remain unchanged.[25]

Schutz begins with the intersubjectivity of the world of everyday interaction. On this level of intersubjectivity we are oriented to other people as subjects; we are not involved with them as natural objects, but rather find ourselves speaking and acting with one another in reciprocally interlocked perspectives and reciprocal roles within the same communicative context. Nor can sociology ever completely emancipate itself from this perspective of communicative experience, except at the price of interpretive access to its data.

It cannot detach the facts in its object domain from the level of intersubjectivity, on which they are constituted. And even when equated with nature for purposes of investigation, society does not completely surrender its identity. The object domain is prestructured in itself by the intersubjective context of sociocultural worlds. Social subjects put forth interpretations of their realm of action. Their manifest behavior is only a fragment of communicative action as a whole. The methodological consequence of this is the requirement of subjectively oriented interpretation. Scientific concepts must be linked to the interpretive schemata of the actor himself. Conceptual constructions both draw from and reconstruct the stock of traditional knowledge which guides and interprets the conduct of everyday life. Scientific constructs are second-order constructs.[26]

The point of departure for the reconstruction of the lifeworld is the biographical situation. It is egocentrically structured, with multidimensional reference systems of the here and the there, the familiar and the strange, the remembered, the present, and the anticipated. I find myself in these coordinates of my life history, among contemporaries and in the midst of traditions that have been handed down by my ancestors and that we shall hand on down to those who come after us. As children we grow into these traditions in order to win from them our individual life plan with its specific expectations, based on accumulated experience and on memories selected and stored from a certain perspective. The everyday knowledge with which tradition provides us equips us with interpretations of the people and events within the scope of our immediate or potential experience.[27]

Schutz speaks of the "stock of knowledge at hand," of the "commonsense knowledge" to which the "everyday world" conforms. The foreknowledge handed down in everyday language is intersubjective; in it is constituted the world in which I can take the perspective of the other. This foreknowledge consists of prescriptions for what I can typically expect in interaction with others and in encounters with the natural environment. It also orients me to the relevance of behaviors and events. Thus the lifeworld is articulated in culturally determined and differentially distributed contexts of meaning that circumscribe the scope of intentionality within which social action can occur. They determine the scope of

possible action projects and actual motivating schemata of interpretation. The type concepts of interpretive sociology must accord
with this basic stock of typifications. Its theoretical framework may
no more transgress against the structure of the sociocultural world
that phenomenology has made visible than may its techniques of
investigation.[28]

6.3 The phenomenological grounding of interpretive sociology
bursts the bounds of a general methodology of the empirical
sciences. This is not due to the specific procedures for gathering
data; interpretive sociology is intended not to exclude but to make
possible adequate measurement of social facts. But sociology now
acquires its own status vis-à-vis the natural and behavioral sciences.
It stands in principle on the same level as transcendental investigations; what it grasps empirically are relationships between interrelated social lifeworlds that prestructure the object domain. Social
reality is the totality of the events that take place on the level of
intersubjectivity.

In an exchange with Nagel and Hempel, Schutz points out that
this level of intersubjectivity disappears in the hands of positivism,
which must nevertheless presuppose it, without discussion, on the
level of theory formation:

All forms of naturalism and logical empiricism simply take for granted this
social reality, which is the proper object of the social sciences. Intersubjectivity, interaction, intercommunication, and language are simply
presupposed as the unclarified foundation of these theories. They assume,
as it were, that the social scientist has already solved his fundamental problem, before scientific inquiry starts. To be sure, Dewey emphasized, with a
clarity worthy of this eminent philosopher, that all inquiry starts and ends
within the social-cultural matrix; to be sure, Professor Nagel is fully aware
of the fact that science and its self-correcting process is a social enterprise.
But the postulate of describing and explaining human behavior in terms of
controllable sensory observation stops short before the description and
explanation of the process by which scientist B controls and verifies the
observational findings of scientist A and the conclusions drawn by him. In
order to do so, B has to know what A has observed, what the goal of his
inquiry is, why he thought the observed fact worthy of being observed, i.e.
relevant to the scientific problem at hand, etc. This knowledge is commonly called understanding. The explanation of how such a mutual understanding of human beings might occur is apparently left to the social
scientist.[29]

What in the empirical-analytic sciences is surreptitiously presupposed by participants in the research process as the basis of their mutual understanding, is reclaimed by interpretive sociology as its proper domain. The communicative context and the experimenting community of the researchers operate on the level of the inter-subjectivity of the background knowledge articulated in ordinary language. The strict empirical sciences remain within this horizon without questioning it; the task of sociology is to comprehend it by thematizing it. Consequently, sociology cannot separate the language-immanent level of interaction, on which theoretical assumptions are made, discussed, and tested, from the language-transcendent level of facts in the same way the empirical sciences can: the transcendental level is also the level of its data. In the phenomenological approach, the paradoxical implication that Neo-Kantianism saw itself forced to draw arises again. A cultural science like interpretive sociology is concerned with objectivations in which the objectivating subjectivity has renounced transcendental consciousness. Although these facts are symbolically mediated, they are not produced in accordance with logical rules but rather first encountered contingently. Thus a sociology that does not objectivistically project its facts onto the level of natural events is required to perform an empirical analysis from a transcendental perspective.

In America, Schutz found disciples who took up his constitutional analysis of the lifeworld without concerning themselves about its transcendental-logical level; they submitted his theories to experimental testing. Cicourel reports on tests stemming primarily from the work of Harold Garfinkel.[30] Garfinkel conceives the structures of the lifeworld as the general rules of interpretation in accordance with which actors define everyday-life situations and themselves. These rules are as stable or as transient as the world in which the socialized individual lives. We can understand them as transcendental conditions for the social ordering of a life-historical situation. They establish the individual reference points in terms of which the normality of events is measured. The transcendental structure of a person's social lifeworld is shown in what the person considers to be "perceivedly normal":

The notion of perceivedly normal events directs the researcher's attention to (1) the typicality of everyday events and their likelihood of occurrence,

(2) the ways in which they compare with events in the past and suggest how future events might be evaluated, (3) the actor's assignment of causal significance to events, (4) the ways events fit into an actor's or society's typical means-end relationships, and (5) the ways events are deemed necessary to an actor's or society's natural or moral order. How the actor perceives his environment is rooted in a culturally defined world. Practiced and enforced norms or rules of conduct would vary by typicality, comparability, likelihood, causal significance, means-end schema, and the nature of the natural or moral order.[31]

Garfinkel's strategy in the experiments he undertakes to isolate the basic pattern of the social lifeworld that provides stability is simple. He starts with situations that are considered normal, either informally on the basis of everyday experience or formally through rules of the game (chess or bridge), and systematically alters the conditions until situations arise that the experimental subject finds first abnormal, then disorienting, and finally chaotic: the controlled collapse of a world supposedly reveals the conditions of its stability.

In order to evaluate the logical status of these unusual experiments, we must bear in mind the function that they are to have. Cicourel hopes to overcome in this way the discrepancy between social facts and the measuring instruments applied to them and thereby to satisfy the immanent claim of communicative experience. If it is possible to lay bare the constitutive ordering of the world that experimental subjects owe to their own interpretive rules, then the process of translation between them and the observer can be done away with. The experimenter can make use of those rules from the outset in determining the research design:

If the experimental variations are not accepted or perceived by the subject as intended by the experimenter, a common basic order operating for the experimenter and subject(s) may still be presumed to hold. This common order is present before the experiment, is temporarily "dropped" or "suspended" during the experiment, and is adopted again after the experiment is concluded. If the experimental order is a simulation of the common order, then the former can be understood only by references to properties of the latter. The constitutive order or set of rules provides the actor with the basis for assigning meaning structures so that he can understand what has happened or what is happening.[32]

Cicourel makes experimental comprehension of the transcendental structure of lifeworlds the precondition for any reliable measurement in social research. In so doing, he entangles himself in a circular argument. For it is not evident how the basic biographical pattern is to be adequately measured if only these measurements can provide the criteria for the adequacy of measuring instruments. One also asks oneself what domains an interpretive sociology would still need to measure once it had completed the prior task of a descriptive understanding of particular sociocultural worlds. These contradictions are the consequence of a misunderstanding of the phenomenological approach, which draws its strength from the reflective representation of constructive subjectivity and cannot be turned outward in experiments. If phenomenological description has meaning in methodological terms, then the meaning is certainly that the phenomenological description can be reviewed through individual meditation but not tested intersubjectively. Garfinkel's experiments could fulfill their declared intention if all the experimental subjects were trained phenomenologists who brought their own interpretive rules to awareness under varied conditions; but in that case, the test would be superfluous, and we could return to the private methods of Husserl, who demanded that every phenomenologist be his own experimenter and vary the conditions of a situation through controlled fantasy.

On the other hand, no one can seriously expect an empirical science to consist only of meditations on the transcendental structure of the social world. Clearly, a sociological investigation focused on the level of intersubjectivity cannot be conducted in the classical form of a transcendental analysis of consciousness, whether the analysis be a Neo-Kantian or a phenomenological one. Because the transcendental rules that an interpretive sociology must clarify are altered under empirical conditions, because they can no longer be considered to be invariant properties of a consciousness that transcends phenomena as such, they can be made accessible to empirical investigation. Thus Garfinkel's intention is not false as such. But to carry it out he would have to abandon his phenomenological presuppositions and shift to the realm of linguistics. Then he would be able to understand the interpretive rules in accordance with which the actor defines his situation and his self-understanding as what they are—rules for action-related communication.

The limits of the phenomenological approach become clear when we recall the two tasks that a constitutional analysis of the lifeworld was to perform for sociology. We have already mentioned the first:

it was to eliminate the difficulties that arise in the measurement of social facts. If we know exactly how events and persons are interpreted in the lifeworld of the experimental subjects, we can adapt our measurement standards accordingly. Cicourel's argument rests on this basic assumption. The analysis of the lifeworld is intended to create the preconditions for the objectivity of measurement procedures, something that is unattainable as long as we suppress the filtering layer of subjectivity. But this line of argument is deceptive. It proceeds from the implicit assumption that the analysis of the lifeworld is not bound to precisely the same translation process that it is supposed to enable us to bypass.

Phenomenologists have always proceeded from the experience of their own individual lifeworld in order to reach, through abstraction and generalization, the accomplishments of the subjectivity that creates meaning. The constitution of the lifeworld in its abstract universality can be investigated in this way. But by this method we shall not encounter a single historically concrete lifeworld except that of the phenomenologist himself. We may describe phenomenologically how there can in general be only lifeworlds that are inalienably individual. But this abstract statement does not help us to cross the line that separates a phenomenological description of the structure of the social lifeworld as such from the comprehension of every possible individual lifeworld, whether it be that of an individual or that of a social group. In this case generalization from one's own experience, which Schutz, as a good student of Husserl, never went beyond, is no longer sufficient. Now the phenomenologically oriented sociologist must converse with the Other. He must engage in a communication that links him with an other, and that, if the individuality of the lifeworld is of any importance, is also the only way to encounter the particular through the mediation of general categories; for the spoken language in which we maintain our own identity and that of others is the only medium in which the dialectic of the general and the particular is carried out every day. We do not satisfy the methodological conditions of communicative experience by evading them phenomenologically. If this experience is not to be prematurely cut off through seeming objectivation, it requires training in an already constituted realm, that of the intersubjectivity of acting subjects who live together and interact with one another; it demands, then, the learning of concrete language patterns.

The constitutional analysis of the lifeworld cannot deliver what Cicourel hoped for from it in methodological terms. A sociology enlightened by reflection on the prior decisions involved in the practice of everyday life can no longer naively impose its standards of measurement on social facts. But reflection on the preconditions of communicative experience cannot relieve us of the methodological constraints of this communication itself; at best, we can systematically adapt to them. We grasp the structure of individual lifeworlds only through communication experienced in a social context; one learns the specific rules of communication through systematic participation and not, as Schutz assumes, through phenomenological intuition or, as Cicourel and Garfinkel assume, through phenomenologically guided experiments.

Sociology's recourse to phenomenology has more than the function of justifying the so-called subjective approach in opposition to the objectivism of the usual ways of proceeding. It is also intended to help differentiate this approach so that interpretive sociology can do without a functionalist frame of reference, without thereby having to become a history of ideas. The descriptions of cultural values and the analyses of roles are directed to the explication of subjectively intended meaning. But since role analyses are clearly inadequate for causal explanation or prediction of the actual outcome of social actions, it seems unavoidable that we either limit ourselves to the systematic history of ideas or return to objectively oriented analysis. A functionalism that includes nonnormative conditions and that attempts to represent role systems in their objective context takes this path. Phenomenology, in contrast, seems likely to preserve the claim to exclusivity of the subjective approach in social-scientific analysis.

Role analysis presumes that social action is motivated by sanctioned behavioral expectations. What in groups is institutionalized in the form of typical expectations takes the form of obligation in the individual. To explain the deviation of actual behavior from behavioral norms, with which we must always reckon, it is sufficient to shift the point of view: instead of recurring to the objective contexts that reshape or permeate the motivating force of subjectively intended meaning, we need only, or so it seems, deepen the subjectively oriented aspect of the analysis. If we distinguish the role as a social norm from the actual role performance, the biographical situation of the actor provides the key to the explanation of the unavoidable incongruence. As soon as we analyze role behavior from the perspective of the actor relating to his own roles, deviations from the norm can be explained phenomenologically. Erving Goffman, who through his ingenious studies was the first to gain acclaim in sociology for an eye sharpened by phenomenology, and who is thus considered a representative of the new "West Coast approach,"[33] distinguished "role" from "role performance" or "role enactment" in this sense:

Role may now be defined, in this corrected version, as the typical response of individuals in a particular position. Typical role must of course be distinguished from the actual role performance of a concrete individual in a given position. Between typical response and actual response we can usually expect some difference, if only because the position of an individual, in the terms now used, will depend somewhat on the varying fact of how he perceives and defines his situation. Where there is a normative framework for a given role, we can expect that the complex forces at play upon individuals in the relevant position will ensure that typical role will depart to some degree from the normative model, despite the tendency in social life to transform what is usually done to what ought to be done. In general, then, a distinction must be made among typical role, the normative aspects of role, and a particular individual's actual role performance.[34]

Roles are situated in each case in the social lifeworld of the actor. The situated role is not equivalent to the role norm.[35]

Goffman examined this incongruence primarily in terms of the notion of role distance.[36] With a great degree of role distance comes mastery of the repertoire of behavioral expectations; then we can juggle roles, put them into play for manipulative purposes, play them out, refract them ironically, or retract them. With a high degree of role identification, in contrast, we are dependent; we are scarcely equal to the demands of the roles; we live according to their dictates. Cicourel gives other dimensions of the embeddedness of social roles in the context of the lifeworld. In all cases, the subjective interpretation of the action situation determines role-taking. The context of the role, and thus the conditions for the translation of prevailing norms into motivations for action, can thus again be clarified only through lifeworld analysis. We have to move back from the typically intended meaning of the sanctioned behavioral expectations to inquire about the rules of interpretation in terms of which the actor defines his situation and his self-understanding:

> Patterns of the responses may enable us to infer the existence and substantive properties of norms, but these patterns do not tell us how the actor perceives the role of the other and then shapes his self-role accordingly. They do not explain the differential perception and interpretation of norms and their practiced and enforced character in everyday-life .... "Typical," and often unstated conceptions about what is appropriate and expected provide the actor with an implicit model for evaluating and participating in (practiced and enforced) normative behavior. An empirical issue which sociology has barely touched is how the actor manages the discrepancies between the formally stated or written rules, his expectations of what is expected or appropriate, and the practical and enforced character of both the stated and unstated rules.[37]

Cicourel emphasizes the distinction between rules of conduct and basic rules of everyday life; the transcendental rules in terms of which the social lifeworld of an individual is structured thus attain the status of transformational rules for the translation of prevailing norms into motives for action. They determine the action situation in which norms are "taken up."

These rules of interpretation are not part of the invariant equipment of the conduct of life by either individuals or groups; they change constantly with the structures of the lifeworld, sometimes through continual inconspicuous shifts and sometimes in a discontinuous and revolutionary way. They are expressly claimed as an object of empirical research. They are not something ultimate but rather are themselves the product of social processes that it is important to understand. Clearly, the empirical conditions under which transcendental rules are formed and that establish the constitutive order of the lifeworld are themselves the result of processes of socialization. Thus I cannot see how these processes can be understood without reference to social norms. But if this is the case, the rules of interpretation can in principle not be distinguished from the rules of social action. Without recourse to social norms, neither the origin of nor change in the "constitutive order" of a lifeworld could be understood; and yet the latter is the basis for the individual translation of norms into actions, which in turn allow us to tell what is accepted as a norm.

There is a good reason for analytically distinguishing between rules of interpretation and social norms. But the two categories of rules cannot be analyzed independently of one another; both are moments of the same social life-context. But if the analysis of the lifeworld is no longer given priority, which strictly speaking is appropriate only in a transcendental-logical investigation, then those background rules of interpretation are the same as the grammatical rules of a language in whose categories the actor defines his situation and his self-understanding. In the obscure relationship between basic rules and rules of conduct we can recognize the relationship between an internalized ordinary language and role systems. The two, language and practice, are linked in communicative action. Wittgenstein calls this the relationship between language game and form of life.

The phenomenological approach remains within the limits of the analysis of consciousness. This is why Cicourel and Garfinkel do not take the obvious step from analysis of the lifeworld, the logical status of which remains dubious within the frame of reference of an empirical science, to linguistic analysis. They are not able to recognize the obvious rules of the grammar of language games in the structures of consciousness. It is easy to show the systematic basis for this incapacity in the work of Schutz; the trail leads directly to Husserl.[38] Following closely Husserl's *Cartesian Meditations* and *Experience and Judgment*, Schutz describes the symbolic structure of the lifeworld. It is constituted on all levels as a referential context in which every element perceived is grasped within a halo of other elements that are also given but not immediately intuited. What is given is apperceived within the horizon of what is merely cogiven: "Experience by appresentation has its particular style of confirmation; each appresentation carries along its particular appresented horizons, which refer to further fulfilling and confirming experiences, to systems of well-ordered indications, including new potentially confirmable syntheses and new nonintuitive anticipations.[39]

Because primary experience is characterized by relationships of appresentation in this way, there can be systems of signs that become autonomous on the level of symbols in the form of a language. Just as for Cassirer language, as *one* symbol system among others, is grounded in the representational function of consciousness, and the structuring of consciousness cannot be derived from linguistic communication, so for Husserl and Schutz as well, linguistic symbols are grounded in the comprehensive appresentational activity of the transcendental ego. Monadological consciousnesses spin linguistic intersubjectivity out of themselves. Language has not yet been understood as the web to whose threads subjects cling and through which they develop into subjects in the first place.

7 The Linguistic Approach

7.1 Today the problem of language has taken the place of the traditional problem of consciousness: the transcendental critique of language takes the place of that of consciousness. Wittgenstein's life forms, which correspond to Husserl's lifeworlds, now follow not the rules of synthesis of a consciousness as such but rather the rules of the grammar of language games. In consequence, linguistic philosophy no longer grasps the connection between intention and action, as does phenomenology, in terms of the constitution of meaning contexts, that is, within the transcendental frame of reference of a world constructed from acts of consciousness. The linking of intentions, a problem that the study of intentional action also encounters, is now explained not in terms of a transcendental genesis of "meaning" but rather in terms of a logical analysis of linguistic meanings. Like the phenomenological approach, the linguistic approach leads to the grounding of an interpretive sociology that examines social action on the level of intersubjectivity. But intersubjectivity is no longer produced by the reciprocally interlocked and virtually interchangeable perspectives of a lifeworld; rather, it is given with the grammatical rules of symbolically regulated interactions. The transcendental rules in accordance with which lifeworlds are structured now become graspable through linguistic analysis in the rules of communication processes.

This shift of analytic approach has as a consequence a transposition of the level of investigation: social actions can now be analyzed in the same way as the internal relationships between symbols. The paradoxical requirement of an empirical investigation from a transcendental perspective no longer needs to lead to misunderstandings; it can easily be fulfilled by linguistic analysis. For the linguistic rules in accordance with which symbols are connected are on the one hand accessible to empirical analysis, as subject matter to be grasped descriptively, but on the other hand they are higher-order data that are constituted not on the level of facts but on the level of propositions about facts. Linguistic investigations have always been empirically directed logical analyses. Now interpretive sociology is also directed to this level; this focus has the advantage of being unambiguous. Transcendental-logical methods of proceeding, which had been reserved to philosophy and had proved themselves only within a specific tradition, are no longer needed. The possibility of a confusion between this level of reflection and the level of experimentally testable propositions is excluded. As an analysis of concepts, linguistic analysis is unmistakably distinguished from a testing of hypotheses.

The linguistic approach owes this lack of ambiguity to its extreme contrast with behaviorism. Whereas the latter identifies society with nature by reducing action to behavior and takes a decidedly agnostic position on structural distinctions between object domains, linguistics removes any trace of nature from symbolically mediated modes of behavior and idealistically sublimates society to a context of symbols. It puts social facts completely on the side of symbol systems. Both positions appeal to the same basis for sociology as an empirical science—a strict distinction between propositions and facts. The internal connections among signs are logical; the external connections among events are empirical. The behavioral approach claims social actions for the one side, and the linguistic approach claims them for the other; in this respect the two are complementary. The identification of social relationships with internal relationships would be even less convincing than the positivist identification of them with external relationships if linguistic philosophy conceived of language merely as a system of signs. The approach of linguistic analysis to the realm of social action is plausible only if internal relationships among symbols always imply relationships among actions. The grammar of languages would then be, in accordance with its immanent sense, a system of rules that determines connections between communication *and* possible praxis: "It will seem less strange that social relations should be like logical relations between propositions once it is seen that logical relations between propositions themselves depend on social relations between men." [40]

Linguistic analysis could become relevant for the methodology of an interpretive sociology only after logical positivism had passed through *two stages of self-criticism*; both stages are in evidence in the work of *Wittgenstein*. The *Tractatus* points out the transcendental status of the intended universal scientific language. The *Philosophical Investigations* reveals this transcendental "language as such" to be a fiction and discovers in the grammars of ordinary language communication the rules in accordance with which life forms are constituted. We can distinguish between the transcendental stage of reflection and the sociolinguistic one. At a turning point in Wittgenstein's biography a systematic transition is evident that does not appear in the analogous development of phenomenology in the work of Schutz. From this point on, Wittgenstein's work sheds light on problems that would have been posed if a sociologically oriented phenomenology had become aware in such a fundamental way of the gap between the transcendental analysis of the lifeworld as such and the analysis of the constitution of specific empirically existing lifeworlds.

The *linguistic transcendentalism* of the early Wittgenstein is analogous in many respects to Kant's transcendental philosophy of consciousness, as Stenius has seen and Apel has discussed:[41] the universal language that depicts the world corresponds to transcendental consciousness as such. The logical form of this language establishes a priori the conditions of possible statements about states of affairs. If they exist, states of affairs are facts; the totality of all facts is the world—in Kantian terms, the world of phenomena. To the categories of the intuition and the understanding, as the transcendental conditions of the objectivity of possible experience and knowledge, corresponds the syntax of the universal scientific language, which establishes the pattern and the limits within which empirically meaningful statements about what is the case are a priori possible. This linguistic transcendentalism recapitulates the critique of pure reason in linguistic-analytic form. At the same time, it brings to completion the old nominalistic critique of language that was taken up by neopositivism.

The critique of language was always concerned with making ordinary language, which is a vexation to pure thought, more precise. It is based on the presupposition of a difference between the form of thought and the structure of expression in ordinary language. The later Wittgenstein reckons candidly with a transcendental illusion that results from the fact that we use linguistic categories in ways broader than the logical relationships that are the only context in which they can be meaningful. On the level of a critique of language, the critique of pure reason takes the form of a "struggle against the enchantment of our understanding by means of our language." In contrast to his later view, however, the Wittgenstein of the *Tractatus* is convinced that the logical form of the understanding, which provides the criterion for the correct working of language, should not be sought in the established grammars of ordinary language itself: "It is not humanly possible to gather immediately from it (everyday language) what the logic of language is. Language disguises thought. So much so, that from the outward form of the clothing, it is impossible to infer the form of the thought beneath it, because the outward form of the clothing is not designed to reveal the form of the body, but for entirely different purposes." [42]

Ordinary-language formulations can, however, be judged by the standard of an ideal language that depicts the world, and the logical structure of which determines the universe of possible empirically meaningful statements. Thus for every sentence in ordinary language there is one and only one complete analysis; it is equivalent in meaning to the reconstruction of the sentence in the logically transparent language of science. All natural sentences that are not capable of this transformation can be eliminated as meaningless.

The *Principia Mathematica* provides the model for a unitary scientific language. The universal language is constructed in atomistic fashion: every complex proposition can be reduced to elementary propositions. It is truth-functional: the truth values of the propositions are dependent on the truth values of their arguments. This language corresponds to reality in the sense of a representational function: every elementary sentence is correlated with a fact. Wittgenstein's actual radicalness shows not so much in his recommendation of such a universal language as in his reflection on its status. Whereas positivism pursues linguistic analysis with a methodological intent and develops it to a formal science, Wittgenstein, opposing the trend to reductionistic thought, raises the epistemological question how language makes knowledge of reality possible. From this point of view the logical syntax of the unitary language reveals itself as a transcendental logic in the strict sense.

Wittgenstein's point of departure is the nominalistic conception that excludes reflexivity of language: "No proposition can make a statement about itself, because a propositional sign cannot be contained in itself."[43] He makes epistemological use of Russell's theory of types in applying it to the universal language: "Propositions can represent the whole of reality, but they cannot represent what they must have in common with reality in order to be able to represent it—logical form. In order to be able to represent logical form, we should have to be able to station ourselves with propositions somewhere outside logic, that is to say outside the world. Propositions cannot represent logical form; it is mirrored in them. . . . What expresses *itself* in language, *we* cannot express by means of language."[44]

The propositions permitted in the universal language correspond exclusively to states of affairs that, if they exist, are facts in the world. Propositions that, like those in the *Tractatus*, are intended to express the logical form in which we can meaningfully represent states of affairs are reflexively related to the universal language and thus cannot belong to it. They do not fulfill the logical conditions of empirically meaningful statements. By formulating the inexpressible, they draw attention to the transcendental status of language.

Like Husserl, Wittgenstein uses the analogy of the horizon: everything that can be perceived optically is given in a field of vision, but we do not see the perspective, the body-centered view of the seeing eye, as such; it shows itself in the horizon of what is perceived. It is the same with the logic of language; in establishing the logical form for all conceivable statements about what is in the world, it also establishes the structures of the world itself: "The limits of my language mean the limits of my world."[45] But the truth of these metalinguistic propositions shows itself in their logical impossibility: because the logic of language establishes with transcendental necessity the framework of our conception of what is in the world, that is, what the world as such is, that cannot be expressed in this language itself: "Logic pervades the world: the limits of the world are also its limits. So we cannot say in logic, 'The world has this in it, and this, but not that.' For that would appear to presuppose that we were excluding certain possibilities, and this cannot be the case, since it would require that logic should go beyond the limits of the world; for only in that way could it view those limits from the other side as well. . . ; so what we cannot think we cannot *say* either."[46]

Wittgenstein avoids Hegel's dialectic of the limit, because it is only in a self-critical form that he repeats Kant's critical restriction of the use of reason to knowledge gained through the understanding: the language of his own transcendental philosophy is no longer affirmative.

Wittgenstein explains the principle that logic is transcendental with the proposition, "Logic is not a body of doctrine but a mirror-image of the world." [47] This does not mean that it can be formulated as a system of propositions that would represent the world as a whole the way elementary propositions represent individual facts, for logic is precisely not a doctrine. Rather, in the use of propositions, the structure of the world is reflected in logical forms, as something also given, something that shows itself in speaking but cannot be expressed in propositional form. In this sense of ineffable speculation, Wittgenstein says in the *Philosophische Bemerkungen*, which prepare the transition to his later philosophy, "What belongs to the essence of the world cannot be said. And if philosophy could say anything, it would have to describe the essence of the world. The essence of language, however, is an image of the essence of the world; and philosophy as the mistress of grammar can actually grasp the essence of the world, but not in sentences in language but in rules for this language that exclude meaningless connections of signs." [48]

By demonstrating the meaninglessness of metaphysical propositions, the critique of language makes us aware that what cannot be said may very well be shown: "It will signify what cannot be said, by presenting clearly what can be said." [49] In conformity with mystical traditions, Wittgenstein recommends the practice of the critique of language as an exercise that allows the one who has thus been silenced to see the inexpressible essence of the world. He is enough of a positivist to continue the relentless expulsion of reflection in the name of understanding and to leave no middle ground between the coercion of deductive representation and the pathos of unmediated intuition. But the early Wittgenstein also broke the positivist spell insofar as he became aware of the logic of language as a transcendental net woven around the block of facts. He notices that the purgative efforts of the critique of language must themselves make use of a language that is just as metaphysical as the one against which they are directed, and that at the same time refers to experiences that are not nothing. On this self-negating path of the mystic who speaks indirectly, Wittgenstein comes again to the transcendental-philosophical insight: "The subject does not belong to the world; rather it is a limit of the world." [50]

The unity of this transcendental subject breaks down along with the unity of the universal language. The program that Wittgenstein grounded epistemologically in the *Tractatus* and that was translated on the methodological level into the program of a unified science proved incapable of being carried out. There is no need to recapitulate here the difficulties of principle that confront a reductive analysis of linguistic expressions.[51] No basis for independent *elementary propositions* can be found; clearly even the elementary components of a language are meaningful only as parts of a system of propositions. The requirement of *truth-functionality* can be fulfilled only at the price of physicalism. No rules can be given, however, in accordance with which intentional statements can be translated into an extensional language. Finally, the *representational function* of the unitary language is understood to be a metaphysical assumption. The nominalistic conception of language, which allows only a descriptive correlation of signs and states of affairs, clearly does not do justice to the irreducible multiplicity of linguistic modes. There is no *one* privileged way of applying propositions to reality:

There are countless ... different kinds of use of what we call "symbols," "words," "sentences." And this multiplicity is not something fixed, given once for all; but new types of language, new language-games, as we may say, come into existence, and others become obsolete and get forgotten.... It is interesting to compare the multiplicity of the tools in language and of the ways they are used, the multiplicity of kinds of word and sentence, with what logicians have said about the structure of language. (Including the author of the *Tractatus Logico-Philosophicus*.)[52]

Naming, which as a form of descriptive correlation is all that nominalism considers valid, is in addition a derived mode: "We may say: only someone who already knows how to do something with it can significantly ask a name."[53] The representational function presupposes elementary modes of application of language that vary along with the language itself: "Commanding, questioning, recounting, chatting, are as much a part of our natural history as walking, eating, drinking, playing."[54]

The ideal language that Wittgenstein once had in mind does not result in a descriptively compelling way from a transcendental "language as such." We can of course produce formalized languages in accordance with conventional rules. Carnap continued linguistic analysis along this route of constructing scientific languages. In this form, linguistic analysis is content with the status of an auxiliary science to methodology. But no path leads back to positivism from the transcendental-logical level of reflection that the *Tractatus* reached. Even the hierarchy of possible formalized languages presupposes ordinary language as an unavoidably ultimate metalanguage. A reflective linguistic analysis takes up this residual level and attempts to do what the *Tractatus* declared to be humanly impossible: to derive the logic of language from ordinary language itself: "How strange if logic were concerned with an ideal language and not with our own. For what would this ideal language express? Probably what we now express in our ordinary language; then logic has to investigate it. Or something else: but then how am I to know what that is?—The logical analysis of something we have, not of something we don't have. It is thus the analysis of sentences as they are. (It would be strange if human society had spoken up until now without putting together a correct sentence.)"[55] Only with this shift does linguistic analysis acquire significance for the grounding of an interpretive sociology.

7.2 The development of the universal language had as its methodological implication only the delimiting of "the much disputed sphere of natural science."[56] With respect to the sciences, the *Tractatus* set for philosophy only the purgative task of making sure "to say nothing except what can be said, i.e. propositions of natural science—i.e. something that has nothing to do with philosophy."[57] The meaning of statements allowable in terms of the logic of language was determined in accordance with the model of natural-scientific propositions; consequently, linguistic analysis, which has the task of eliminating nonsense, remains negatively related to the natural sciences. Near the end of the *Tractatus* there is a strange remark that further clarifies this idea. Since propositions that transcend possible facts are not allowed, there can be no meaningful ethical propositions: "Propositions can express nothing that is higher."[58] Ethical propositions have normative meaning; no facts in the world correspond to these norms. Postulates are directed to the will of acting subjects; these subjects do not have the character of something in the world. Thus ethical sentences can characterize a world as a whole. If there were an ethics, it would be transcendental: "If the good or bad exercise of the will does alter the world, it can alter only the limits of the world, not the facts—not what can be expressed by means of language. In short the effect must be that it becomes an altogether different world. It must, so to speak, wax and wane as a whole. The world of the happy man is a different one from that of the unhappy man."[59]

This hypothetical consideration has the status of a thought experiment that is to clarify once again the limits of the universal language, and thereby of meaningful language as such, using the example of ethical propositions. Ethical propositions establish a normative order. In a language that permits only statements about facts, they can have no meaning. They could have meaning on the transcendental level if the projected ethical order had at the same time the binding force of a grammatically necessary order. This thought is absurd as long as the relationship between language and reality is fixed once and for all as one of picturing or representation. Only if this presupposition is eliminated does a dimension become visible in which the application of language to reality can change along with the grammar of the language. In that case, the transcendentalism of language becomes to a certain extent ethical; grammar acquires the power to determine the limits of my world, which in principle are capable of being altered.

When Wittgenstein had to give up the idea of a unitary language and a world of facts that would be represented positivistically in that language, he took that thought experiment seriously. If empirical languages establish different and variable conceptions of the world in a transcendentally binding fashion, then a linguistically fixed world loses its exclusively theoretical meaning. The relationship of the logic of language to reality becomes a practical one. The world as determined by grammar is now the horizon within which reality is interpreted. Interpreting reality differently does not mean giving different selective interpretations of describable facts within the same system of reference; rather, it means projecting different systems of reference. These are no longer determined in accordance with a theoretical standard of correspondence between sign and state of affairs. Rather, each frame of reference establishes in a practical way attitudes that prejudge a specific relationship of signs to states of affairs; there are as many types of "states of affairs" as there are grammars. On this transcendental-linguistic level, to interpret reality differently does not mean "only" to interpret it differently; it means to integrate reality into different forms of life. In Wittgenstein's late philosophy, the disempowered monopolistic language of the natural sciences has given way to a pluralism of natural languages that no longer capture reality theoretically within the framework of a single worldview, but rather practically within different lifeworlds. The rules of these language games are the grammars both of languages and of life forms. To every ethics or life form there corresponds its own logic, namely, the grammar of a particular and irreducible language game. Ethical propositions are still inexpressible, but now grammar, which I can make transparent through linguistic analysis, is itself ethical; it is no longer the logic of a unitary language and of the universe of facts but rather the constitutive order of a social lifeworld.

With this conception, positivist linguistic analysis reaches the *second stage*, the stage of *sociolinguistic self-reflection*. The critique of language completes the transition from the critique of pure reason to the critique of practical reason. In fact, with the identification of language and life form, practical reason becomes universal; even the language of the natural sciences is now constituted within the framework of life-practice as *one* language game among many. On this level, linguistic analysis loses the significance for the philosophy of science that it was able to claim in the *Tractatus*. It no longer delimits the controversial area of the natural sciences. Instead, it acquires special meaning for the social sciences: it not only delimits the sphere of social action; it opens it up.

Logical clarification of the universal language could have only a propaedeutic function for research—that of delimiting the realm of possible empirically meaningful statements with the rules of an empiristic language. In contrast, in the grammar of life forms, the logical analysis of ordinary language touches the object domain of the social sciences themselves. As the "mistress of grammar," philosophy grasps, even if only indirectly, the essence of the world. This world was once the world of nature; the facts in the world were natural events and thus the object of the natural sciences. The latter are concerned with what is in the world, not with the "essence of the world." After the renunciation of the *Tractatus*, linguistic analysis includes many grammars; the essence of the world is reflected in them. If society, however, is constituted from such lifeworlds, the latter are themselves the "facts" with which sociology must be concerned. Consequently, social facts have a different status than natural events, and the social sciences have a different status than the natural sciences. Whereas linguistic analysis once could and was intended only to clarify the transcendental-logical presuppositions of the natural sciences, which were identified with science as such, now it is equivalent in its structure to an interpretive sociology. Both analyze the rules of language games as forms of social lifeworlds.

This is the point of departure for the linguistic grounding of interpretive sociology that Peter Winch, following Wittgenstein, undertakes:

It is true that the epistemologist's starting point is rather different from that of the sociologist but, if Wittgenstein's arguments are sound, that (i.e. the concept of a "form of life") is what he must sooner or later concern himself with. That means that the relations between sociology and epistemology must be different from, and very much closer than, what is usually imagined to be the case.... The central problem of sociology, that of giving an account of the nature of social phenomena in general, itself belongs to philosophy...; this part of sociology is really misbegotten epistemology. I say "misbegotten" because its problems have been largely misconstrued, and therefore mishandled, as a species of scientific problem.[60]

We can distinguish the objective regularities under which a behavior, for example, the conditioned behavior of a trained dog, can be subsumed, as under natural laws, from the rules with which actors orient themselves. Rule-guided action of this type is always communicative action, because rules cannot be private rules for one individual but rather must have intersubjective validity for a life form in which at least two subjects participate. An action regulated by norms is not the same thing as behavior determined by natural laws and correspondingly predictable. A norm can be violated, but in principle a natural law cannot be. An action can be correct or incorrect with respect to a governing norm; a natural law is refuted by faulty predictions: "I want to say that the test of whether a man's actions are the application of a rule is not whether he can formulate it but whether it makes sense to distinguish between a right and a wrong way of doing things in connection with what he does. Where that makes sense, then it must also make sense to say that he is applying a criterion in what he does even though he does not, and perhaps cannot, formulate that criterion."[61]

The application of a criterion requires not only the reproduction of the same behavior (or sign) in comparable circumstances, but the production of new modes of behavior *in accordance with* a rule. We proceed synthetically and not merely repetitively:

It is only when a past precedent has to be applied to a new kind of case that the importance and nature of the rule become apparent. The court has to ask what was involved in the precedent decision and that is a question which makes no sense except in a context where the decision could sensibly be regarded as the application, however unselfconscious, of a rule. The same is true of other forms of human activity besides law, though elsewhere the rules may perhaps never be made so explicit. It is only because human actions exemplify rules that we can speak of past experience as relevant to our current behaviour. If it were merely a question of habits, then our current behaviour might certainly be influenced by the way in which we had acted in the past; if I am told to continue the series of natural numbers beyond 100, I continue in a certain way because of my past training. The phrase "because of," however, is used differently of these two situations: the dog has been conditioned to respond in a certain way, whereas I know the right way to go on on the basis of what I have been taught.[62]

It is not sufficient, of course, simply to impute a rule to a series of observable segments of behavior. We can be certain that we have identified rule-guided behavior only when we ourselves could continue the sequence of actions *in the place of* the actor, without meeting objections. Only from the reactions of those involved can we infer whether or not we have found the guiding rule. The concept of "following a rule" includes the intersubjectivity of the validity of rules. Monitoring rule-guided action is thus possible only on the level of intersubjectivity: "It suggests that one has to take account not only of the actions of the person whose behaviour is in question as a candidate for the category of rule-following, but also the reactions of other people to what he does. More specifically, it is only in a situation in which it makes sense to suppose that somebody else could in principle discover the rule which I am following that I can intelligibly be said to follow a rule at all."[63]

Winch draws conclusions from the linguistic approach that are largely identical with those of phenomenology. Actions are constituted in contexts of linguistically mediated interactions in such a way that an intersubjectively valid meaning is "embodied" in the observable modes of behavior. Thus an interpretive sociology proceeds essentially in the manner of linguistic analysis; it conceives norms that guide action in terms of rules of communication in everyday language. The result of this is again the dependence of theory formation on the self-understanding of the acting subjects. Like Schutz, Winch emphasizes the logical distinction between natural and social sciences:

Mill's view is that understanding a social institution consists in observing regularities in the behaviour of its participants and expressing these regularities in the form of generalizations. Now if the position of the sociological investigator (in a broad sense) can be regarded as comparable, in its main logical outlines, with that of the natural scientist, the following must be the case. The concepts and criteria according to which the sociologist judges that, in two situations, the same thing has happened, or the same action performed, must be understood in relation to the rules governing sociological investigation. But here we run against a difficulty; for whereas in the case of the natural scientist we have to deal with only one set of rules, namely those governing the scientist's investigation itself, here what the sociologist is studying, as well as his study of it, is a human activity and is therefore carried on according to rules. And it is these rules, rather than those which govern the sociologist's investigation, which specify what is to count as "doing the same kind of thing" in relation to that activity." [64]

Winch too points out that in sociology the relationship of the researcher to the object domain must be established on the level of intersubjectivity. The natural scientist enters upon this only when he communicates with others participating in the research process. [65]

Winch's thinking is quietly radical: he dissolves sociology into a specialized linguistic analysis. And he does not hide the idealism that this approach contains. Human beings act as they speak; consequently, social relations are of the same nature as relations between sentences: "If social relations between men exist only in and through ideas, then, since the relations between ideas are internal relations, social relations must be internal relations." [66] These internal relations, however, are not merely symbolic relations of symbol systems. What we are able to reconstruct in formal languages is already an abstraction that disregards precisely the fact that languages, as symbolic contexts, represent at the same time empirical contexts. Grammatical rules are always also rules of ongoing communication and the latter in turn takes place only in the social context of life forms. Thus the connection between language games and life forms is central to the grounding of interpretive sociology in terms of linguistic analysis.

Certainly, the assertion that symbolic relations in the framework of ongoing language games are at the same time objective relations of social interaction requires substantiation. Winch must be able to demonstrate that linguistic communication logically points to social action. The connection between language and praxis is the same one that pragmatist linguistic analysis saw in communicative action within role systems. But linguistic philosophy takes the opposite path. It does not proceed genetically on the basis of organic adaptive behavior, as in Mead's linguistic pragmatism, but rather tries to derive the embeddedness of language in social institutions logically. Winch's analysis leads from the question how a meaning can be identified to the problem of the application of criteria, and ends with Wittgenstein's concept of rule-guided behavior. But it does not go beyond the intersubjectivity of the validity of linguistic rules; it leaves the connection between grammar and life form as it was, in darkness. Winch could have taken a better cue from Wittgenstein, who does not discuss this complex of issues directly.

7.3 Wittgenstein conceives language games as a complex of language and praxis. He envisions a primitive use of language as one party calling out the words and the other acting accordingly: "The children are brought up to perform *these* actions, to use *these* words as they do so, and to react in *this* way to the words of others."[67] The model of the language game puts language into relation with communicative action; in it are included the use of symbols, the reaction to behavioral expectations, and an accompanying consensus about the fulfillment of expectations that, if it is disturbed, requires restoration of the agreement that is lacking. Otherwise, the interaction is interrupted and it disintegrates. The language game then no longer functions. In Wittgenstein's definition: "I shall ... call the whole, consisting of language and the actions into which it is woven, the 'language-game.'"[68] If Wittgenstein were the pragmatist that he seems to be to observers who are superficial or preoccupied, he would not have derived the web that binds language and praxis together logically from the conditions of the understanding of language itself, but rather empirically from the connection between behavior and the use of signs. In apparent agreement with pragmatism, Wittgenstein demands over and over that one study language in the ways it is applied, and derive the meaning of words from the functioning of sentences. But the functional context that

Wittgenstein has in mind is a language game in which symbols and activities are already linked under the reciprocal supervision of an accompanying consensus of all participants.

The internal connection between language and praxis can be demonstrated logically through an unusual implication of the understanding of meaning. In order to "understand" a language, we must "have a command of" it. Thus understanding means to be skilled in something, to be able to do or to have a command of something that one has practiced and learned: "The grammar of the word 'knows' is evidently closely related to that of 'can,' 'is able to.' But also closely related to that of 'understands.' ('Mastery' of a technique.)"[69]

Understanding a language and being able to speak indicate that one has gained skills, has learned how to perform certain activities. The repeated expression "mastery of a technique" is misleading, it is true, because in this context Wittgenstein is not thinking of instrumental action but rather by "technique" means the rules of a game, thus rules of communicative interaction. Be that as it may, understanding a language clearly has a practical meaning. Wittgenstein notes that early on: "Strangely enough, the problem of understanding language is related to the problem of the will. Understanding a command before one carries it out has a connection with intending an action before one carries it out."[70]

Understanding is connected with the virtual anticipation of actions that in turn presume learning processes. The understanding of language indicates an ability to take certain actions, whereby this communicative action itself is linked to a symbolized expectation of behavior: language and action are moments of the same model of the language game.

The connection between these two moments becomes understandable in the kind of learning processes that are linked to the understanding of meaning: to understand means to have learned to be skilled at something in practical terms. Within the horizon of the understanding of language there is no such thing as a "pure" grasp of symbols. Only formalized languages, which are monologically structured, that is, in the form of calculi, can be understood abstractly, without regard to practical learning processes. For the understanding of such languages requires the reproduction of series of signs according to formal rules, a solitary symbolic operation that in many respects resembles the monological use of instruments. What is specific to the understanding of everyday language is precisely the achievement of communication. There we do not use signs as such but rather adhere to reciprocal behavioral expectations. The processes through which I learn to speak imply then learning to act. There is an element of repression involved in them, as there is in all procedures through which norms are internalized. Wittgenstein speaks of training: "The teaching of language is not explanation, but training."[71] The fact that language *in its immanent meaning* is dependent on praxis is apparent in this moment of force in the processes of learning to speak—provided that a logical connection between understanding a language and learning to speak, between grasping symbolically expressed meaning and training in the correct use of symbols, actually exists.

According to the *Tractatus*, we can understand sentences produced in ordinary language as unanalyzed expressions. Everything that can be said at all can be said with complete clarity. Under these presuppositions, understanding language would be limited to reductive linguistic analysis, that is, to transformation into expressions in the universal language. The relationship to the ideal language itself would depend only on understanding its grammar. The latter could be given in the form of metalinguistic instructions for permissible symbolic operations. Wittgenstein himself, however, was doubtful about the conditions of possibility of a metalanguage. Consequently, he withdrew descriptive validity from the language used for linguistic analysis; but he depended on the evocative power of this inauthentic metalanguage in the certainty that it would make the grammatical rules evident. We shall not consider this problem further at this point. What is crucial is that the grammatical rules of the ideal language were to be comprehensible on a level of "pure" symbolic relationships—whether, as Wittgenstein assumed at the time, this syntax is intuitively accessible, "reveals" itself phenomenologically, so to speak; or whether, as Carnap then proposed, it is produced operationally and is therefore also completely transparent. In the form of reductionist linguistic analysis, the understanding of language implies no practical meaning whatsoever.

This implication becomes logically inescapable as soon as the unitary-language system of reference has to be abandoned.

Without a binding ideal language, reduction can no longer be substituted for the understanding of language. Anything like a final analysis of our linguistic forms is no longer possible. The attempt to formalize expressions at any price is seen to be a positivistic misunderstanding:

"Inexact" is really a reproach, and "exact" is praise. And that is to say that what is inexact attains its goal less perfectly than what is more exact. Thus the point here is what we call "the goal." Am I inexact when I do not give our distance from the sun to the nearest foot, or tell a joiner the width of a table to the nearest thousandth of an inch?

No *single* idea of exactness has been laid down; we do not know what we should be supposed to imagine under this head—unless you yourself lay down what is to be so called.[72]

It cannot be a question of either discovering a universal language that will guarantee exactness or constructing formal languages in place of it: "On the one hand it is clear that ... we are not *striving after* an ideal, as if our ordinary vague sentences had not yet got a quite unexceptionable sense, and a perfect language awaited construction by us.—On the other hand it seems clear that where there is sense there must be perfect order.—So there must be perfect order even in the vaguest sentence."[73]

The understanding of language, then, means the analysis of this order that is immanent in natural language. Evidently, the order consists in grammatical rules. But this syntax is no longer accessible on the same level, that is, "understandable" in the way the grammar of the unitary language was. We cannot formalize everyday language and then define it metalinguistically without destroying it *as* everyday language. Nor can we trust an inauthentic metalanguage that leads us to the threshold of intuitive understanding; that is plausible only in relation to a transcendental "language as such" of a species subject.

Linguistic analysis has now been deprived of a metalanguage in both its forms; it falls back on the reflexive use of language and can analyze a traditional language only with the expressions of that language. But then the understanding of language is trapped in a circle; it always has to have already understood the context. Reflexive linguistic analysis cannot follow the path of reductive linguistic analysis. Analyzing an unclear expression can no longer mean transforming it and reconstructing it in a precise language. The reliable logical connection that once seemed to exist between traditional linguistic forms and a completely transparent language has been severed. Every language now carries its own order, which is to be made transparent within it as a natural grammar. These grammars can be elucidated only "from within," that is, through the application of the grammars themselves. This very circularity indicates with compelling logic the connection of language to practice. For how can grammatical rules and semantic meanings be explicated at all under these circumstances? By our imagining possible situations in which symbols are used: "Suppose you came as an explorer into an unknown country with a language quite strange to you. In what circumstances would you say that the people there gave orders, understood them, obeyed them, rebelled against them, and so on? The common behaviour of mankind is the system of reference by means of which we interpret an unknown language." [74]

It is not sufficient, of course, to observe modes of behavior. The anthropologist entering a country with an unknown language imputes a rule to the interactions he observes on the basis of his own linguistic preunderstanding. He can test his supposition only by at least virtual participation in the observed communication, in order to see whether it functions when he behaves according to this rule. The criterion for the accuracy of his assumption is his successful participation in ongoing communication. If I behave in such a way that the interactions are not disturbed, I have understood the rule. I can ascertain this only within communication itself: "It is what human beings *say* that is true and false; and they agree in the *language* they use. That is not agreement in opinions but in form of life." [75]

The truth that must be confirmed through the tacit consensus of the participants refers to the "functioning" of an interplay of symbols and activities, to the "mastery" of the rules that organize not opinions but a life form. The attempt to explicate linguistic rules leads with immanent necessity to their basis in life-practice. We analyze an unclear expression by considering situations in which it might be used. We must recall possible situations of its use; we cannot simply project them. Ultimately, this recall will bring us back to the situation in which we ourselves learned the expression in question. Linguistic analysis recapitulates the learning situation in a certain way. In order to make an expression comprehensible it recalls to consciousness the manner of instruction, the procedure of practice: "In such a difficulty always ask yourself: How did we *learn* the meaning of this word ('good' for instance)? From what sort of examples? In what language-games?" [76]

Thus logical analysis of the understanding of language shows that we can ascertain the grammatical rules of an everyday language only by remembering the training through which we ourselves learned these rules. Understanding language is the virtual recapitulation of a process of socialization. For this reason Wittgenstein introduced the term "language game" with reference to the process of learning to speak: "We can also think of the whole process of using words . . . as one of those games by means of which children learn their native language. I will call these games 'language-games. . . .'" [77]

In language games symbolic validity cannot be logically distinguished from the origin of meaning. The grammatical rules according to which the "perfect order" of a traditional language form is determined have a peculiar status: they are not metalinguistic rules for combining symbols but didactic rules for teaching language. Strictly speaking, the grammar of language games contains the rules through which children are inducted through training into an existing culture. Because everyday language is the ultimate meta-language, it itself contains the dimension within which it can be learned; but for this reason it is not only language but also practice. This connection is logically necessary; otherwise, everyday languages would be hermetically sealed; they could not be passed on. This connection can be logically demonstrated through the implications of the understanding of language. But if the grammatical rules establish not only the connection between symbols but also the interactions through which the connection can be learned, then such a syntax must refer to the "whole of language and the activities with which it is interwoven"—and to imagine a language is to imagine a form of life. [78]

7.4 Winch did not demonstrate the internal connection between language game and life form by means of a logical analysis of what it is to understand a language. Had he done so, he would have had to reflect on the conditions of possibility of a sociology proceeding through linguistic analysis: linguistic analysis is only an explicit form of understanding language.

If every statement is meaningful only in the context of its language game, and if, on the other hand, linguistic analysis makes monadic language games transparent through considering their family resemblances, then the question arises what language game this analysis itself is making use of. Wittgenstein was not able to give a consistent answer to this question of the metalanguage game of linguistic analysis. But he did not need to answer it; he could dismiss it. The question arises only if we accord descriptive value to linguistic analysis. According to Wittgenstein, it has only therapeutic value; it is not a theory but an activity. Strictly speaking, its "results" cannot be expressed but only effected, used as aids in seeing the working or nonworking of a particular language game. The revocation of his own propositions with which Wittgenstein concludes the *Tractatus* occurs with the *Philosophical Investigations* as well. This expedient is not open to Winch. He has to pose the problem of translation if he is to recommend linguistic analysis for an ethnography of language games from a transcendental point of view, or as he understands it, for an interpretive sociology.

Winch makes a theoretical claim. He thus considers possible a metalanguage in which I can describe the grammar of a language game as the structure of a lifeworld. How is this language possible, when the dogmatism of existing language games demands a strictly immanent interpretation and excludes the derivation of the grammars of different language games from a general system of rules? Winch prefaces his investigation with a motto taken from Lessing's *Anti-Goeze*: "It may indeed be true that moral actions are always the same in themselves, however different may be the time and however different the societies in which they occur; but still, the same actions do not always have the same names, and it is unjust to give any action a different name from that which it used to bear in its own times and amongst its own people."[79]

This sentence anticipates the historicism of the following century. Winch seems to be contemplating a linguistic version of Dilthey. From his free-floating position the linguistic analyst can slip into the grammar of any language game without being himself bound by the dogmatism of his own language game, which would be obligatory for linguistic analysis as such. Winch relies as naively as Schutz on the possibility of pure theory. The phenomenologist too makes use of the interpretive schemata through which acting subjects construct their lifeworlds in an ego-centered manner; he himself, however, is detached from the social world. This change in perspective from that of the participant caught up in his environment to that of the observer of a social world is itself acquired prescientifically, and thus it never became problematic for Schutz. The linguist, however, should no longer share this naiveté after Wittgenstein's penetrating analysis of the conditions of communicative experience.

When we practice linguistic analysis with a descriptive intent and forgo the therapeutic restriction, the monadic structure of language games must be penetrated and the context in which the pluralism of language games is originally constituted must be reflected upon. And then the language of the analyst can no longer simply be equated with the object language in question. A translation must take place between the two language systems, just as it does between the language games being analyzed. Wittgenstein defines this task as the analysis of similarities or family resemblances. Linguistic analysis must see commonalities and mark distinctions. But if this activity is not to be turned back into something therapeutic, systematic points of reference for comparison are needed; the linguistic analyst in the role of the comparative interpreter must always presuppose a concept of language games as such and a concrete preunderstanding in which various languages converge. The interpreter mediates between different patterns of socialization; at the same time, in this translation he relies on the pattern in which he was socialized. Actually, reflective linguistic analysis accomplishes a communication between different language games; the example of the anthropologist in a country with a foreign culture and language is not fortuitously chosen. Wittgenstein does not analyze it adequately when he points out in it only the virtual repetition of socialization processes in the context of other forms of life. Getting to know a foreign culture is possible only to the extent to which a successful translation between it and one's own culture has taken place.

With this we arrive at the field of hermeneutics, which Wittgenstein did not enter. Winch could avoid the hermeneutic self-reflection of linguistic analysis and interpretive sociology, which he wants to establish as a special form of linguistic analysis, only under one condition: if he found a metalanguage for theory into which the grammar of any everyday language whatsoever could be translated. Then the translation of the primary language in question into the language of the analyst, and thus the translation of one analyzed language into another, could be formalized and undertaken in accordance with general transformational rules. The circle in which the reflexivity of everyday language, as the ultimate metalanguage, places us would then be broken through. Linguistic analysis would no longer be tied to the practice of language games; it could be made theoretically fruitful for sociology without needing hermeneutics.

Fodor and Katz have developed a program for a metatheory of language linked to the work of Chomsky.[80] At present it is only the elaboration of an idea—an idea that, however, is just as ambitious as Wittgenstein's program of a unitary language. Whereas the universal language of neopositivism was to represent a language system that would establish the formal conditions of empirically meaningful statements with the rigor of a grammar, Fodor and Katz envision an empirical-scientific theory that will explain actual linguistic behavior in relation to linguistic rules. This transformational grammar must be independent of any grammar connected with everyday language; it is a general system, in the sense not of a universal language but rather of a theoretical language. The descriptions of all the syntactic and semantic rules that one has at one's command when one knows a traditional language must be derivable from the theory. Linguistic rules are rules of synthesis: they enable one who has internalized them to understand and generate an unspecified number of sentences. We understand and form not only sentences we have heard and have learned, but also sentences we have never heard before, as long as they are formed in accordance with learned rules. The descriptions of such generative rules form the object domain of a theory that, because its objects are themselves grammars or theories, can be called a metatheory of language: "Linguistic theory is a metatheory dealing with the properties of linguistic descriptions of natural language. In particular, linguistic theory is concerned with whatever such descriptions have in common—with universals of linguistic description."[81] Fodor and Katz must, of course, presume the systematic independence of the language of theory from the generative rules that it is to be used to explain. This assumption is not discussed.

Fodor and Katz show only that a general linguistics, which would enable us to derive a descriptively appropriate grammar for any possible ordinary language, without itself relying on any traditional language—that is, in purely theoretical expressions—would be able to avoid the complementary difficulties of constructive linguistic analysis on the one hand and therapeutic linguistic analysis on the other:

The ordinary-language and positivist approaches present incompatible conceptions of the nature and study of language. Positivists contend that the structure of a natural language is illuminatingly like that of a logistic system and advocate that natural languages be studied through the construction of logistic systems. Ordinary-language philosophers deny that a logistic system can capture the richness and complexity of a natural language. Language, they contend, is an extremely complicated form of social behavior and should be studied through the detailed analysis of individual words and expressions. Thus, positivists tend to emphasize the need for rational reconstruction or reformulation at precisely those points where ordinary-language philosophers are most inclined to insist upon the facts of usage.[82]

And further:

Disagreements between positivists and ordinary-language philosophers shade into differences of emphasis on various points. Thus, ordinary-language philosophers have by and large tended to occupy themselves with the study of the use of words, while positivists have been primarily concerned with the analysis of sentences and their inference relations. This difference does not simply represent a disagreement about research priorities. Rather, it reflects the ordinary-language philosopher's concern with the function of language in concrete interpersonal situations, as opposed to the positivist's interest in the structure of the logical syntax of the language of science. The conflict behind this difference is between the belief that language is best viewed as an articulate system with statable rules and the belief that talking about language is, at bottom, talking about an indefinitely large and various set of speech episodes.[83]

A general theory of ordinary language would combine both points of view: the advantages of a formalized language on the theoretical level, and respect for natural language games on the level of the data. It is not a question of formalizing ordinary language; in a reconstruction, ordinary language as such would be liquidated. The aim is, rather, a formalized representation of ordinary language, that is, the deduction of the rules at the basis of the communication possible in a given language. So far, constructive linguistic analysis has kept as its model the *Principia Mathematica* and produced examples of context-free languages that are occasionally appropriate for the representation of empirical-scientific theories but are in principle not appropriate for the representation of ordinary-language grammars. Therapeutic linguistic analysis, on the other hand, renounces theory altogether. It limits itself to the differentiation of everyday-language intuition. It has a contingent character, for it can only clarify on a case-to-case basis whether a use of language in concrete circumstances violates the institutionalized rules of communication or not. Fodor and Katz take up the counterarguments of both sides: "The ordinary-language philosopher correctly maintains against the positivist that a formalization is a revealing theory of a natural language only insofar as its structure reflects that of the language. What is needed is a theory based upon and representing the full structural complexity of a natural language, not one which reflects the relatively simple structure of some arbitrarily chosen artifical language." [84] And the complementary objection:

One must agree with the positivist's charge against the ordinary-language philosopher that any account of a natural language which fails to provide a specification of its formal structure is ipso facto unsatisfactory. For it is upon this structure that the generative principles which determine the syntactic and semantic characteristics of a natural language depend. These principles determine how each and every sentence of the language is structured and how sentences and expressions are understood. It is his failure to appreciate the significance of the systematic character of the compositional features of language which accounts for the ordinary-language philosopher's disregard of the study of sentences and sentential structure. [85]

However plausible this indication of the complementary weaknesses of the two approaches to linguistic analysis may be, it can make understandable why a general theory of ordinary language is desirable, but it does not provide an argument for the practicality of this program. I cannot discuss here the contributions to a transformational grammar that have appeared to this point; it seems as if they are of great consequence for the operationalization of assumptions in the area of comparative linguistics and sociolinguistics. It is questionable, however, whether such an idea can be not only sketched out and furnished with examples but also brought to empirical fulfillment. This attempt touches on the relativity theorem, which was first advanced on the level of intellectual history, in historicism, and has now been revived on the linguistic level in the wake of the work of Sapir and Whorf. [86] Does not the language of the metatheory remain tied to the grammar of specific ordinary languages? Or can a categorial framework independent of culture be found that will not only allow correct descriptions of linguistic structures but also make possible the identification of that set of formal properties that systematically distinguish every traditional language from an arbitrary or accidental sequence of structural descriptions?

I would like to mention one difficulty of principle that is of interest in our methodological context. For reasons that Chomsky has set forth convincingly (see above, chapter II, section 4.4.), a general theory of ordinary-language structures cannot proceed behavioristically. It is dependent on data that are given only in communicative experience. Linguistics must ground its constructions in the intuitive experiences of the normally socialized members of a linguistic community; the linguistic sense of these "native" speakers provides the criteria by means of which correctly formed sentences are distinguished from those that are grammatically deviant. Theoretical assumptions in turn must also be tested by means of the same linguistic intuitions: "It is sometimes assumed that operational criteria have a special and privileged position, in this connection, but this is surely a mistake. For one thing, we can be fairly certain that there will be no operational criteria for any but the most elementary notions. Furthermore, operational tests, just as explanatory theories, must meet the condition of correspondence to introspective judgment, if they are to be at all to the point."[87]

The experiential basis, however, is not adequately defined as "linguistic intuition" and "introspective judgment." In actuality it is a matter of the experience of the intersubjective validity of communication rules. Judgment of the "correctness" of linguistic forms in the frame of reference of traditional linguistic communities is based on the experience of whether they are parts of functioning language games and ensure a smooth course of interaction. The so-called linguistic intuitions of "native" speakers are not private experiences at all; the collective experience of the consensus that tacitly accompanies every functioning language game is stored in them. The intersubjectivity of the validity of communication rules is confirmed in the reciprocity of actions and expectations. Whether this reciprocity occurs or fails to occur can be discovered only by the parties involved; but they make this discovery intersubjectively.

There can be no disagreement about it, because it is formed in the agreement of the partners about the success or failure of the interaction. This indicates the precise dimension within which reflective linguistic analysis operates. But if the construction and verification of a general linguistics are dependent on decisions in this dimension, the reflective process outlined by Wittgenstein can scarcely be omitted. Fodor and Katz are well aware of the danger:

One of the main dangers encountered in the construction of the rules of a linguistic theory is that they may be formulated so as to be workable only when an appeal to linguistic intuition is made. This means that in order for the rules to serve their intended purpose it is necessary that a fluent speaker exercises his linguistic abilities to guide their application. This, then, constitutes a vicious circularity: the rules are supposed to reconstruct the fluent speaker's abilities, yet they are unable to perform this function unless the speaker uses these abilities to apply them. As much of the abilities of the speaker as are required for the application of the rules, so much at least the rules themselves fail to reconstruct.[88]

The two authors recognize not only the danger but also its source; but the proposed way to avert the danger is not quite plausible:

The intuitions of fluent speakers determine the data for which a linguistic theory must account .... Such intuitions establish sets of clear cases: of grammatically well-formed strings of words on the one hand, and of ungrammatical strings on the other. Clear cases, intuitively determined, provide the empirical constraints on the construction of a linguistic theory. The appeal to linguistic intuition is question begging when intuitions replace well-defined theoretical constructs in an articulated system of description, or when intuitions are permitted to determine the application of rules. Intuition in its proper role is indispensable to the study of language, but misused, it vitiates such a study.[89]

Because Fodor and Katz do not clarify what is hidden under the name "intuition," the so-called feeling for language, they trust naively to the tools of the empirical sciences somehow to cope with it. Linguistic intuitions, however, not only pose a general problem involved in testing linguistic theories—a problem that might be dealt with through research techniques; they also pose a problem that is systematically related to theory construction itself. Since theoretical expressions are not formulated in the primary language, general rules of application are required. Normally those rules take the form of instructions for measurement. Now, the data through which a general linguistics must be confirmed are given only in the communicative experience of the parties to a language game. Anyone wanting to verify the structural descriptions of the theory must appeal to this experience. Consequently, the measuring instruments cannot exclude the possibility that the "native" speaker being questioned will himself undertake the translation of the theoretical language into his own language. In doing so, however, he will adhere to the grammar of his own language. Hence it is unavoidable that "linguistic intuitions also determine the rules of application."

8 The Hermeneutic Approach

8.1 General linguistics is, however, not the only alternative to a linguistic analysis that proceeds historically and immerses itself in the plurality of language games without being able to justify the language of analysis itself. To break through the grammatical boundaries of individual linguistic totalities we need not follow Chomsky and leave the dimension of ordinary language. It is not only a theoretical language's distance from the primary languages that can guarantee the unity of analytic reason in the pluralism of language games. Clearly, every ordinary-language grammar opens up the possibility of also transcending the language that it establishes, the possibility, that is, of translating into other languages and from other languages. The ordeal of translation certainly brings an especially vivid awareness of the objective connection between linguistic structure and worldview, the unity of word and subject matter. Getting a hearing for a text in a foreign language often enough requires a new text rather than a translation in the ordinary sense of the term. Since Humboldt, the sciences of language have been guided by the idea of demonstrating a close correlation between linguistic form and worldview. But even this evidence of the individuality of language structure, even the resignation before the "untranslatability" of familiar expressions, is based on the everyday experience that we are never enclosed within a single grammar. Rather, the first grammar that one masters also enables one to step outside it and interpret something foreign, to make something that is incomprehensible intelligible, to put in one's own words what at first eludes one. The relativity of linguistic worldviews and the monadology of language games are both illusory. For the boundaries that the grammar of ordinary languages draw around us are also brought to awareness by means of this grammar. Hegel's dialectic of the limit is a formulation of the experience of the translator. The concept of translation is itself dialectical: only where rules of transformation that allow a deductive relationship between languages to be produced through substitution are lacking and an exact "translation" is not possible is the kind of interpretation that we usually call translation necessary. It expresses in a language a state of affairs that is not literally expressed in it and nevertheless can be rendered "in other words." Hans-Georg Gadamer calls this experience, which is the basis of hermeneutics, the hermeneutic experience:

Hermeneutic experience is the corrective by means of which thinking reason escapes the prison of language, and it is itself constituted linguistically .... Certainly the variety of languages presents us with a problem. But this problem is simply how every language, despite its difference from other languages, is able to say everything it wants. We know that every language does this in its own way. But we then ask how, amid the variety of these forms of utterance, there is still the same unity of thought and speech, so that everything that has been transmitted in writing can be understood.[90]

Hermeneutics defines its task in contrast to linguistic descriptions of different grammars. But it does not preserve the unity of reason in the pluralism of languages by means of a metatheory of ordinary-language grammars, as the program of general linguistics claims to do. It has no trust in a mediation of ordinary languages and does not step outside the dimension of ordinary language; rather, it uses the tendency to self-transcendance that is inherent in the practice of language. Languages themselves contain the potential for a rationality that, expressing itself in the particularity of a specific grammar, reflects the limits of that grammar and at the same time negates them in their specificity. Reason, which is always bound up with language, is also always beyond its languages. Only by destroying the particularities of *languages*, which are the only way in which it is embodied, does reason live in *language*. It can purge itself of the residue of one particularity, of course, only through the transition to another. This mediating generality is attested to by the act of translation. Formally, it is reflected in the trait that all traditional languages have in common and that guarantees their transcendental unity, namely, the fact that in principle they can all be translated into one another.

Wittgenstein the logician understood "translation" as a trans-formation in accordance with general rules. Since the grammars of language games cannot be reconstructed in terms of general rules, he conceived the understanding of language in terms of socializa-tion as training in a cultural life form. It makes sense to think of learning "language as such" in terms of this model. But initially we can study the problem of understanding language in terms of the less fundamental process of learning a foreign language. Learning a language is not identical with learning to speak; it presupposes the mastery of at least one language. Along with this primary language we have learned rules that make it possible not only to achieve understanding within the framework of this one grammar, but also to make foreign languages understandable. In learning a particular language we have also learned how one learns languages in general. We appropriate foreign languages through translation. As soon as we know them, of course, we no longer require translation. Trans-lations are only necessary in situations where understanding is dis-turbed. On the other hand, difficulties of understanding also arise in conversations within one's own language. Communication takes place in accordance with rules that the partners to the dialogue have mastered. These rules, however, not only make consensus pos-sible; they also include the possibility of setting situations right in which understanding is disturbed. Talking with one another means two things: understanding one another in general and making one-self understandable in a given instance. The role of the partner in dialogue contains in virtual form the role of the interpreter as well, that is, the role of the person who not only makes his way within a language but can also bring about understanding between lan-guages. The role of the interpreter does not differ in principle from that of the translator. Translation is only the most extreme variant of an accomplishment on which every normal conversation depends:

Thus the case of translation makes us aware of linguisticality as the medium in which understanding is achieved; for in translation under-standing must first be artfully produced through an explicit contrivance. This kind of conscious process is undoubtedly not the norm in conversa-tion. Nor is translation the norm in our attitude to a foreign language .... If we really master a language, then no translation is necessary—in fact, any translation seems impossible. The understanding of a language is not yet of itself a real understanding and does not include an interpretative process; it is rather an accomplishment of life. For you understand a language by living in it—a statement that is true, as we know, not only of living, but also of dead languages. Thus the hermeneutical problem is not one of the correct mastery of language, but of the proper understanding of that which takes place through the medium of language .... Only when it is possible for two people to make themselves understood through language by talking together can the problem of understanding and agreement even be raised. Dependence on the translation of an interpreter is an extreme case that duplicates the hermeneutical process of conversation: there is that between the interpreter and the other as well as that between onself and the interpreter.[91]

As a limiting case in hermeneutics, which also provides the model case of scientific interpretation, translation reveals a form of reflection that we perform implicitly in every linguistic communication. In naive conversation it is concealed, for in reliably institutionalized language games understanding rests on an unproblematic basis of agreement—it is "not an interpretive process but a life process."

Wittgenstein analyzed only this dimension of the language game as a life form; for him, understanding was limited to the virtual recapitulation of the training through which "native" speakers are socialized into their form of life. For Gadamer this understanding of language is still not a "real understanding," because the accompanying reflection on the application of linguistic rules becomes thematized only when a language game becomes problematic. Only when the intersubjectivity of the validity of linguistic rules is disturbed does a process of interpretation come into play to restore consensus. Wittgenstein assimilated this hermeneutic understanding to the primary process of learning to speak; that corresponds to his conviction that learning a foreign language has the same structure as learning one's mother tongue. He was forced to these identifications because he lacked a dialectical concept of translation. In translation we are not concerned with a transformation that permits statements in one language system to be reduced to statements in another. The act of translation points rather to a productive accomplishment to which language always empowers those who have mastered its grammatical rules: assimilating what is foreign and thereby further developing one's own language system. This occurs every day in situations in which the dialogue partners must first find a "common language." This language is the result of having reached an understanding, a process that is similar in structure to translation:

Reaching an understanding in conversation presupposes that both partners are ready for it and are trying to recognise the full value of what is alien and opposed to them. If this happens mutually, and each of the partners, while simultaneously holding on to his own arguments, weighs the counterarguments, it is finally possible to achieve, in an imperceptible but not arbitrary reciprocal translation of the other's position (we call this an exchange of views), a common language and a common judgment. Similarly, the translator must respect the character of his own language, into which he is translating, while still recognizing the value of the alien, even the antagonistic character of the text and its expression. Perhaps, however, this description of the translator's activity is too abbreviated. Even in these extreme situations, in which it is necessary to translate from one language into another, the subject matter can scarcely be separated from language. Only that translator can succeed who gives voice to the subject matter disclosed in the text; but this means finding a language which is not only his, but is also adequate to the original.[92]

In grammatical rules Gadamer sees not only institutionalized forms of life but also delimitations of horizons. Horizons are open, and they shift; we wander into them and they in turn move with us. This Husserlian concept offers a way of emphasizing the assimilative and generative powers of language in contrast to its structuring achievements. The lifeworlds established by the grammar of language games are not closed life forms, as Wittgenstein's monadological conception suggests.

Wittgenstein showed how the rules of linguistic communication imply the conditions of the possibility of their own application. At the same time, they are rules for the instructional practice through which they are internalized. But Wittgenstein failed to recognize that the same rules also include the conditions of the possibility of interpretation. To the grammar of a language game belongs not only the fact that it defines a form of life, but also that it defines a life form in relation to other life forms as one's own in contrast to those that are foreign. Because every world articulated in a language is a totality, the horizon of a language also includes what the language is not; the language shows itself as something particular among particulars. Consequently the limits of the world that it defines are not irrevocable. The dialectical confrontation of what is one's own with what is foreign leads, usually inconspicuously, to revisions. Translation is the medium in which these revisions take place and language is continuously developed further. The rigid reproduction of language and life form on the part of a person not yet mature is only the limiting case of an elastic renewal to which a traditional language is always subject as those who already have mastered it restore disturbed communication, respond to new situations, assimilate what is foreign—and find a common language for diverse tongues.

Translation is necessary not only on a horizontal level, between competing linguistic communities, but also between generations and epochs. Tradition, as the medium in which languages reproduce themselves, takes place as translation, that is, as a bridging of the distances between the generations. The process of socialization through which the individual learns his language is the smallest unit in the process of tradition. Against this background we see the foreshortened perspective to which Wittgenstein succumbed: the language games of the young do not simply reproduce the practice of the old. With the first basic linguistic rules the child learns not only the conditions of possible consensus but also the conditions of possible interpretation of the rules, which enables him to overcome and *thereby also to express* a distance. Hermeneutic understanding, which is only articulated in situations of disturbed consensus, is as fundamental to the understanding of language as is primary consensus.

Hermeneutic self-reflection goes beyond the sociolinguistic level of linguistic analysis marked out by the later Wittgenstein. When the transcendental conception of language as such broke down, language gained a dimension in the pluralism of language games. A grammar of language games no longer governs only the linking of symbols but also their institutionalized application in interaction. But Wittgenstein still has too narrow a conception of this dimension of application. He sees only invariant contexts of symbols and activities and fails to appreciate the fact that the application of rules includes their interpretation and further development. In opposition to positivist bias, Wittgenstein certainly first brought to awareness the fact that the application of grammatical rules is not in turn defined by general rules on the symbolic level but rather can only be learned as a connection between language and practice and internalized as part of a form of life. But he remained positivistic enough to think of this training process as the reproduction of a

fixed pattern, as though socialized individuals were wholly subsumed under their language and activities. The language game
congeals in his hands into an opaque oneness.

In actuality, language spheres are not monadically sealed but
porous, in relation both to what is outside and to what is inside. The
grammar of a language can contain no rigid pattern of application.
He who has learned to apply its rules has learned not only to express himself in a language but also to interpret expressions in this
language. Translation with respect to what is outside and tradition
with respect to what is inside must both, in principle, be possible.
Along with their possible application, grammatical rules also imply
the necessity of an interpretation. Wittgenstein did not see this.
Conseqently, he also conceived the practice of language games
ahistorically. With Gadamer, language acquires a third dimension:
grammar governs an application of rules that in turn gives further
historical development to the system of rules. The unity of language,
which disappeared in the pluralism of language games, is dialectically restored in the context of tradition. Language exists only as
something traditional, for tradition mirrors on a large scale the life-
long socialization of individuals in their language.

Despite the abandonment of an ideal language, the concept of a
language game remains bound to an implicit model of formalized
languages. Wittgenstein linked the intersubjectivity of ordinary-
language communication to the intersubjective validity of grammatical rules: following a rule means applying it in an identical
way. The ambiguity of ordinary language and the imprecision of its
rules are an illusion; every language game is completely ordered.
The linguistic analyst can rely on this order as the standard for his
critique. Even if ordinary language cannot be reconstructed in a
formal language without being destroyed as such, its grammar is no
less precise and unequivocal than that of a calculus. This assumption
is plausible only to someone who, in opposition to Wittgenstein's
own intention, is preoccupied with the authority of formalized languages. For someone who connects linguistic analysis with the self-
reflection of ordinary language, the opposite is obvious. The lack
of ambiguity in calculus languages is achieved by means of their
monadological structure, that is, by means of a construction that
excludes dialogue. Strictly deductive connections permit derivations, not communications. Dialogue is replaced by the transfer of

information. Only languages free of dialogue are perfectly ordered. Ordinary languages are imperfect and do not ensure lack of ambiguity. For this reason the intersubjectivity of communication in ordinary language is continually interrupted. It exists because consensus is, in principle, possible; and it does not exist, because reaching an understanding is, in principle, necessary. Hermeneutic understanding begins at the points of interruption; it compensates for the discontinuous quality of intersubjectivity.

A person who takes as his starting point the normal case of the speech situation and not the model of formalized language understands the open structure of ordinary language immediately. Continuous, seamless intersubjectivity in the prevailing grammar would certainly make possible identity of meaning and thus constant relations of understanding, but at the same time it would destroy the identity of the ego in communication with others. Klaus Heinrich has investigated ordinary-language communication from the point of view of the dangers of a complete integration of the individual.[93] Languages that are no longer inwardly porous and have hardened into rigid systems eradicate the breaks in intersubjectivity and at the same time the hermeneutic distance of individuals from one another. They no longer make possible the delicate balance between separation and union in which the identity of every self must engage. The problem of an ego-identity that can be established only through identifications, and that means precisely through alienation of identity, is at the same time the problem of linguistic communication that makes possible the crucial balance between mute union and mute isolation, between the sacrifice of individuality and the isolation of the solitary individual. Experiences of threatened loss of identity refer to experiences of the reification of linguistic communication. In the nonidentity maintained in successful communication, the individual can construct a precarious ego-identity and preserve it against the risks of both reification and formlessness. Heinrich analyzes primarily one aspect of this: the conditions of protest against the self-destruction of a society that is sinking into indifference and that destroys the distance between individuals through forced integration. This is the situation of enforced regulation of language and uninterrupted intersubjectivity that abolishes the subjectives field of application. It is in this way that what Wittgenstein conceived as a language game would have to be realized. For a regimented language that had sealed all its internal gaps would have to close itself monadically to the outside. Protest in speech is thus the reverse side of hermeneutic understanding, which bridges the distance maintained and prevents communication from being broken off. In translation lies the power of reconciliation. In it the unifying power of speech proves successful against disintegration into many unrelated languages that would be condemned in their isolation to unmediated oneness.[94]

8.2 Gadamer uses the image of the horizon to capture the fundamental hermeneutic character of every concrete language: it is so far from having a closed boundary that it can in principle incorporate everything that is linguistically foreign and at first unintelligible. Each of the partners between whom communication must be established, however, lives within a horizon. Thus Gadamer represents the hermeneutic process of coming to an understanding with the image of a fusion of horizons. This is true both for the vertical plane, on which we overcome a historical distance through understanding, as well as for the process of understanding on a horizontal plane, which mediates a linguistic distance that is geographical or cultural. The appropriation of tradition through understanding follows the model of translation: the horizon of the present is not extinguished but rather fused with the horizon from which the tradition stems:

Understanding a tradition ... undoubtedly requires an historical horizon. But it is not the case that we acquire this horizon by placing ourselves within a historical situation. Rather, we must always already have a horizon in order to be able to place ourselves within a situation. For what do we mean by 'placing ourselves' in a situation? Certainly not just disregarding ourselves. This is necessary, of course, in that we must imagine the other situation. But into this situation we must also bring ourselves. Only this fulfills the meaning of 'placing ourselves.' If we place ourselves in the situation of someone else, for example, then we shall understand him, that is, we shall become aware of the otherness, the indissoluble individuality of the other person, by placing ourselves in his position. This placing of ourselves is not the empathy of one individual for another, nor is it the application to another person of our own criteria, but it always involves the attainment of a higher universality that overcomes, not only our own particularity, but also that of the other. The concept of the 'horizon' suggests itself because it expresses the wide, superior vision that the person who is seeking to understand must have. To acquire a horizon means that one learns to look beyond what is close at hand—not in order to look away from it, but to see it better within a larger whole and in truer proportion. It is not a correct description of historical consciousness to speak, with Nietzsche, of the many changing horizons into which it teaches us to place ourselves. If we disregard ourselves in this way, we have no historical horizon. . . . It requires a special effort to acquire an historical horizon. We are always affected, in hope and fear, by what is nearest to us, and hence approach, under its influence, the testimony of the past. Hence it is constantly necessary to inhibit the overhasty assimilation of the past to our own expectations of meaning. Only then will we be able to listen to the past in a way that enables it to make its own meaning heard. . . . In fact the horizon of the present is being continually formed, in that we have continually to test all our prejudices. An important part of this testing is the encounter with the past and the understanding of the tradition from which we come. Hence the horizon of the present cannot be formed without the past. There is no more an isolated horizon of the present than there are historical horizons. Understanding, rather, is always the fusion of horizons we imagine to exist by themselves.[95]

That this interpenetration of horizons cannot be eliminated through methodology, but rather is among the conditions of hermeneutic work itself, is shown in the circular relationship of pre-understanding and the explication of what is understood. We can decipher the parts of a text only if we anticipate an understanding, however diffuse, of the whole; and conversely, we can correct this anticipation only by explicating individual parts. "The circle, then, is not formal in nature, it is neither subjective nor objective, but describes understanding as the interplay between the movement of tradition and the movement of the interpreter. The anticipation of meaning that governs our understanding of text is not an act of subjectivity, but proceeds from the common bond that links us to the tradition. But this common bond is constantly being developed in our relationship to tradition."[96]

The interpreter is a moment in the same context of tradition as his object. He carries out the appropriation of tradition from within a horizon of expectation that has already been formed by this tradition. Consequently, in a certain way we have always already understood the tradition with which we are confronted. And only for this reason is the horizon given with the interpreter's language not merely a subjective horizon that distorts our comprehension. In contrast to the theoretical use of linguistic analysis, hermeneutics insists that we learn to understand a language game from within the horizon of the language that is already familiar to us. In a certain way, we repeat virtually the same learning process through which a native-born person is socialized into his own language. We are drawn into this learning process, however, not without mediation, but rather through the mediation of the rules that we have internalized in our own socialization processes. Hermeneutics understands the mediation of what the interpreter brings with him and what he appropriates as a further development of the same tradition that the interpreter is concerned with appropriating. Hermeneutics avoids the embarrassment of linguistic analysis, which cannot justify its own language game; for hermeneutics proceeds on the assumption that training in language games never succeeds abstractly but only on the basis of the language games the interpreter has already mastered. Hermeneutic understanding is the interpretation of texts with the knowledge of texts that have already been understood. It leads to new processes of development within the horizon of developmental processes that have already taken place. It is a new piece of socialization linked to socialization that has already been undergone—by appropriating tradition, it continues it. Because hermeneutic understanding itself belongs to the objective context that is reflected in it, its overcoming of temporal distance should not be thought of as a construction of the knowing subject. The continuity of tradition has in fact already bridged the interpreter's distance from his object.

From the point of view of hermeneutic self-reflection, the phenomenological and linguistic foundations of interpretive sociology belong with historicism. Like the latter, they fall prey to objectivism, for they claim a purely theoretical attitude for the phenomenological observer and the linguistic analyst when in fact both of them are bound up with their object domain through communicative experience and thus can no longer lay claim to the role of the uninvolved observer. Objectivity can be assured only by reflective participation, that is, through the control provided by the initial situation, the sounding board from which hermeneutic understanding cannot be detached. On the level of communication, the possible objectivity of experience is endangered precisely to the extent to which the interpreter is induced by the illusion of objectivity to conceal his indissoluble bond with the initial hermeneutic situation. Gadamer's excellent critique of the objectivistic self-understanding of the *Geistes-*

wissenschaften applies to historicism and to the false consciousness of its phenomenological and linguistic successors as well. The pluralism of lifeworlds and language games is only a distant echo of the worldviews and cultures that Dilthey projected onto a hypothetical plane of simultaneity.

In the second part of his book, Gadamer discusses the romantic theory of empathy in hermeneutics and its application to history: Schleiermacher and Droysen. He uses the example of Dilthey to demonstrate the aporias in which historical consciousness becomes entangled when, having abandoned the psychology of understanding expressions for analysis of contexts of meaning, it remains caught in the deceptive enthusiasm that claims to be able to reproduce traditional contents from its own knowledge, regardless of the form in which they are encountered. To Schleiermacher's and Dilthey's aestheticization of history and their anaesthetization of historical reflection, Gadamer applies, subtly but relentlessly, Hegel's insight that the restitution of life that is past is possible only to the extent of a reconstruction of the present from its past. The illusory reproduction of the past is replaced by its reflective mediation with present life:

Subsequent understanding is in principle superior to the original production and hence can be described as a "better understanding." This does not depend so much on a subsequent consciousness-raising that places us on the same level as the author (as Schleiermacher thought), but denotes rather the inevitable difference between the interpreter and the author that is created by the historical distance between them. Every age has to understand a transmitted text in its own way, for the text is part of the whole of the tradition in which the age takes an objective interest and in which it seeks to understand itself. The actual meaning of the text, as it speaks to the interpreter, does not depend on the contingencies of the author and those whom he originally wrote for. At least it is not exhausted by them, for it is always partly determined also by the historical situation of the interpreter and hence by the totality of the objective course of history. A writer like Chladenius, who does not yet see understanding in terms of history, is saying the same thing in a naive, ingenuous way when he says that an author does not need to know the real meaning of what he has written, and hence the interpreter can, and must, often understand more than he. But this is of fundamental importance. Not occasionally only, but always, the meaning of a text goes beyond its author. That is why understanding is not merely reproductive, but always productive as well.[97]

Objectivism conceals the complex of historical influences in which historical consciousness itself stands. The principle of the history of a text's influence (*Wirkungsgeschichte*) attains for Gadamer the status of a methodological principle for the interpretation of the text itself. It is not an auxiliary discipline that supplies supplementary information but is rather research fundamental to the interpretation itself. For the history of the text's influence is only the chain of past interpretations through which the interpreter's preunderstanding is objectively mediated with his object, even if this occurs without the interpreter's awareness. Historical events and documents that have been handed down do not acquire their "meaning," the descriptive comprehension of which is the aim of hermeneutic understanding, independently of the events and interpretations that follow them. The meaning is an aggregate of the meanings that are continuously sedimented as the result of new retrospective viewpoints. Thus the traditional meaning is in principle incomplete, that is, open to accretions derived from future retrospection. Historians and philologians who reflect with a view to historical influence take into account the fact that the horizon of meaning cannot be closed off. They anticipate that the continuation of events will bring out new aspects of meaning in their object. That is the rational core of the philological experience that the content of traditional texts is "inexhaustible."[98] It corresponds to the historian's experience that it is in principle not possible to give an adequate description of any event: "Completely to describe an event is to locate it in all the right stories, and this we cannot do. We cannot because we are temporally provincial with regard to the future."[99]

Danto confirms Gadamer's principle of historical influence through an analysis of the form of historical statements. These statements are called narrative because they present events as elements of stories. Stories have a beginning and an end; they are held together by a plot. Historical events are reconstructed within the frame of reference of a story: they cannot be represented without being related to other events that follow them in time. Narrative statements are generally characterized by the fact that they refer to at least two events occurring at different points in time, the earlier of these events being the subject of the description. Narrative events describe an event with the aid of categories in terms of which the event could not have been observed. The statement "The Thirty Years War began in 1618" presupposes at least the occurrence of events relevant to the history of that war up to the Peace of Westphalia, events that no observer could have described at the time of the outbreak of the war. But depending on the context, the expression "the Thirty Years War" could mean not only a military event extending over thirty years but: the political collapse of the German Empire, the postponement of capitalist development, the end of the Counter-Reformation, the theme of the Wallenstein drama, etc., etc. The predicates with which an event is represented in narrative form require the appearance of later events in the light of which the event becomes a historical event. Consequently, with the passage of time historical description of events becomes richer than empirical observation at the time of occurrence permits it to be.

Within the frame of reference of empirical-scientific theories, events are described only in terms of categories that can also be used in making a protocol of the observation of the event. An event that is scientifically predicted can be designated only in an observational language that is neutral with respect to the time of occurrence. A historical representation of the same event, a solar eclipse, for example, must relate to the interpretive languages of all those for whom the event has acquired historical significance, that is, relevance in the framework of a story. If the historian wanted to proceed like the astronomer or the physicist in his description of events and choose an observational language that is neutral with respect to time, he would have to assume the role of the ideal chronicler. Danto introduces this fiction: he places at the disposal of the historian a machine that records all events at every moment and stores them for retrieval. This ideal eyewitness records in a language of observation what occurs historically and how it occurs. This wondrous machine, however, would be almost valueless for our historian, for these perfect eyewitness reports would be meaningless unless they were the constructions of at least one living eyewitness who could use narrative statements. The Ideal Chronicler is not in a position to describe intentional action, for that would presuppose the anticipation of events beyond the time of observation. He is incapable of establishing causal relationships, for that would involve describing an event retrospectively. The observation of a subsequent event is a necessary condition for identifying a preceding event as its cause. The Chronicler cannot narrate a single story, because the relationships of events at different points in time evade his observation. He cannot see the beginning, the turning point, and the end of an action-complex because there is no point of view for possible interpretation.

Naturally, even the descriptions of the ideal eyewitness would have to be interpretations. But a temporally neutral language of observation excludes interpretations through which alone an observed event can be grasped as a historical event. Only within the retrospective frame of reference of acting subjects who assess current conditions with regard to anticipated future conditions can two successive historical events be understood as the relationship of a past-present to a past-future. When we speak of the outbreak of the Thirty Years War, we are thinking about the events of the year 1618 from the retrospective point of view of the war that ended thirty years later. This expression could have had only prospective significance for someone in 1618. Thus we are describing the event in categories that would be relevant to the contemporary not as an observer but as an actor able to anticipate something in the future. To represent events historically, that is, in the form of narrative statements, means that we understand them in terms of the schema of possible action.

In doing so, of course, the historian restricts himself to the actual intentions of the actor. As someone living at a later time, he will always have already transcended the horizon of history as it appears to the actor. But to the extent to which they enter into the historical horizon of one who comes later, the unintended components and the indirect results of intentional contexts are also grasped from the standpoint of possible intentionality. Gadamer used this point to illustrate the transition from the psychological to the hermeneutic foundations of the *Geisteswissenschaften*: "The real historical problem is not so much how continuity in general is experienced and known but how a continuity that no one has experienced can be known." [100] Danto discusses this relationship between subjectively intended meaning and objective meaning in terms of the example of the romantic features subsequently recognized in the works of classicism:

It is a discovery for which we require the concept of romanticism, and criteria for identifying the romantic. But a concept of romanticism would naturally not have been available in the heyday of classicism. . . . Whatever in classical writings turns out to fall under the concept of romanticism was doubtless put in those works intentionally. But they were not intentional under the description "putting in romantic elements," for the authors lacked that concept. This is an important limitation of the use of *Verstehen*. It was not an intention of Aristarchus to anticipate Copernicus, nor of Petrarch to open the Renaissance. To give such descriptions requires concepts which were only available at a later time. From this it follows that even having access to the minds of men whose action he describes will not enable the Ideal Chronicler to appreciate the significance of those actions.[101]

The historian does not observe from the perspective of the actor. Rather, he describes events and actions from within the experiential horizon of a history that transcends the actor's horizon of expectations. But the meaning that thus accrues to the events retrospectively emerges only in terms of the schema of possible action, namely, as if the meaning, incorporating the knowledge of those born later, had been intended. The language in which the historian represents events thus expresses not primary observations but rather the relationship of interpretations at different stages.

The interpretation made by contemporary observers is the last rung on a ladder of interpretations. Its first rung is the historian's frame of reference, which, insofar as he is himself an acting subject, cannot be independent of his own horizon of expectations. The ladder itself is the context of tradition, which binds the historian to his object. It is formed from the retrospective projections of those who come later, who, knowing better, have reconstructed what has happened in terms of the schema of possible action. The historian is not a chronicler limited to observation. His experiences are communicative ones. Uninvolved recording of events is replaced by the job of hermeneutic understanding. It proves to be meaningless to try to distinguish something like chronological description from interpretation on the plane of historical representation. Danto criticizes that kind of conception,

which, in a way, accepts the ideal of imitation of the past, but wants to insist that there is something beyond giving accounts, even perfect accounts, of the past, or parts of the past, which it is also the aim of history to do. For in addition to making true statements about the past, it is held, historians are interested in giving interpretations of the past. And even if we had a perfect account, the task of interpretation would remain to be done. The problem of just giving descriptions belongs to a humbler level of historical work: it is, indeed, the work of chroniclers. This is a distinction I am unable to accept. For I wish to maintain that history is all of a piece. It is all of a piece in the sense that there is nothing one might call a pure description in contrast with something else to be called an interpretation. Just to do history at all is to employ some overarching conception which goes beyond what is given. And to see that this is so is to see that history as an imitation or duplication of the past is an impossible ideal.[102]

A series of events attains the unity of a story only from a point of view that cannot be derived from the events themselves. The actors are caught up in their histories; when they tell their own stories, they too become aware only after the fact of the point of view from which the events can take on the coherence of a story. The story, of course, has significance only for those who are capable of action in the first place.

As long as new points of view emerge, the same events can appear in other stories and take on new meanings. We could give the definitive and complete description of a historical event only if we could be sure that no further new points of view would appear—that is to say, that we could anticipate all relevant points of view that would emerge in the future. In this sense, the philosophy of history anticipates the point of view that would guide the last historian after the close of history. Since we cannot anticipate the future course of things, we also have no grounds on which to anticipate the point of view of the last historian. On the other hand, without a philosophy of history no historical event can be fully represented:

Any account of the past is essentially incomplete. It is essentially incomplete, that is, if its completion would require the fulfillment of a condition which simply cannot be fulfilled. And my thesis will be that a complete account of the past would presuppose a complete account of the future, so that one could not achieve a complete historical account without also achieving a philosophy of history. So that if there cannot be a legitimate philosophy of history, there cannot be a legitimate and complete historical account. Paraphrasing a famous result in logic, we cannot, in brief, consistently have a complete historical account. Our knowledge of the past, in other words, is limited by our knowledge (or ignorance) of the future. And this is the deeper connection between substantive philosophy of history and ordinary history.[103]

Incompleteness of description is not a deficiency as long as the choice of descriptive expressions is determined by a theoretical frame of reference. Because, however, historians do not have at their disposal theories like those in the empirical sciences, their incomplete descriptions are in principle also arbitrary:

Completely to describe an event is to locate it in all the right stories, and this we cannot do. We cannot because we are temporally provincial with regard to the future. We cannot for the same reasons that we cannot achieve a speculative philosophy of history. The complete description then presupposes a narrative organization, and narrative organization is something that we do. Not merely that, but the imposition of a narrative organization logically involves us with an inexpungable subjective factor. There is an element of sheer arbitrariness in it. We organize events relative to some events which we find significant in a sense not touched upon here. It is a sense of significance common, however, to all narratives and is determined by the topical interests of this human being or that.[104]

These conclusions are plausible, however, only if we accept the ideal of complete description as meaningful for history. Danto develops this *idea of all possible histories* in connection with the hypothetical role of the last historian. But for the last historian, as for every historian before him, the series of past events takes shape as a story only in terms of a point of view that cannot be derived from the events themselves. Only if he himself acts from within a horizon of expectations can he project the last of all possible systems of reference for the representation of historical events. But as soon as the historian acts at all, he creates new contexts that from a new retrospective point of view are joined to create a further story. The definitive and complete description would thereby be subjected in turn to revision. A qualification that is incompatible with the end of history as such would be required for the historical representation of the story as a whole. The ideal of complete description cannot be imagined with logical consistency. It attributes to history a claim to contemplation that it not only cannot fulfill but that is illegitimate as a claim.

Every historian is in the role of the last historian. Hermeneutic discussion of the inexhaustibility of the horizon of meaning and the new interpretations of future generations remains empty: it has no consequences for the historian's task. For he does not organize his knowledge in terms of the criterion of pure theory at all. What he can know historically cannot be grasped independently of the framework of his own life-praxis. In this context, what is in the future exists only within the horizon of expectations. And these expectations form the fragments of previous tradition into a hypothetical totality of preunderstood universal history. In the light of this history every relevant event can in principle be as completely described as is possible for the practically effective self-understanding of a social lifeworld. Every historian implicitly operates as Danto would like to forbid the philosopher of history to operate. He anticipates from a practical perspective end states in terms of which the multiplicity of events is easily organized into action-orienting histories. It is precisely the openness of history, thus the situation of the actor, that permits the hypothetical anticipation of history as a whole without which the retrospective interpretation of the parts would not be forthcoming. Dilthey understood this:

We grasp the significance of a moment in the past. It is meaningful insofar as in it a connection with the future was made, through an act or an external event.... The individual moment has significance through its connection with the whole, through the connection between past and future, between individual existence and humanity. But in what does the particular nature of this connection between whole and part within life consist?— It is a connection that is never completely made. One would have to wait until the end of one's life and then in the hour of death look back at the whole in which the connection of its parts could be seen. One would have to wait for the end of history in order to possess complete material for the determination of its meaning. On the other hand, the whole exists for us only insofar as it is intelligible through its parts. Understanding always moves between these two ways of looking at things. Our conception of the meaning of life is constantly changing. Every life-plan is the expression of a conception of the meaning of life. What we posit as our goal for the future conditions our determination of the meaning of the past.[105]

These goals that are posited, that is, the hermeneutic anticipations rooted in the interests of life-practice, are not arbitrary. For they can be maintained only to the extent to which things do not elude their grasp. In addition, it is the particular achievement of hermeneutic understanding that in relation to the successful appropriation of tradition it has also made clear and accessible to reflection the prejudices that attach to the initial situation of the interpreter.

8.3 Historical accounts that take the form of narrative statements can appear incomplete and arbitrary in principle only when measured against a false ideal of description. Empirical-scientific statements also fail to meet this standard of contemplative comprehension and corresponding representation. Their accuracy is measured in terms of criteria that establish the validity of technologically exploitable knowledge. If, correspondingly, we examine the validity of hermeneutic statements in the appropriate framework of practically effective knowledge, what Danto considers a deficiency proves to be the transcendental condition of possible knowledge. Like interpretations of parts, which can be deciphered as fragments in relation to an anticipated totality, interpretations of events can be organized backward from the projected end point into a story. Only because we can thus project the provisional closure of a frame of reference from within the horizon of a life-practice can interpretations of events have any informational content at all for that life-practice. I see Gadamer's real accomplishment as his demonstration that hermeneutic understanding is necessarily related, on the transcendental level, to the articulation of an action-orienting self-understanding.

The immanent connection between understanding and application can be seen in the cases of theology and jurisprudence. In a sermon, the interpretation of the Bible, like the interpretation of positive law in adjudication, serves at the same time as an interpretation of the application of the facts in a given situation. Their practical life-relationship to the self-understanding of those addressed, the congregation or the legal community, is not added to the interpretation afterward. Rather, the interpretation is realized in its application. According to Gadamer, this constitutive connection between understanding and its practical transformation does not hold only for certain traditions that, like the sacred texts of a canonical tradition or the prevailing norms of positive law, already have institutional validity. He wants not only to extend the connection to the interpretation of works of art and the explication of philosophical texts. He convinces us that the applicative understanding of eminent traditions bearing authoritative claims provides the model for hermeneutic understanding as such:

The original close connection between these forms of hermeneutics depended on the recognition of application as an integral element of all understanding. In both legal and theological hermeneutics there is the essential tension between the text set down—of the law or of the proclamation—on the one hand and, on the other, the sense arrived at by its application in the particular moment of interpretation, either in [legal] judgment or in preaching. A law is not there to be understood historically, but to be made concretely valid through being interpreted. Similarly, a religious proclamation is not there to be understood as a merely historical document, but to be taken in a way in which it exercises its saving effect. This includes the fact that the text, whether law or gospel, if it is to be understood properly, that is, according to the claim it makes, must be understood at every moment, in every particular situation, in a new and different way. Understanding here is always application. We started from the point that understanding, as it occurs in the cultural disciplines, is essentially historical, that in them a text is understood only if it is understood in a different way every time. This was precisely the task of an historical hermeneutics, to consider the tension that exists between the identity of the common object and the changing situation in which it must be understood.[106]

Gadamer explains the applicative knowledge to which hermeneutic understanding leads in terms of the Aristotelian determinations of practical knowledge.[107] Hermeneutic knowledge has three moments in common with the political-ethical knowledge that Aristotle distinguishes both from science and from technique.[108] *First,* practical knowledge has a reflexive form: it is also "self-knowledge." For this reason, we experience errors in areas of practical knowledge personally, on our own person. False opinions have the habitual form of false consciousness. Lack of insight has the objective force of blindness. This is connected with the *second* moment: practical knowledge is internalized. It has the power to determine drives and to shape passions. Technical knowledge, in contrast, remains external. We forget technical rules as soon as we are out of practice. In contrast, practical rules, once mastered, become a part of the personality structure. Consequently, in addition, practical reason cannot be gained without presuppositions, as theoretical knowledge can; it has to be connected to a structure of prejudgments. Only a listener who has already acquired foreknowledge on the basis of traditions he has assimilated and situations he has experienced will find lectures in practical philosophy instructive. Practical knowledge links up with and continues a process of socialization. This makes the *third* moment understandable as well: practical knowledge is global. It does not refer to particular goals that can be determined independently of the means of their realization. The goals that orient action are moments of the same life form (*bios*) as the pathways through which they can be realized. This life form is always a social life form that is developed through communicative action. Practical knowledge orients one to the rules of interaction. These traditional rules are acquired through training, but the historically changing conditions of application require an application that in turn further develops the rules through interpretation. If the hermeneutic sciences occupy with respect to tradition the position of a practical philosophy that, instructed by historical consciousness, has renounced ontologically grounded natural law, then the Aristotelian definition can also be applied to hermeneutics as well:

The interpreter dealing with a traditional text seeks to apply it to himself. But this does not mean that the text is given for him as something general, that he understands it as such and only afterwards uses it for particular applications. Rather, the interpreter seeks no more than to understand this general sense, the text, to understand what this piece of tradition says, what constitutes the meaning and importance of the text. In order to understand that, he cannot disregard himself and his particular hermeneutic situation. He must relate the text to this situation, if he wants to understand it at all.[109]

By its very structure, hermeneutic understanding aims at gaining from traditions a possible action-oriented self-understanding for social groups and clarifying it. It makes possible a form of consensus on which communicative action depends. It dispels the dangers of a communication breakdown in two directions: in the vertical direction of one's own tradition, and in the horizontal direction of the mediation between the traditions of different cultures and groups. If these flows of communication are interrupted and the intersubjectivity of the process of understanding either becomes rigid or falls apart, an elementary condition of survival is destroyed: the possibility of unconstrained agreement and recognition.

The dialectic of the general and the particular, which pervades the appropriation of traditions and the corresponding application of practical rules, reveals once again the discontinuity of intersubjectivity. The fact that there even is such a thing as tradition has in it a moment of flexibility: what has been handed down must also be subject to revision, for otherwise the nonidentical moment in the group identity being maintained would be destroyed. Ego-identities can be formed and maintained in linguistic communication in relation to a group identity only if the latter can itself be constituted in relation to the collective otherness of its own past as something simultaneously identical to and different from it. Consequently the global generality of practical rules requires a concretizing application through which it is determined in a given situation as a concrete generality with intersubjective validity.

A technical rule is general in an abstract way. It can be compared to a theoretical proposition whose conditions of application are formulated in general terms. Intersubjectivity is established on the theoretical level through a provisional definition of fundamental predicates, and on the operational level through invariant rules of application. The identification of states of affairs to which the proposition can be applied does not affect its semantic content. Thus we can subsume cases under an abstract universal. But it is otherwise with practical rules. We compare them with traditional meanings that have been understood only when we have established consensus about their meaning. Only then do they have intersubjective validity within a social group. In this case, understanding becomes a problem because two things are lacking: the binding definition of the fundamental predicates and the invariant rules of application. A preunderstanding guides us in the search for states of affairs in connection with which the meaning can be made precise. But this identification of the domain of application qualifies the semantic content in turn. The global universal, which we must have already understood diffusely, determines the subsumed particular only to the extent to which it itself is concretized through this particular. Only thus does it gain intersubjective recognition in a given situation. It is bound to this situation. A new situation requires a renewal of intersubjectivity through repeated understanding. It is not created arbitrarily but is rather the result of mediation of the past with present life through thought.

In this connection Hegel, of course, had more right to speak of thought than Gadamer does. It is difficult to fix the moment of cognition in hermeneutic understanding independently of the absolute movement of reflection. When the context of tradition as a whole is no longer thought of as a production of reason's self-apprehension, the further development of tradition, which hermeneutic understanding sees itself as being, cannot in itself be considered rational.

A critique, however, that took the logical dependence of interpretation on application and the interlocking of normative anticipations with cognitive experiences as cause to banish hermeneutic understanding from the realm of solid research and possible knowledge would be rash. On the plane of hermeneutic understanding, the mobile process that makes knowledge possible at all—the formation of standards, and description in accordance with standards—has not yet come to a stop. The methodology of the empirical sciences is what separates theoretical constructions from the observations on which they can founder. But both moments are precoordinated in a transcendental framework. Protophysics makes an interpretation of reality binding. Reality has been preconstituted in terms of the concept of possible objects of technological exploitation. With this, the rules in accordance with which theoretical propositions can be applied to facts have already been decided; consequently, within the sciences they are unproblematic. Their application, on the other hand, is problematic, and as such it is inseparable from interpretation wherever the transcendental framework that coordinates propositions and facts has not been predetermined once and for all but rather is involved in a process of transformation and has to be determined in an ad hoc fashion.

The appropriation of meanings provided by tradition takes place on the level on which the schemata of possible conceptions of the world are decided. This decision is not made independently of whether or not such a schema proves effective in a given and pre-interpreted situation. Thus it is meaningless to classify hermeneutic understanding as either theory or experience. It is both, and yet not completely either. What we have called communicative experience usually takes place within a language whose grammar is used to establish connections among such schemata. But the discontinuity of intersubjectivity makes the continuous determination of a common schema an ongoing task. Only in extreme cases does this continuous unobtrusive reconstruction and development of the transcendental schemata of worldviews become a matter for hermeneutic understanding to deal with explicitly. Such cases occur when traditions are interrupted or when they encounter foreign cultures—or when we analyze familiar traditions and cultures as though they were foreign. Controlled distancing (*Verfremdung*) can raise understanding from a prescientific practice to the status of a reflective process. Hermeneutic procedures enter into the social sciences in this way as well. They are inevitable when data are collected on the level of communicative experience. They are just as important in the choice of a categorial framework if we do not want our relationship to the unavoidable historical content of even the most general categories to be a naive one.

Gadamer, to be sure, involuntarily makes concessions to the positivist devaluation of hermeneutics. He concurs with his opponents in the view that hermeneutic experience "transcends the sphere of control of scientific method."[110] In the preface to the second edition of his work, Gadamer sums up his study as follows: "My thesis is that the element of historical influence is operative in all understanding of tradition, even where the methodology of the modern historical sciences has been largely adopted, which makes what has grown historically and has been transmitted historically into an object to be established like an experimental finding—as if tradition were as alien and, from the human point of view, as unintelligible, as an object of physics."[111] This accurate critique of a false objectivistic self-understanding cannot, however, lead to the suspension of the methodological distancing of the object that distinguishes a reflective understanding from every communicative experience. The confrontation of "truth" and "method" should not have led Gadamer to an abstract opposition between hermeneutic experience and methodical knowledge as a whole. It is the basis of the hermeneutic sciences; and even if it were a question of completely removing the humanities from the sphere of science, the sciences of action would not be able to avoid joining empirical-analytic methods and hermeneutic ones. The claim that hermeneutics legitimately brings to bear on the absolutism of a general methodology of the empirical sciences, which has practical consequences as well, does not relieve it of the business of methodology as such—this claim, we must fear, will be effective either *in* the sciences or not at all. The ontological (in Heidegger's sense) self-understanding of hermeneutics, which Gadamer expresses in the aforementioned preface, does not seem to me to be appropriate to the intention of the matter:

I did not wish to elaborate a system of rules to describe, let alone direct, the methodical procedure of the human sciences. Nor was it my aim to investigate the theoretical foundation of work in these fields in order to put my findings to practical ends. If there is any practical consequence of the present investigation, it certainly has nothing to do with an unscientific "engagement"; instead, it is concerned with the "scientific" integrity of acknowledging the engagement involved in all understanding. My real concern was and is philosophic: not what we do or what we ought to do, but what happens to us over and above our wanting and doing.[112]

The basis for this thesis is expressed in the proposition, "Understanding is not to be thought of so much as an action of one's subjectivity, but as the placing of oneself within a process of tradition, in which past and present are constantly fused. This is what must be expressed in hermeneutical theory, which is far too dominated by the idea of a process, a method." [113]

Gadamer sees living traditions and hermeneutic research fused in a single point. Against this stands the insight that the reflective appropriation of tradition breaks the quasi-natural substance of tradition and alters the positions of subjects within it. Gadamer knows that the hermeneutic sciences were first developed in reaction to a decline in the binding character of traditions. Even though he emphasizes that traditions are not disempowered by historical consciousness,[114] he overlays his justified criticism of the false self-understanding of historicism with the unjustified expectation that historicism will have no consequences. Certainly, Scheler's thesis that historical traditions lose their quasi-natural effectiveness through scientific objectivation[115] is falsely based, methodologically speaking. And certainly in contrast the hermeneutic insight is correct that understanding, however controlled, cannot simply leap over the traditional contexts of the interpreter. This structural affiliation of understanding with the traditions it continues to develop through appropriation does not, however, justify the conclusion that the medium of tradition has not been profoundly transformed as a result of scientific reflection. Even in a tradition that has never lost its effectiveness what is at work is not simply an authority detached from insight, making its way blindly. For every tradition must be woven with a broad enough mesh to permit its application, that is, its judicious transformation in consideration of altered circumstances. But the methodological cultivation of such judiciousness in the hermeneutic sciences shifts the balance of authority and reason. Gadamer fails to recognize the power of reflection that unfolds in *Verstehen*. There reflection is no longer blinded by the illusion of an absolute, self-grounded antonomy, and it does not detach itself from the ground of the contingent on which it finds itself. But when reflection understands the genesis of the tradition from which it proceeds and to which it returns, the dogmatism of life-praxis is shaken.

Gadamer turns his insight into the structure of prejudgments (or prejudices: *Vorurteilsstruktur*) in *Verstehen* into a rehabilitation of prejudgment as such. But does it follow of itself from the unavoidability of hermeneutic anticipation that there are legitimate prejudgments? In his conviction that true authority need not be authoritarian, Gadamer is motivated by the conservatism of the first generation, by the impulse of a Burke not yet directed against the rationalism of the eighteenth century. True authority, according to Gadamer, distinguishes itself from false authority through being acknowledged; "indeed, authority has nothing to do with obedience, but rather with knowledge."[116] This very harsh sentence expresses a fundamental philosophical conviction that coincides not so much with hermeneutics as with its absolutization.

Gadamer has in mind the type of educational process through which what is handed down is translated into individual learning activities and appropriated as tradition. Here the person of the educator legitimates prejudgments that are inculcated into the learner with authority—and this means, however we want to look at it, under the potential threat of sanctions and with a view to gratifications. Identification with the role model creates the authority through which an internalization of norms, and thus a sedimentation of prejudgments, is made possible. The prejudgments in turn are the preconditions of possible knowledge. This knowledge is raised to the status of reflection when it makes transparent the normative framework within which it moves. In this way hermeneutics brings into awareness what in acts of understanding has always been historically prestructured through inculcated traditions. At one point, Gadamer characterizes the task of hermeneutics as follows: it has to retrace the path of Hegel's phenomenology of spirit in such a way as to demonstrate in all subjectivity the substantiality that determines it.[117] What is substantial in what is historically given, however, does not remain untouched by the fact that it is taken up into reflection. Made transparent, the prejudgment structure can no longer function as prejudgment. But that is precisely what Gadamer seems to imply. For authority to converge with knowledge would mean that tradition, working behind the back of the educator, so to speak, legitimates the prejudgments inculcated into the person growing up; these prejudgments could then be confirmed only in the reflection of that person. As the person, having become mature, confirmed the structure of prejudgments, he would transfer, in reflected form, the once involuntary acknowledgment of the personal authority of the guardian to the objective authority of a context of tradition. Yet it would remain authority, for reflection would be able to move only within the limits of the facticity of what was handed down. The act of recognition, mediated by reflection, would not have altered the fact that tradition as such remained the only basis for the validity of prejudgments.

Gadamer's prejudice in favor of the legitimacy of prejudices (or prejudgments) validated by tradition is in conflict with the power of reflection, which proves itself in its ability to reject the claim of traditions. Substantiality disintegrates in reflection, because the latter not only confirms but also breaks dogmatic forces. Authority and knowledge do not converge. Certainly, knowledge is rooted in actual tradition; it remains bound to contingent conditions. But reflection does not wear itself out on the facticity of traditional norms without leaving a trace. It is condemned to operate after the fact; but, operating in retrospect, it unleashes retroactive power. We are not able to reflect back on internalized norms until we have first learned to follow them blindly through coercion imposed from without. But as reflection recalls that path of authority through which the grammars of language games were learned dogmatically as rules of worldview and action, authority can be stripped of that in it that was mere domination and dissolved into the less coercive force of insight and rational decision.

This experience of reflection is the permanent legacy bequeathed to us by German Idealism from the spirit of the eighteenth century. One is tempted to use Gadamer against himself and show him hermeneutically that he is ignoring that legacy because he has adopted an undialectical concept of enlightenment from the limited perspective of the German nineteenth century, and with it an attitude that has raised a dangerous claim to superiority on behalf of our German tradition and separated us from Western tradition as a whole. But it is not so simple as that: Gadamer has a systematic argument on hand. The right of reflection requires that the hermeneutic approach limit itself. It requires a system of reference that transcends the context of tradition as such. Only then can tradition be criticized as well. But how is such a system of reference to be legitimated in turn except through the appropriation of tradition?

IV

Sociology as Theory of the Present

Wittgenstein subjected linguistic analysis first to a transcendental and then to a sociolinguistic self-reflection. Gadamer's hermeneutics marks a third stage of reflection: historical reflection, which conceives the interpreter and his object as moments of the same context. This objective context takes the form of tradition or historical influence. Through it, as a medium of linguistic symbols, communications are transmitted historically. We call this process historical because the continuity of tradition is preserved on a large scale only through translation, through a philology that takes place in a quasi-natural manner. The intersubjectivity of ordinary-language communication is discontinuous and must be reestablished at intervals. Thus this productive achievement of hermeneutic understanding, whether accomplished implicitly or explicitly, is from the outset motivated in turn by tradition, which continues itself in this way. Tradition is not a process that we learn to master but a transmitted language in which we live:

The mode of being of tradition is not sensible immediacy. It is language, and in interpreting its texts the hearer who understands it relates its truth to his own linguistic being-in-the-world. This linguistic communication between present and tradition is, as we have shown, the event that takes place in all understanding. The hermeneutical experience must take as a genuine experience everything that becomes present to it. It does not have freedom to select and discard before the fact. But neither can it claim absolute freedom in that tolerant neutrality that appears to be specific to understanding. It cannot undo the event that it is itself.[1]

The hermeneutic self-reflection of linguistic analysis overcomes the transcendental view that Wittgenstein had maintained even in the face of the diversity of grammars of language games. As tradition, language encompasses all particular grammars and creates unity in the empirical multiplicity of transcendental rules. At the level of objective spirit, language becomes a contingent absolute. It can no longer conceive itself as absolute spirit; it is only to subjective spirit that it makes itself felt as absolute power. This power becomes objective in the historical transformation of the horizons of possible experience. Hegel's experience of reflection shrinks to the consciousness that we are delivered over to a process, itself irrational, in which the conditions of rationality change with time and place, epoch and culture.

Hermeneutic self-reflection, however, gets lost in this irrationalism only when it posits hermeneutic experience as an absolute and fails to acknowledge the transcending force of reflection that is also at work in it. Certainly, reflection can no longer reach beyond itself to an absolute consciousness that it then claims to be. The path to absolute idealism is barred to a transcendental consciousness that is hermeneutically mediated and has fallen back into the contingent content of traditions. But must it for that reason remain on the path of relative idealism?

The objectivity of a process of tradition that takes place in the medium of symbolic meaning is not objective enough. Hermeneutics comes up against the limits of the context of tradition from the inside. Once these limits have been experienced and recognized, it can no longer consider cultural traditions absolute. There is good reason to conceive language as a kind of metainstitution on which all social institutions depend. For social action is constituted only in ordinary-language communication.[2] But clearly this metainstitution of language as tradition is dependent in turn on social processes that cannot be reduced to normative relationships. Language is *also* a medium of domination and social power. It serves to legitimate relationships of organized force. Insofar as the legitimations do not articulate the power relationship whose institutionalization they make possible, insofar as that relationship is merely manifested in the legitimations, language is *also* ideological. In that case it is not so much a matter of deceptions in language as of deception with language as such. Hermeneutic experience, encountering this dependence of symbolic context on actual relationships, becomes a critique of ideology.

The nonnormative forces that enter into language as a metainstitution derive not only from systems of domination but also from social labor. The instrumental sphere of action monitored by success structures experiences that can give rise to specific linguistic interpretations and subject traditional patterns of interpretation to the constraints of the labor process. A change in the mode of production entails a restructuring of the linguistic worldview. This can be studied in, for example, the extension of the realm of the profane in primitive societies. Certainly, revolutions in the conditions of the reproduction of material life are in turn linguistically mediated. But a new practice is not set in motion by a new interpretation. Rather, old patterns of interpretation are also attacked and overthrown "from below" by new practices.[3]

Today the institutionalized research practice of the empirical sciences guarantees a flow of information that was formerly accumulated prescientifically in systems of social labor. This information concerns natural or contrived experience constituted in the functional sphere of instrumental action. I suspect that the institutional changes brought about by scientific and technical progress exercise an indirect influence on the linguistic schemata of worldviews of the same kind once exercised by changes in the mode of production; for science has become the foremost of the forces of production. But the empirical sciences do not represent an arbitrary language game. Their language interprets reality from the viewpoint of possible technological exploitation, a viewpoint that is, anthropologically speaking, deeply anchored. Through that language the actual constraints of the natural circumstances of life enter into society. Even the propositional systems of empirical-scientific theories may well refer to ordinary language as the ultimate metalanguage; but conversely, the system of activities that those theories make possible, the technologies for the domination of nature, in turn have an effect on the institutional context of society as a whole, and alter language.

An interpretive sociology that hypostatizes language as the subject of life forms and of tradition binds itself to the idealist presupposition that linguistically articulated consciousness determines the material being of life-practice. But the objective context of social action is not reducible to the dimension of intersubjectively intended and symbolically transmitted meaning. The linguistic infrastructure of society is a moment in a complex that, however symbolically mediated, is also constituted by the constraints of reality: by the constraint of external nature, which enters into the procedures of technological exploitation, and by the constraint of inner nature, which is reflected in the repressions of social relationships of power. These two categories of constraint are not only the object of interpretations; behind the back of language, so to speak, they affect the very grammatical rules in accordance with which we interpret the world. *The objective context in terms of which alone social actions can be understood is constituted conjointly by language, labor, and domination.* The process of tradition is relativized both by systems of labor and by systems of authority; it appears as an absolute power only to an autonomous hermeneutics. Sociology may therefore not be reduced to interpretive sociology. It requires a system of reference that on the one hand does not disregard the symbolic mediation of social action in favor of a relationship that is merely sign-controlled and stimulus-produced, but on the other hand does not fall prey to a linguistic idealism and completely sublimate social processes to cultural tradition. Such a frame of reference would no longer be able to leave tradition as something undefined and all-encompssing, but would rather make tradition as such, and tradition in its relationship to other moments of the social life context, comprehensible, so that we can indicate the conditions external to tradition under which transcendental rules of worldview and action change empirically.

Gadamer, whose work derives from the Marburg school of Neo-Kantianism, is prevented by the residues of Kantianism retained in Heidegger's existential ontology from drawing the conclusions suggested by his own analyses. He avoids the transition from the transcendental conditions of historicity to the universal history in which these conditions are constituted. He does not see that in the process of tradition he must consider as already mediated what in terms of its ontological difference is not capable of mediation: linguistic structures and the empirical conditions under which they change historically. Only because of this can Gadamer also conceal from himself the fact that the practical connection between understanding and the initial hermeneutic situation of the interpreter requires a hypothetical anticipation of a philosophy of history with practical intent.[4]

9 The Limits of Linguistically Oriented Interpretive Sociology

9.1 So far as I know there are no sociological studies that expressly claim a foundation in linguistic analysis or linguistic hermeneutics. But in the past decade interesting work belonging within the framework of a linguistically oriented interpretive sociology (*sprachverstehende Soziologie*) has come out of the school of symbolic interactionism, which goes back to Cooley, Thomas, and especially Mead,[5] and which later integrated impulses from the work of Cassirer's emigration period. Anselm Strauss,[6] in particular, has purged linguistic pragmatism of its behavioristic origins so thoroughly that today it can be enlisted for the scientific program proposed by Winch and further differentiated by Gadamer's work.[7]

Strauss understands social action in the context of a series of interpretations. Each new interpretation provides a revised picture of the past in the light of an anticipated future. Individual life history appears from the perspective of a continually repeated hermeneutic effort. New situations and problematic events make necessary a changed application or extension of traditional language. In this process, the new vocabulary must be confirmed in interaction with reference persons. Conversely, a change in reference persons or in group membership requires adaptation to new terminologies. The actor's situations and his own identity are reinterpreted within the framework of the new terminologies. Turning points in the socialization process are indicated by a shift in terminologies and by the effort to replace interpretations that have lost their credibility with more appropriate ones. The loss of a language means the loss of a world. This is the linguistic concept of alienation, to which there corresponds in the social-psychological sphere the concept of a disturbance of ego-identity:

Under certain social conditions a man may undergo so many or such critical experiences for which conventional explanations seem inadequate, that he begins to question large segments of the explanatory terminology that has been taught him. In the internal rhetorical battle that ensues, his opponents may be conceived as lying or manipulating events to their own advantage, as wrong, or as duped. But a man cannot question his own basic terminology without questioning his own purposes. If in large measure he rejects the explanations he once believed, then he has been alienated and has lost a world. He has been "spiritually dispossessed." If he embraces a set of counter-explanations or invents a set of his own, then he has regained the world, for the world is not merely "out there" but is also what he makes of it.[8]

The same thing is true of social groups whose identity is threatened:

Alienation and repossession generally are not occurrences that happen merely to isolated sufferers, but simultaneously to particular sectors of the population. Certain alienated persons eventually discover that others are facing similar problems and experiences, and the new terminologies arising out of these discoveries are shared products. These take the form of new philosophies, new interpretations of the world, of situations, persons, and acts. Such radical transvaluation is equivalent to new vision, a re-seeing of the meanings and ends of human life.[9]

Social processes can be adequately analyzed as changes in language. This change itself, however, is unfathomable. Strauss seems to envision a linguistically creative spontaneity on the part of the ego that responds to unforessen situations by drafting new terminologies. In this he recalls Mead's study of the "I" and the "me":

Such a novel reply to the social situation involved in the organized set of attitudes constitutes the "I" as over against the "me." The "me" is a conventional, habitual individual. It is always there. It has to have those habits, those responses which everybody has; otherwise the individual could not be a member of the community. But an individual is constantly reacting to such an organized community in the way of expressing himself, not necessarily asserting himself in the offensive sense but expressing himself, being himself in such a co-operative process as belongs to any community. The attitudes involved are gathered from the group, but the individual in whom they are organized has the opportunity of giving them an expression which perhaps has never taken place before.[10]

Society, however, seems to be such an unresisting medium for new language projects and playful revisions of worldviews that the idealism of this interpretive sociology reminds one of a sociolinguistic offshoot of Sartre's existential philosophy. Whether the context of tradition is conceived as the aggregate of the creative linguistic accomplishments of socialized individuals, or their products are seen in turn as continuations of traditions that mediate themselves with themselves through the living hermeneutic of individuals—the absolutization of language is the same; and the irrationalism also remains the same. Linguistically oriented interpretive sociology dissolves into linguistic analysis; but at the same time, because it does not allow itself to transcend the dimension of traditional symbols, it has to forgo explanations of changes in language. Thus the movement of power, which moves everything else, eludes investigation.

The limitations of a linguistically oriented interpretive sociology are the limitations of its concept of motivation. It explains social action in terms of motives that are identical with the actor's own interpretations of situations, and thus identical with the linguistically oriented meaning in terms of which the actor orients himself. The subjective approach, whether it is grounded in phenomenology, linguistics, or hermeneutics, thus rules out a distinction between observed segments of behavior and the actors' interpretations:

What is the distinction then, if any, between a motivational statement and the overt action which follows? It is clear that they are not separate units, like a hand which throws a ball. The verbal (spoken to oneself, or more usually, merely thought) statement is an integral part of the entire activity. The act does not begin with its overt expression, the motivational statement merely preceding or accompanying the visible motions. Assessment of situation, persons, and self enter into the organization of an act, and are part of its structure.[11]

Thus new terminologies create new motivations:

Motive avowal and motive imputation are not radically different acts; they differ only insofar as motives are assigned to myself or to others. But the only motives that can be imputed are those which I myself can understand. I cannot attribute to others, any more than to myself, motives not dreamed of; neither can I attribute motives that I place no credence in, as for instance compacts with the devil or secret possession by spirits. We use the vocabularies of motive which we have learned to use, whether on ourselves or on others. When a man comes into contact with groups new to him and thus learns new terminologies, his assignments of motives become affected. He learns that new kinds of motivation exist, if not for himself then for others. Having admitted that such grounds for action do exist, it is often but a step to ascribe them to himself.[12]

A sociology that conceives motivation in this way must restrict itself to interpretive explication. The explanations it can provide are equivalent to linguistic descriptions and hermeneutic exegeses; it has to forgo causal explanations. Thus to represent motives does not means to identify causes. Linguistically oriented interpretive sociology is not a nomological science.

A. J. Ayer has criticized the distinction between motives and causes inspired primarily by Wittgenstein.[13] He begins by repeating the most important arguments for this distinction:

> The most simple of them is that motives operate a fronte whereas causes operate a tergo; to put it crudely, that causes push while motives pull. A more sophisticated argument is that cause and effect are distinct events: so, if the motive for an action caused it, it would have to be a separate occurrence which preceded the action or at any rate accompanied it; but in many, perhaps in most, cases of motivated actions, such separate occurrences are simply not discoverable; the specification of the motive is part of the description of the action, not a reference to anything outside it, and certainly not a reference to any distinct event.... Finally, a point is made of the fact that motivated action often consists in following or attempting to follow a rule; that is to say, the action may be one to which normative criteria are applicable; the question arises whether it has been performed correctly; but this means, so it is argued, that we somehow impoverish the motive if we regard it merely as a cause.[14]

Ayer's counterarguments amount to an attempt to circumvent the intentionality of behavior by recourse to dispositions that can be defined as end-states of self-regulating systems. This is a modernized version of the old physicalist proposal to characterize motives not in terms of an intended meaning but as needs that we measure by organic states. Given this presupposition, we can describe the behavior to be analyzed without reference to the motive; the motive, which is also represented in observable behavior, can be understood as the intial condition in a lawful hypothesis and identified as the cause of the motivated behavior. I do not see, however, how the organic states, the needs, or the systemic conditions that represent end-states, thus the motives, are supposed to be describable at all on the level of social action without reference to transmitted meaning. Since, however, the description of motivated behavior itself also implies this meaning, that description cannot be given independently of motive. The proposed distinction between motive for behavior and motivated behavior itself remains problematic.

Ayer, to be sure, does not seriously consider the level of social action. For him, social facts have the same status as events in the object domain of the natural sciences; in the final analysis, they too are movements of bodies. A theory that permits contexts of action to be explained causally thus operates reductionistically. It describes actions in an analytic framework that does not provide for actions as such—for example, in physiological terms. The concept of rule-governed action cannot be used for causal analysis in the social sciences. If we describe modes of behavior with reference to norms, we are choosing a form of representation that does not meet scientific criteria. We can understand social facts in their normative content; but we can also make them the object of a causal explanation—one has as little to do with the other as an aesthetic judgment about a rainbow has to do with the optical analysis of its wavelengths. In different social systems of reference a movement of the hand may have a different meaning (as a traffic signal, greeting, farewell, refusal, etc.). But this does not mean that it needs to be *explained* with reference to norms. If and to the extent to which the context of these rules determines behavior, that context will enter into the actor's motivation, which can be analyzed independently of normative contents:

If the motives which impel men to act are, let us say, projections of the state of their brains, there is no reason why this should not apply to their social responses as much as to anything else. But surely no purely physiological account could be an adequate description of an action. Obviously it could not; even if the study of the agent's brain could give us all the information that we needed beyond the observation of his physical movements, we should still have to decode it. But this is not an objection to holding that actions can be explained in these terms, any more than the fact that to talk about wave-lengths is not to describe colours is an objection to the science of optics.[15]

The problem that theory seeks to avoid through the choice of a physicalistic frame of reference recurs on the level of the data. Ayer sees that we still have to decode, as social actions, the sequence of physical movements to which such a theory is applied. The weak analogy between the observation of color qualities and the understanding of symbolic contents conceals the actual difficulty that Ayer's presentation involuntarily betrays. The reduction of qualitative observation to controlled observation cannot simply be equated to the translation of communicative experience into the observation of measured data. The necessity for an additional process of decoding shows that the object domain has been previously coded in terms of the fundamental theoretical assumptions. When we analyze the colors of the rainbow in terms of physical expressions, we can scarcely speak of a coding of the actual subject matter. We are analyzing an event that is initially experienced qualitatively from the point of view of possible technological disposition. When we interpret social subject matter in terms of a physical frame of reference with the same intent, that way of speaking makes sense. For the application of a theory that operates reductionistically to the domain of social action requires translation and retranslation. And this is precisely the point that gave rise to the problematic of the understanding of meaning. Ayer concludes his discussion at the point at which Cicourel took it up (see section 6.2).

The positivist procedure of substituting causes for motives is not the only alternative to a linguistically oriented interpretive sociology. *Freud's concept of unconscious motivation* permits us to expand approaches oriented to the subjective understanding of meaning, without having to ignore the intentionality of action or pass over the layer of symbolic meanings as such. Unconscious motives, like conscious ones, take the form of interpreted needs; thus they are given in symbolic contexts and can be understood hermeneutically. Dream analysis proceeds hermeneutically, as does the interpretation of hysterical symptoms or compulsive behavior. On the other hand, these motives are not given to the acting subject; they are excluded from consciousness through repression. This is why the patient needs the doctor who helps him bring unconscious motives to consciousness. On the one hand, unconsciously motivated actions are objectively meaningful; they can be interpreted. On the other hand, these motives have the status of causes, because they prevail outside the subjects' awareness, They are dispositions acquired in early childhood situations of denial and conflict. Thus the behavior that is being analyzed can be described without reference to the underlying motives. It is the analyst who makes the connection. When the interpretations, which at first exist only for the doctor, are acknowledged as correct by the patient himself as well, the unconscious motive can be dissolved. Unconscious motives are disguised, as it were, as causes; but only in this disguise do they have motivating force.

9.2 In a study of Freud's theory of the unconscious, Alasdair MacIntyre has examined the connection between the study of motivation and causal explanation.[16] He attempts to purge Freud's concept of unconscious motivation from misleading connotations and reduce it to the usual meaning of "motive." Like motives in general, an unconscious motive consists of action-orienting meaning. It is the object of linguistic analysis, not the object of causal analysis. The actor can reject ascriptions of motive in normal behavior as well. If he admits the motive, we are confirmed; if he denies it, we do not take that as adequate falsification. It is sufficient if the addressee can be brought at all and in principle to acknowledge what is imputed to him. It does not seem to be any different with the unconscious motivations that Freud investigated:

Unless the patient will in the end avow his intention the analyst's interpretation of his behaviour is held to be mistaken. "In the end" is a phrase that covers the multitude of almost interminable turnings and twistings of which an analysis may consist. Of course, it is a feature of the psychoneuroses that the patient will in the short run deny, and often deny vehemently, the analyst's interpretations of his conduct. Sometimes this denial may go on for a very long time. And there are unsuccessful analyses. So that it will not do for the psychoanalyst to make it a necessary criterion of a correct interpretation of the motivation of an action that the patient should in fact avow the correctness of the interpretation within any particular period of time. But the psychoanalyst means by a correct interpretation of an action an interpretation that the patient would avow if only certain conditions were to be fulfilled. What these conditions are depends on the character of the patient's disorder and its aetiology. Thus a patient's intention or purpose in his neurotic behaviour is something which both is betrayed in his behaviour and is what he would, if he were not prevented by his disorder, avow. Thus the meaning of "intention" is elucidated by a categorial reference to behaviour supplemented by a hypothetical reference to avowals. This surely is how the concept of intention and kindred concepts ought to be understood in ordinary pre-Freudian usage.[17]

MacIntyre considers Freud's identification of unconscious motives with causes to be a mere confusion. In actuality, psychoanalysis serves to reinterpret a previously binding interpretation of the patient's life history. The doctor offers the patient a new terminology. In this framework new interpretations of the biographical situation are produced and new motivations can develop: "So that what the analyst provides is a way of arranging the past that is acceptable to the present. He offers not so much an explanation as an identification and then a classification. And the 'unconscious' functions here as a classificatory label, as a category into which many of those aspects of life which are now brought to the patient's attention can be fitted."[18]

MacIntyre agrees with Ayer that intentional action can be explained causally only through a process of reduction within the framework of general theories: "The neurophysiologists will one day give us their full account, which will itself be reducible to a set of chemical and finally of physical explanations."[19] But unlike Ayer he sees that even comprehensive explanations of this kind, however they may extend our power of technological exploitation to processes of human behavior that are not understood, do not have a particle of meaning that we could use in the practice of life. To that end we do not need technologically exploitable information about natural laws but rather "a different kind of account, the kind of portrayal that the novelist rather than the scientist gives us."[20] From the perspective of linguistic analysis, psychoanalysis appears as a hermeneutic exploration of unconsciously motivated behavior. It has more to do with the critical exegesis of texts than with empirical science. More consistently than Winch, MacIntyre insists on the purely therapeutic significance of linguistic analysis. In so doing, however, he has to rob psychoanalysis, which he has reduced to linguistic analysis, of its claim to theoretical status.

This accords badly, however, with the categorial framework that Freud himself developed. The latter does serve for the reconstruction of life histories, but it is the reconstruction of particular life histories in accordance with a generally binding model. It is to this model that psychoanalysis owes its appearance of being a general theory. In actuality it is a systematically generalized history. Freud's theory provides the outline of a narrative that presents the psychodynamic development of the child from birth to maturity in narrative fashion, as a sequence of actions with a typical distribution of roles, fundamental conflicts appearing in succession, and recurrent patterns of interaction, as well as with dangers, crises, and resolutions. What is most important is that this sequence can proceed normally or deviantly. The definition of the conflicts indicates their correct resolutions. MacIntyre fails to recognize the systematic framework of Freudian hermeneutics, which is thus also more than just hermeneutics.

Whereas the interpreter tests his hermeneutic preunderstanding against the text and corrects it until both "horizons fuse"—thus until his interpretation is successful within the framework of a language common both to himself and to that of his text—Freud established an interpretive framework once and for all in his metapsychology. Once can perhaps see this framework as the result of repeated clinical experiences, which have themselves been accumulated in accordance with the more elastic procedure of hermeneutic anticipations that are confirmed in a circular fashion. Once established, the interpretive framework no longer permits such corrections. In compensation, it offers the advantages of a functionalistic framework. Metapsychology views the developmental process as an orderly sequence of states of a system, so that all biographical variables can be analyzed in relation to the system as a whole. To be sure, the objective-intentional context of life history is not functionalist in the usual sense. The elementary processes are not seen from the instrumentalist point of view of the purposive-rational organization of means or the adaptive behavior of the organism. Rather, the functionalist context is now interpreted in terms of drama: the elementary processes are seen as parts of a context of interactions through which a "meaning" is realized.

We cannot equate this kind of meaning with ends that are realized through means. It is not a question of a category of meaning belonging to the sphere of instrumental action, as, for example, the maintenance of a certain state of the system under changing external conditions. It is a question of a meaning formed through communicative action and articulated as biographical experience; it is a meaning constituted within the framework of formative processes (*Bildungsprozesse*). Thus we also speak of the "meaning" revealed in a drama. In a formative process, however, we are both actor and critic at once. Ultimately we who are enmeshed in the drama of a life history must become critically aware of the meaning of the process. Ultimately, the subject too must be able to narrate his own history; for the end-state of a formative process is not reached until the subject has remembered the sequence of identifications and alienations through which he was constituted. In a formative process we only learn as much about the world as we simultaneously experience in ourselves as the learning subject. This dialectic of knowledge of the world and knowledge of oneself is the *experience of reflection* whose course Hegel sketched in the *Phenomenology of Spirit*. In like manner, Freud represented the individual life history as one pathway of the experience of reflection.

We can think of Freud's interpretive framework as a narrative background against which interrupted formative processes can be filled out to form a complete history. The metapsychological model of development enables the doctor to piece together fragmentary information gained in the analytic dialogue in such a way that he can virtually anticipate the experience of reflection of which the patient is not capable. He suggests interpretations of a history that the patient cannot at first narrate but that can be confirmed only when the patient tells it as his own history. Each instance of interpretation is confirmed through the successful continuation of an interrupted formative process; conversely, it cannot be definitively refuted by a failure.

The general interpretive framework is confirmed, of course, through the distribution of clinical successes and failures. But the criteria of success cannot be operationalized. Successes and failures cannot be established intersubjectively, as, for instance, the removal of symptoms can be. The experience of reflection is confirmed only by the completion of the reflection; through it, the objective power of an unconscious motive is broken. The experience of reflection is a proving ground where false hypotheses can founder. But it is not equivalent either to controlled observation or to communicative experience. Thus psychoanalytic assumptions are subject to other logical conditions of falsification. The assumptions inevitably refer to conditions for suspending the very experience through which they must be confirmed. When that does not occur, either the interpretation is false or the therapy is ineffective. Perhaps the therapy cannot prevail over resistances that have been correctly diagnosed. The conditions of therapeutic failure must be capable of theoretical explanation. But in this the empirical confirmation of the theory has already been assumed.

Individual hypotheses can be detached from the metapsychological framework of interpretation and tested independently. For this, translation into the theoretical framework of the strict empirical sciences is necessary. This translation eliminates, of course, the specific context in which covariances between observable events signify not a nexus of natural law but rather a connection that can be dissolved through reflection, thus a quasi-natural nexus. Nevertheless the Freudian theory does contain assumptions that can be interpreted as lawlike hypotheses in the strict sense. Thus it also grasps causal relationships. It cannot be reduced to a hermeneutics of the motives for action, as MacIntyre asserts. Certainly, psychoanalysis is a general interpretive model rather than a general theory. The functionalist relationship of the parts to the whole is determined not by causality and reciprocity, as in the model of a self-regulating system, but rather, as in the dramatic model, through the reflective connection between unconscious and conscious motivation. But the unconscious motivation produces connections between events and modes of behavior that can easily be *understood* as causal. The unconscious is not simply a label under which the parts of a life history that only appear in the light of a new terminology can be subsumed. "The unconscious" designates rather the class of all motivating compulsions arising from those need interpretations that are not socially sanctioned and that are evident in the causal connection between situations of denial and abnormal modes of behavior. The number and gravity of causal motivations for action visible in the behavior of adult patients from the perspective of psychoanalysis is a measure of the disturbance and deviance of the formative process being analyzed.

Freud could apply the action model of linguistically oriented interpretive sociology only to the description of the state in which the formative process culminates, not to the process itself. Only in the final state of a formative process that has been reflected upon do all the motivations for action coincide with the meanings to which the actor himself is oriented, that is, with the intersubjectively valid norms of action. Needs whose satisfaction is socially acceptable are interpreted in terms of these norms. But there are also interpreted needs whose satisfaction is not secured through institutions. We can say that the interpretations of these needs are suppressed. They are subjected to censorship. The image that Freud uses for this process of repression is the "re-pression" of the forbidden interpretations into the unconscious. The needs are not thereby deprived of their motivating force. They do motivate actions, only these actions may not appear under the appropriate interpretations. They are disguised. The suppressed interpretations and fragmented needs no longer appear on the level of acknowledged cultural tradition and prevailing norms; rather, they establish themselves behind the backs, as it were, of the acting subjects—as unconscious motives.

They are still motives, and that means that they are action-orienting meaning. But now they act in the manner of external causes.

The social force of repression, of instinctual renunciation under authority, is transformed into the psychological compulsion of unconsciously motivated actions: into virtual dream actions, into rationalized parapraxes, into compulsion-neurotic substitute actions, into somaticized actions, that is, psychosomatic disturbances, or into the regressive repetition of behavior patterns fixed at an early childhood level. All these actions are subjectively understood in terms of a context other than the one that actually motivates them. In deciphering repressed interpretations as unconscious motives,[21] linguistic analysis transcends the dimension of subjectively intended meaning and cultural tradition. It steps outside language as serving communication and focuses on the causal connections between traumatic experiences and abnormal behavior patterns. As causal analysis, it penetrates into the dimension of a language that, because it is withdrawn from public communication through repression, reacts with a complementary compulsion and subjects intentional action to the power of a second nature. The suppressed intentions become causes that subject communicative action to the causality of quasinatural relationships. This causality reigns through the symbolic means of the spirit. For the same reason it is also subject to being compelled by the force of reflection. MacIntyre sees that the causal relationships that psychoanalysis traces arise with the repression of need interpretations: "The purpose is unconscious if it is not only unacknowledged (that alone would merely make it preconscious) but if the patient is unable by ordinary means to acknowledge it. It is this inability of the patient which introduces a genuine causal element into the explanation of the behavior in question."[22]

But MacIntyre is not able to identify the domination in such acts of repression, which not only do not get a hearing in language but even repress language itself through the prohibition of unconstrained discussion. It is this domination that splits off transmitted meaning from free communication and distorts it into a demonic force of nature.

10 Open Questions

The limitations of a linguistically oriented interpretive sociology direct us once again to functionaism. A functionalist approach has the advantage of systematically grasping objective-intentional contexts. The objective context, in terms of which social action can be understood without sacrificing intentionality, is not woven solely of the threads of transmitted meaning and tradition articulated in language. The dimensions of labor and domination in it cannot be suppressed in favor of subjectively intended symbolic contents. A functionalist framework can also do justice to nonnormative conditions. Cultural tradition here loses the semblance of absolutism that a hermeneutics become autonomous had falsely claimed for it. Tradition can be accorded its place *in the totality*; it can be understood in its relationship to the system of social labor and political domination. Thus it becomes possible to understand the functions that cultural tradition serves in the system as a whole, without them being expressed *in it* and *as such*—ideological relationships, in other words. Language as ideology corresponds to the excommunicated language that is suppressed into a demonic natural force. In a word, functionalism allows analysis of contexts of action from the dual perspective of subjectively determined meaning and objective meaning.

Parsons has worked out a differentiated framework for a functionalist theory of action. Preoccupied with the postulates of a general methodology of the empirical sciences, he suppresses the problematic of access to social facts through understanding meaning. He does not see the implications of communicative experience for theory formation. He wants to apply functionalism in the social sciences as would the biologists. He is thereby forced against his will to a purely normative-analytic approach. The desired end-states of a social system cannot be grasped descriptively; they must be established by definition. If we insist nevertheless on an empirical-analytic understanding of the system, we must concern ourselves with communicative experience and accept a categorial framework that is in principle linked to the self-understanding of acting subjects and that can also be incorporated in turn into that self-understanding. But given this presupposition, the functionalist relationship can no longer be understood in instrumental terms. In place of the desired end-state of a self-regulating system there appears the anticipated end-state of a formative process. A functionalism that is hermeneutically enlightened and historically oriented has as its aim not general theories in the sense of strict empirical science but a general interpretation of the kind that we have examined in the example of psychoanalysis.

Classical social theories from Marx and Comte to Franz Oppenheimer and Max Weber pursued this intention more or less implicitly. These earlier theories, which reflect on the formative process of society as a whole and reconstruct the contemporary situation at any given time through past contexts of interaction, are loosely identified with empirical science, even and precisely by their authors. If one applies this scientific criterion, Popper's critique of these theories is justified.[23] But those social theories are not properly subjected to that criterion. They do not need to place themselves in comparison with strict empirical sciences. They have no defect to conceal. For a historically oriented functionalism does not aim at technologically exploitable information. It is guided by an emancipatory cognitive interest that has reflection as its aim and demands enlightenment about its own formative process. Whether or not it admits this interest, sociology pursues it even today, insofar as it does not dissolve into social-psychological behavioral science, systems research, or the hermeneutics of intellectual history. This is attested to by the substantial work of Riesman, Mills, Lipset, Perroux, Friedmann, Dahrendorf, Marcuse, and others.

Parsons's work has been criticized as exhausting itself in conceptual fetishism. And if one takes Parsons's intention seriously, there is in fact in his work a ridiculous imbalance between the towering heap of empty categorial containers and the slight empirical content housed in them. But we see these categories in a different light when we cease to regard them as preliminary stages in the designing of strict theories. Perhaps the fact that no one has yet been able to develop a single *theory* within this analytical framework is not after all due merely to pragmatic difficulties. For that would simply not be possible if we were in fact dealing with the framework of a general *interpretation*. In this case, the categorial framework of the so-called theory of action would not be merely a proposal on the analytic level. Rather, it would contain the results of long hermeneutic experience and preunderstanding of processes of socialization that had proved reliable. From this point of view, what seems to be a preparatory clarification of categories would itself already be a theory, although one that does not admit its true character and is thus unsatisfactory, even in terms of the criteria of theoretically generalized history. I consider it worthwhile to investigate Parsons's theory in terms of the question whether the useful elements in it are suitable for use in reconstructing the history of social systems. The human species too is constituted as such through formative processes that are embodied in the structural transformation of social systems and that can be reflected upon, in other words, narrated systematically, from the perspective of an anticipated later point in those processes.

A history has a beginning and an end. The beginning can only be reconstructed anthropologically from the ongoing conditions of existence of socialized individuals, as the beginning of the human species.[24] The end can only be anticipated through the experience of reflection, from a point of view specific to a given situation. For this reason, the framework of a general interpretation, however saturated it may be with prior hermeneutic experience and however much it may have been confirmed in individual interpretations, retains a hypothetical moment. The truth of historically oriented functionalism is confirmed not technically but only practically, in the successful continuation and completion of a formative process.

Here we are again confronted with the problem of that singular relationship to theory of practice that since the eighteenth century has appeared wherever the logic of inquiry has involved the intention of enlightenment.

Notes

Preface

1. Completed in April 1966, it was first published as a special volume of *Philosophische Rundschau* in 1967. For a list of reviews, see R. Görtzen, *Jürgen Habermas: Eine Bibliographie* (Frankfurt: 1982), pp. 35–36.

2. Richard Bernstein, *The Restructuring of Social and Political Philosophy* (New York: 1976).

3. Albrecht Wellmer later called this "the linguistic turn in critical theory," in "Communication and Emancipation: Reflections on the Linguistic Turn in Critical Theory," in J. O'Neill, ed., *On Critical Theory* (New York: 1976), pp. 231–263.

4. See the excellent collection edited by F. Dallmayr and T. McCarthy, *Understanding and Social Inquiry* (Notre Dame: 1977).

5. See W. Diederich, ed., *Beiträge zur diachronischen Wissenschaftstheorie* (Frankfurt: 1974).

6. Concerning my exchange with Gadamer, see the collection published by Suhrkamp Verlag under the title *Hermeneutik und Ideologiekritik* (Frankfurt: 1971). See also Paul Ricoeur, "Ethics and Culture. Habermas and Gadamer in Dialogue," *Philosophy Today* 2 (1973): 153ff; J. Mendelsohn, "The Habermas-Gadamer Debate," *New German Critique* 18 (1979): 44ff; D. Misgeld, "Gadamer's Hermeneutics," *Philosophy of Social Science* 9 (1979): 221ff; A. R. How, "The Habermas-Gadamer Debate," *Journal of the British Society for Phenomenology* 11 (1980): 131ff; and U. Nassen, "H. G. Gadamer und J. Habermas: Hermeneutik, Ideologiekritik, Diskurs," in U. Nassen, ed., *Klassiker der Hermeneutik* (Paderborn: 1982), pp. 301ff.

7. J. Habermas, *The Theory of Communicative Action*: Vol. I, *Reason and the Rationalization of Society* (Boston: 1984); Vol. II, *Lifeworld and System: A Critique of Functionalist Reason* (Boston: 1987).

I The Dualism of the Natural and Cultural Sciences

1. For a critique of Popper's philosophy of science, which I cannot discuss systematically here, see A. Wellmer, *Methodologie als Erkenntnistheorie* (Frankfurt: 1967).

2. Exceptions are, among others, H. Skjervheim, *Objectivism and the Study of Man* (Oslo: 1959), and K. O. Apel, *Analytic Philosophy of Language and the Geisteswissenschaften* (Dordrecht: 1967).

3. J. v. Kempski, "Brückenschlag aus Missverständnis," in *Brechungen* (Hamburg: 1964), pp. 221–234.

4. This interest links the two collections: H. Albert, *Theorie und Realität* (Tübingen: 1964), and E. Topitsch, *Logik der Sozialwissenschaften* (Cologne: 1965).

5. W. Dilthey, *Einleitung in die Geisteswissenschaften* (1883), *Gesammelte Schriften*, Vol. I; *Abhandlungen zur Grundlegung der Geisteswissenschaften* (1875–1900), *Gesammelte Schriften*, Vol. V; the later (1907–1910) essays and fragments for the *Aufbau der geschichtlichen Welt in den Geisteswissenschaften, Gesammelte Schriften*, Vol. VII, are already influenced by Husserl's *Logische Untersuchungen*. They are already free of the Kantian approach to the philosophy of science, and they served Heidegger as a point of departure for his philosophical hermeneutics.

6. W. Windelband, *Geschichte und Naturwissenschaft* (Freiburg: 1894).

7. Cf. Rickert's "Die vier Arten des Allgemeinen in der Geschichte," appendix to the 5th ed. of *Die Grenzen der naturwissenschaftlichen Begriffsbildung* (Tubingen: 1929), pp. 739ff, especially pp. 749ff.

8. Cf. K. H. Haag, "Das Unwiederholbare," in *Zeugnisse* (Frankfurt: 1963), pp. 152–161: "Identity is the principle that constituted subjectivity and objectivity and related them to one another. But it is this principle only in that it creates out of existing nature the universal that becomes the soul of both men and things. The great European philosophical tradition declares identity, as what is conceptually graspable, to be what truly exists, while the nonidentical, the singularity of things, which avoided conceptual determination, sinks into nullity. In the ur-history of thought and being, identity is acquired at the price of the insignificance, in regard to content, of the nonidentical. Since classical antiquity, it has no longer been accorded any content in itself but rather acquires content only through subsumption under the universal.... This sacrifice of the particular, which mankind forces itself to make in the transition from the preidentical world to the identical world, however, is productive as well as being a loss. Abstraction from the individual was the presupposition that allowed mankind to identify itself and nature. Without it, however, men would also have remained incapable of perceiving the individual as such. The individual attains significance only as the negative in terms of which men reflect upon themselves" (pp. 152ff). In this context cf. also Theodor Adorno, *Negative Dialectics* (New York: 1973).

9. Rickert took this position in his first treatise, *Kulturwissenschaft und Naturwissenschaft* (Freiburg: 1899).

10. This change in position is clear in the first systematic elaboration of the theory, *Die Grenzen der naturwissenschaftlichen Begriffsbildung.*

11. Cf. *Der Gegenstand der Erkenntnis*, 3rd ed. (Tübingen: 1915), pp. 237ff.

12. This is also true of Wittgenstein's transcendental logic of language (see below, section III, 7). Cf. also the essay by G. Patzig, "Satz und Tatsache," in *Argumentationen, Festschrift für J. König* (Göttingen: 1964), pp. 170ff. Patzig conceives facts as the fulfilled truth conditions of propositions. He does not, however, consider different classes of possible truth conditions, each of which could be interpreted as a transcendental framework of possible experience.

13. E. Cassirer, *The Philosophy of Symbolic Forms*, Vol. 1 (New Haven: 1953), p. 78.

14. Ibid., p. 111.

15. An analogous difficulty is evident in present-day French structuralism; cf. L. Sebag, *Strukturalismus und Marxismus* (Frankfurt: 1966).

16. Cassirer, *Fünf Studien zur Logik der Kulturwissenschaften* (Darmstadt: 1961).

17. Cf. E. Cassirer, *The Philosophy of Symbolic Forms*, Vol. 3 (New Haven: 1957), pp. 58ff, 191ff.

18. Cassirer (1961), pp. 39, 56ff.

19. Cf. the proceedings of the 15th German conference of sociologists, O. Stammer, ed., *Max Weber and Sociology Today* (New York: 1971).

20. M. Weber, *Economy and Society*, G. Roth and C. Wittich, eds. (New York: 1968), vol. I, p. 4.

21. Ibid., pp. 7–8.

22. M. Weber, *Aufsätze zur Wissenschaftslehre* (Tübingen: 1922), p. 591. English: "Science as a Vocation," in H. H. Gerth and C. W. Mills, eds., *From Max Weber* (New York: 1946), pp. 129–156.

23. Ibid., pp. 174ff. English: "Objectivity in Social Science and Social Policy," in M. Weber, *The Methodology of the Social Sciences* (New York: 1949), pp. 49–112.

24. Ibid., p. 171.

25. Rickert (1929), pp. 693ff.

26. Weber, *Wissenschaftslehre*, p. 214.

27. H. Albert, "Wertfreiheit als methodisches Prinzip," in Topitsch (1965), pp. 181ff. In opposition to the positivist view, W. G. Runciman discusses the problem of value judgments within the dimension in which Max Weber posed it. He criticizes the postulate of value freedom as inadequate on the basis of Weber's own presuppositions. W. G. Runciman, *Social Science and Political Theory* (Cambridge: 1963), p. 59: "We have seen that Weber believes, against the extreme positivistic view, that the social sciences differ in kind from the natural. Even leaving aside the problem of the arbitrariness of basic points of view, the uniqueness of historical sequences and the meaningfulness of human behavior mean that there is a latitude of interpretation always confronting the social scientist which the natural scientist is luckily denied. Weber's procedure in the face of this situation breaks down not because he fails to concede that a sociological inquiry cannot be framed in valueneutral terms, but because this concession doesn't buy as much immunity from the remaining problems as he thinks. The arbitrariness of standpoints cannot merely be conceded in the original choice of terms, after which, with this sole limitation, the inquiry conducted can be kept value-free. The infection of values cannot all be passed off on to the questions asked and thereby kept away altogether from the answers given. The evaluative terms will have to be used in inquiries within which— and this is my point—no matter how rigorous the techniques of validation applied there will still be some interpretative latitude." Runciman understands the connection of the problem of value judgments with the choice of a theoretical language suitable for an object domain that is itself linguistically structured: "The point is, of course, the same as that which underlies Weber's whole position on 'value-relevance', and which derives from the fundamental differences between persons and actions on the one hand and objects and events on the other. But the fact that, as Weber saw, we are always confronted with a choice of terms, whether in

sociological or philosophical discussion, need not entail the further implication that any such choice is inherently unarguable. It is this further assumption of Weber which I am concerned to dispute. It is in fact possible to attack or defend the application of particular terms to a given case in such a way that one or other of the parties to the dispute may be induced to change his mind. Moreover, this will require an appeal both to the sociological evidence and to the philosophical presuppositions underlying the praise or blame which it is suggested that the evidence should evoke" (ibid., p. 173).

28. Cf. my contribution to the discussion in *Max Weber and Sociology Today*, pp. 59ff, in which I developed points of view from the older Weber scholarship: K. Löwith, *Max Weber and Karl Marx* (London: 1982); S. Landshut, *Kritik der Soziologie* (Leipzig: 1928); H. Freyer, *Soziologie als Wirlichkeitswissenschaft* (Berlin: 1930). For more recent literature on Weber see R. Bendix, *Max Weber* (New York: 1960) and E. Baumgarten, *Max Weber* (Tübingen: 1964).

29. J. Ritter, "Die Aufgabe der Geisteswissenschaften in der modernen Gesellschaft," in the annual publication of the Gesellschaft zur Forderung der Westfälischen Wilhelmsuniversität zu Münster (1961), pp. 11–39, 31ff.

30. J. Ritter, *Hegel and the French Revolution* (Cambridge, MA: 1982).

31. Ibid., p. 78.

32. See my essay, "Hegel's Critique of the French Revolution," in *Theory and Practice* (Boston: 1973), pp. 121–141.

33. Ritter (1961), p. 34.

34. H. Schelsky, "Einsamkeit und Freiheit," in *Rowohlts Deutsche Enzykopädie* (Hamburg: 1963), pp. 222–228, 278–295; cf. also Schelsky's outline "Grundzüge einer neuen Universität," in Mikat and Schelsky, *Grundzüge einer neuen Universität* (Gütersloh: 1966), pp. 35–70.

35. Schelsky (1963), p. 280.

36. Ibid., p. 225.

37. On what follows, see the appendix to my *Knowledge and Human Interests* (Boston: 1971), pp. 301–317.

38. Cf. Herbert Marcuse, *One Dimensional Man* (Boston: 1964; London: 1964).

39. Schelsky, *Ortsbestimmung der deutschen Soziologie* (Düsseldorf: 1959), pp. 86–109.

40. Ibid., p. 67.

41. Rescuing subjectivity from the power of institutions is a theme that stems from Gehlen, but is now used by Schelsky against his teacher. Cf. Schelsky (1959), p. 105.

42. H. Schelsky, *Der Mensch in der wissenschaftlichen Zivilisation*, Arbeitsgemeinschaft für Forschung des Landes Nordrhein-Westfalen, No. 96 (Cologne: 1961).

43. Ibid., p. 37.

44. Schelsky (1964), p. 299; cf. also my essay, "Vom sozialen Wandel der akademischen Bildung," in *Merkur* (May 1963).

45. The scientific method is invariant in relation to its objects. On the theoretical level, distinctions between object domains are reflected only in terminology, not in the logical form of statements.

46. E. Topitsch, "Das Verhältnis zwischen Sozial- und Naturwissenschaften," in Topitsch (1965), pp. 57–69.

47. See the essays "Seelenglaube und Selbstinterpretation" and "Motive und Modelle der Kantischen Moralmetaphysik," in E. Topitsch, *Zwischen Sozialphilosophie und Wissenschaft*, pp. 155–200, 201–234.

48. Cf. my critique of it in "Der befremdliche Mythos: Reduktion oder Evokation?" in *Philosophische Rundschau* 6 (1958): 215ff.

49. G. H. Mead, *Mind, Self and Society from the Standpoint of a Social Behaviorist*, 7th ed. (Chicago: 1948).

50. K. R. Popper, *The Open Society and Its Enemies*, Vol. II (Princeton: 1966), p. 264; cf. also Popper, "Naturgesetze und theoretische Systeme," in Albert (1964), pp. 87–102.

51. C. G. Hempel, "The Function of General Laws in History," in H. Feigl and W. Sellars, *Readings in Philosophical Analysis* (New York: 1949), pp. 459–471. P. L. Gardiner makes a noteworthy attempt to test this thesis against the writings of historians themselves, and thus to modify it, in his *The Nature of Historical Explanation* (Oxford: 1952). In contrast, the essay by V. Kraft, "Geschichtsforchung als strenge Wissenschaft" in Topitsch (1965), pp. 72–84, does not advance the argument.

52. E. Nagel, *The Structure of Science* (London: 1961), p. 558. Cf. chapter 15 of that volume, "Problems in the Logic of Historical Inquiry," pp. 545ff. In contradistinction to Nagel, M. Scriven does not consider it possible, given the effects, to deduce statements about their causes from probabilistic assumptions of trivial content. Statements of this sort, with which we must be content for pragmatic reasons, in lieu of statements of universal laws, can serve as a basis for a critical justification of explanations. Cf. M. Scriven, "Truisms as Grounds for Historical Explanations," in P. Gardiner, ed., *Theories of History* (Glencoe, IL: 1959); Scriven, "Explanations, Predictions and Laws," in H. Feigl and G. Maxwell, eds., *Scientific Explanation, Space and Time* (Minneapolis: 1962), pp. 170ff; and Nagel (1961), p. 558.

53. Ibid., pp. 570–571.

54. Popper (1966), p. 266.

55. Cf. H.-G. Gadamer, *Truth and Method* (New York: 1975), pp. 274ff.

56. For a discussion of Collingwood, see A. Donagan, *The Later Philosophy of R. G. Collingwood* (Oxford: 1962), especially pp. 173–209.

57. W. Dray, *Laws and Explanation in History* (Oxford: 1964), p. 35.

58. Ibid., pp. 102ff.

59. Ibid., p. 104.

60. Ibid., p. 132. Applying this to the example of the loss of popularity, Dray says, "The force of the explanation of Louis XIV's unpopularity in terms of his policies being detrimental to French interests is very likely to be found in the detailed description of the aspirations, beliefs,

and problems of Louis's subjects. Given these men and their situation, Louis and his policies, their dislike of the king was an appropriate response" (ibid., p. 134).

61. A. C. Danto, *Analytical Philosophy of History* (Cambridge: 1965).

62. This approach is similar to the phenomenological one of W. Schapp, *In Geschichten verstrickt, Zum Sein von Mensch und Ding* (Hamburg: 1953).

63. Danto (1965), pp. 230ff.

64. Ibid., p. 226.

65. Cf. Danto (1965), chapter 9, pp. 233ff.

66. *A Report of the Committee on Historiography*, Social Science Research Council Bulletin 54 (New York: 1946); cf. also *The Social Sciences in Historical Study, a Report of the Committee on Historiography*, Social Science Research Council Bulletin 64 (New York: 1954).

67. W. J. Cahnmann and A. Boskoff, eds., *Sociology and History* (Glencoe, IL: 1964).

68. Cf. L. Gottschalk, ed., *Generalization in the Writing of History, A Report of the Committee on Historical Analysis*, Social Science Research Council (Chicago: 1963).

69. T. C. Cochran, "The Historian's Use of Social Role," in Gottschalk (1963), pp. 103ff.

70. For a critical perspective, see Hofstadter, "History and the Social Science," in F. Stern, ed., *The Varieties of History* (New York: 1956), pp. 359ff; for the opposing point of view, D. M. Potter, "Notes on the Problem of Historical Generalization," in Gottschalk (1963), pp. 178ff.

71. For examples see, among others, the contributions of Birnbaum, Heberle, and Baltzell in Cahnmann and Boskoff, eds. (1964).

72. Max Weber's studies of capitalism are an example of this; on them, cf. R. W. Green, ed., *Protestantism and Capitalism: The Weber Thesis and Its Critics* (Boston: 1959); also see F. v. Hayek, ed., *Capitalism and the Historians* (Chicago: 1954).

73. Cf. S. M. Lipset, "Bermerkungen zum Verhältnis von Soziologie und Geschichtswissenschaft," in Topitsch (1965), p. 477; for a more thorough discussion, see Lipset, Trow, und Coleman, *Union Democracy* (Glencoe, IL: 1956), pp. 17–32, 339–401.

74. Cf., among others, the contributions of Gilmore, Firey, Marsh, and especially Jacobs, in Cahnmann and Boskoff, eds. (1964).

75. Zollman and Hirsch, eds., *Explorations in Social Change* (London: 1963).

76. Willer and Zollschan, "Prolegomenon to a Theory of Revolutions," in Zollschan and Hirsch (1963), pp. 125ff; also R. Dahrendorf, "Elemente einer Theorie des sozialen Konflikts," in his *Gesellschaft und Freiheit* (Munich: 1961), pp. 197ff.

77. R. Bendix and P. Berger, "Images of Society and Concept Formation in Sociology," in L. Gross, *Symposium on Sociological Theory* (New York: 1959), pp. 92ff; this citation is from pp. 97ff.

78. C. W. Mills, *The Sociological Imagination* (New York: 1959), especially chapter 8, "Uses of History," p. 143ff; this citation is from p. 153.

79. A. Malewski, "Two Models of Sociology," in Albert (1964), pp. 103ff.

80. Mills (1959), p. 146.

81. Cf. also B. Moore, *Political Power and Social Theory* (Cambridge: 1958), and I. L. Horowitz, ed., *The New Sociology* (New York: 1964).

82. Mills (1959), pp. 150–151.

83. K. R. Popper, *The Poverty of Historicism* (London: 1957).

84. Cf. section 10.

II On the Methodology of General Theories of Social Action

1. P. Lazarsfeld, "Wissenschaft und empirische Sozialforschung," in Topitsch (1965), pp. 37ff.

2. J. v. Kempski, "Handlung, Maxime und Situation," in Albert (1964), pp. 233ff; this citation is from p. 235.

3. J. v. Kempski, "Der Aufbau der Erfahrung und das Handeln," in *Brechungen* (Hamburg: 1964), pp. 295ff; this citation is from pp. 299ff.

4. Cf. *Brechungen*, p. 231; cf. also J. v. Kempski, *Recht und Politik, Studien zur Einheit der Sozialwissenschaft* (Stuttgart: 1965).

5. V. Kempski, "Zur Logik der Ordnungsbegriffe," in Albert (1964), pp. 209ff; this citation is from p. 230.

6. Cf. v. Kempski, "Die Logik der Geisteswissenschaften und die Geschichte," in *Brechungen*, pp. 79ff, especially pp. 96ff.

7. In 1944 F. Kaufmann published a completely revised English version of his *Methodenlehre der Sozialwissenschaften* (Vienna: 1936): *Methodology of the Social Sciences*, 2nd ed. (New York: 1958)—cf. especially chapters 6, 10, and 17.

8. L. Robbins, in *An Essay on the Nature and Significance of Economic Science*, 2nd ed. (London: 1946), already refers to the analytic form of the statement of a law in pure economics.

9. H. Albert, "Modellplatonismus, Der neoklassische Stil des ökonomischen Denkens," in Topitsch (1965), pp. 406ff; cf. also H. Albert, "Probleme der Theorienbildung," the introduction to Albert (1964), especially pp. 22–38.

10. Albert, "Modellplatonismus," pp. 421ff.

11. Ibid., p. 422; cf. T. Parsons, "The Motivation of Economic Activities," in Parsons, *Essays in Sociological Theory* (Glencoe, IL: 1958), pp. 50–68.

12. E. Grunberg, "Notes on the Verifiability of Economic Laws," in Albert (1964), pp. 137ff.

13. Ibid., p. 149.

14. G. Gäfgen, *Theorie der wirtschaftlichen Entscheidung* (Tübingen: 1963); cf. also O. Morgenstern, "Die Theorie der Spiele und des wirtschaftlichen Verhaltens," in A. E. Ott, ed., *Preistheorie* (Cologne: 1965), pp. 437ff.

15. Gäfgen (1963), p. 46: "In this process, however, goals are linked not only through objective limits on their fulfillment but also directly, in that the fulfillment of one goal can raise the significance of another (complementarity) or lower it (substitutivity of goals)."

16. It is clear that only microeconomic theories can be put into the more general form of a theory of strategic action. This is not possible for theories of economic circulation as a whole. On systems research that makes use of a functionalist frame of reference, see section 5.2.

17. Gäfgen (1963), p. 63.

18. Ibid., p. 51.

19. Cf. also the editor's introduction to the collection *Grundlagen der Wirtschaftspolitik* (Cologne: 1966), ed. G. Gäfgen.

20. In what follows I neglect an interesting attempt to link the normative concept of purposive-rational action with the empirical concept of regulated psychological behavior: Miller, Galanter, and Pribram, *Plans and the Structure of Behavior* (New York: 1960). The authors replace the reflex-arc model of stimulus and response with the feedback-loop model of test-operate-test-exit. Observable behavior is conceived as the result of the execution of a plan. A given value system determines the choice among available plans for a specific situation. See especially chapter 4, "Values, Intentions, and the Execution of Plans," pp. 59ff. I do not see, however, how this "subjective behaviorism" can identify the value systems and the plans, thus the intentional framework of behavior, without immediately becoming involved in the hermeneutic difficulties that mark any action-theoretic approach. On this point, see below, chapter III.

21. R. K. Merton, *Social Theory and Social Structure* (Glencoe, IL: 1957), especially chapter 2, pp. 85ff.

22. W. I. Thomas, *The Unadjusted Girl* (Boston: 1927).

23. T. Parsons, "Wertgebundenheit und Objektivität in den Sozialwissenschaften," in Stammer (1965), p. 50. English: "Value-Freedom and Objectivity," in O. Stammer, ed., *Max Weber and Sociology Today* (New York: 1971), pp. 27–50.

24. T. Abel, "The Operation Called *Verstehen*," in Albert (1964), pp. 177ff.

25. Ibid., p. 181.

26. Ibid., p. 184.

27. Weber, *Wissenschaftslehre*, p. 100.

28. Abel, "The Operation Called *Verstehen*," p. 186: "It is an accepted fact that, in formulating hypotheses, we start with some 'hunch' or 'intuition.' Now it appears highly probable that the hunches which lead us to certain hypotheses concerning human behavior originate from the application of the operation of *Verstehen*."

29. E. Nagel, "Problems of Concept and Theory Formation in the Social Sciences," in Albert (1964), pp. 159ff; this citation is from p. 172; cf. also Nagel (1961), chapter 13, iv, pp. 473ff.

30. Cf. A. Pap, *Analytische Erkenntnistheorie* (Vienna: 1955), pp. 13ff, and R. Carnap, "On Belief Sentences," in McDonald, ed., *Philosophy and Analysis* (Oxford: 1954), pp. 129ff; in connection with Wittgenstein's *Tractatus*, see K. O. Apel, *Analytic Philosophy of Language and the Geisteswissenschaften* (Dordrecht: 1967); with regard to the phenomenological approach, see H. Skjervheim, *Objectivism and the Study of Man* (Oslo: 1959), especially chapter 5, "The Thesis of Extensionality."

31. Cf. J. B. Watson, *Behaviorism* (New York: 1930).

32. Nagel (1961), p. 477.

33. C. Morris, *Signs, Language and Behavior* (New York: 1955); on Morris cf. K. O. Apel, "Sprache und Wahrheit," in *Philosophische Rundschau* 1959, pp. 161ff.

34. Morris (1955), p. 17.

35. Ibid., p. 44.

36. Mead (1948), p. 69.

37. Morris (1955), pp. 45ff.

38. P. F. Strawson, "Critical Notice," in *Mind* LXIII: 84ff; this citation is from p. 85.

39. P. Winch, *The Idea of a Social Science* (London: 1958), pp. 34–35.

40. B. F. Skinner, *Verbal Behavior* (New York: 1957). Hypotheses on verbal behavior in terms of learning theory stem from Miller and Dollard's fundamental research (*Social Learning and Imitation*) from 1941, though they have since been refined.

41. N. Chomsky, "A Review of B. F. Skinner's *Verbal Behavior*," in Fodor and Katz, eds., *The Structure of Language* (Englewood Cliffs, NJ: 1964), pp. 547ff; this citation is from p. 576.

42. N. Chomsky, "Current Issues in Linguistic Theories," in Fodor and Katz (1964), pp. 50ff; this citation is from p. 113.

43. Ibid., p. 52.

44. Ibid.

45. J. Bennett, *Rationality* (London: 1964).

46. A. MacIntyre, "A Mistake about Causality in Social Science," in Laslett and Runciman, eds., *Philosophy, Politics, and Society* (Oxford: 1964), pp. 48ff. I shall not go into the author's problematic interpretation of Marx, Pareto, and Max Weber.

47. Ibid., p. 52; cf. also section 9.2, below.

48. I am setting aside the distinction between two competing approaches to the analysis of behavior, that of the instinct theorists on the one hand and that of the behaviorist learning theorists on the other. The psychological frame of reference of the stimulus-response theories is weaker in content and thus permits a more extensive research strategy in reductionist terms. The biological frame of reference is conceived in more specific terms. It rests on theoretical assumptions concerning evolution and is concerned exclusively with learning processes that serve the preservation of the species. See D. S. Lehrmann, "Problems Raised by Instinct

Theories," *Quarterly Review of Biology* 28 (1953): 337–365; for an opposing view, see K. Lorenz, "Phylogenetische Anpassung und adaptive Modifikation des Verhaltens," in Lorenz, *Über tierisches und menschliches Verhalten, Ges. Abhandlungen,* Vol. II (Munich: 1965), pp. 301–358; see also Lorenz, *Evolution and the Modification of Behavior* (Chicago: 1965).

49. I shall return to this point in the next chapter. An anthology edited by D. Hymes, *Language in Culture and Society* (New York and London: 1964), provides an excellent idea of the relevance and breadth of linguistic studies in cultural anthropology and sociology. See also C. Levi-Strauss, *Structural Anthropology* (New York: 1964).

50. B. Malinowski, "The Functional Theory," in *A Scientific Theory of Culture* (Chapel Hill: 1944), and A. R. Radcliffe-Brown, *Structure and Function in Primitive Society* (London: 1952).

51. Radcliffe-Brown (1952), pp. 179ff.

52. T. Parsons, *The Social System* (Glencoe, IL: 1964, 1951); R. K. Merton, *Social Theory and Social Structure* (Glencoe, IL: 1964, 1949); and Parsons and Shils, eds., *Toward a General Theory of Action* (New York: 1962, 1951).

53. In his *Key Problems of Sociological Theory* (London: 1961), following Weber, Mannheim, and Myrdal, John Rex advances a suggestion for the analytic framework of a theory of action constructed on a nonfunctionalist basis. See especially chapter 5 therein, pp. 78ff. Rex has not convinced me that general theories of nonrational action are possible within this framework.

54. T. Parsons, "An Approach to Psychological Theory in Terms of the Theory of Action," in S. Koch, ed., *Psychology, A Study of a Science,* Vol. III (New York: 1959), pp. 612–712; Parsons, "On the Concept of Influence," in *Public Opinion Quarterly* (1963): 37ff; and Parsons, "Die jüngsten Entwicklungen in der Strukturell-funktionalen Theorie," *Kölner Zeitschrift für Soziologie und Sozialpsychologie* 1 (1964): 30ff; see also his *Beiträge zur soziologischen Theorie* (Neuwied: 1964), with an introduction by D. Rüschemeyer.

55. Parsons, in Koch (1959), p. 631.

56. Cf. Parsons and Smelser, *Economy and Society, a Study in the Integration of Economic and Social Theory* (London: 1956), and Parsons, "Voting and the Equilibrium of the Amerian Political System," in Burdick and Brodbeck, eds., *American Voting* Behavior (Glencoe, IL: 1959), pp. 80ff.

57. I am neglecting the objections raised by sociologists (Dahrendorf, Lockwood, Rex) against the functionalist approach, because they are only indirectly of methodological significance. The thesis that social conflicts and social-structural changes cannot be adequately analyzed within the functionalist frame of reference is difficult to sustain. What is important, however, is the criticism of the methodologically unfounded restriction Parsons sets when he derives disturbances of system equilibrium in principle from external conditions and excludes endogenous causes of the disfunctionality of system states. Cf. R. Mayntz, "On the Use of the Equilibrium Concept in Social System Analysis," *Transactions of the 5th World Congress of Sociology,* Vol. IV, 1964, pp. 133ff.

58. Nagel (1961), p. 403.

59. Ibid., pp. 421ff.

60. C. G. Hempel, "The Logic of Functional Analysis," in L. Gross (1959), pp. 271ff, especially pp. 299ff.

61. Parsons, "Die jüngsten Entwicklungen in der strukturell-funktionalen Theorie" (1964), p. 37.

62. Nagel (1961), p. 530. Cf. the analogous critique in W. G. Runciman, *Social Science and Political Theory*, pp. 109ff, and J. Rex, *Key Problems of Sociological Theory*, chapter 4, pp. 60ff.

63. In his foreword to T. Parsons, *Beiträge zur soziologischen Theorie* (Neuwied: 1964), p. 20.

64. Cf. Don Martindale, ed., *Functionalism in the Social Sciences: The Strength and Limits of Functionalism in Anthropology, Economics, Political Science and Sociology* (Philadelphia: 1965); see also I. C. Jarvie, *The Revolution in Anthropology* (London: 1964), and R. Brown, *Explanation in Social Science* (London: 1963), especially chapter 9, pp. 109ff.

65. The thesis of value-universalism requires proof of the completeness of this table of categories of basic orientations. Parsons attempts to provide this proof in asserting a systematic connection between the four fundamental orientations (universalism/specificity, performance/affectivity, particularism/ diffuseness, quality/neutrality) and the four functions of a self-regulating system (adaptation, goal attainment, integration, pattern maintenance). His extensive technical efforts, however, cannot hide the fact that the correlation between the fundamental value orientations and the necessary system functions remains arbitrary. Parsons develops this idea under the title "Pattern Variables Revisited," in a response to R. Dubin, "Parsons' Actor-Continuities in Social Theory," *American Sociological Review* 25 (1960): 457ff. See also Parsons's afterword to M. Black, ed., *Social Theories of T. Parsons* (New York: 1961), pp. 311ff.

66. Cf. H. Marcuse, *One Dimensional Man* (Boston: 1964).

67. Cf. chapter IV below.

III On the Problem of Understanding Meaning in the Empirical-Analytic Sciences of Action

1. Cf. Oskar Becker, *Grösse und Grenze der mathematischen Denkweise* (Freiburg and Munich: 1959); see also O. Pöggeler, "Hermeneutische und Semantische Phänomenologie," *Philosophische Rundschau* 13 (1965): 1ff.

2. A. Kaplan, *The Conduct of Inquiry, Methodology for Behavioral Science* (San Francisco: 1964).

3. Cf. Kaplan (1964), p. 10: "This reconstruction has been serviceable for some time, chiefly in application to the more advanced parts of physics, though in a few instances also to biological behavioral science. But a reconstructed logic is itself, in effect, a hypothesis. As with other hypotheses, as time goes on it may become more and more awkward to 'fit' the hypothesis to the facts—here, the facts constituted by the logic-in-use. It is not a question of whether the facts can be so construed, but rather whether it is still worthwhile to do so, whether the reconstruction in question continues to throw light on the sound operations actually being used. The 'hypothetico-deductive' reconstruction fails to do justice to some of the logic-in-use, and conversely, some of the reconstructed logic has no counterpart in what is actually in use. The formation of hypotheses is treated as though it were largely an extralogical matter. On the other hand, formal deductions in postulational systems are so seldom found in science that the logician is called upon to construct such systems himself, so as to provide his reconstructions with a subject-matter."

4. Ibid., p. 136.

5. Ibid.

6. Ibid., p. 32.

7. Ibid., p. 362.

8. Ibid., pp. 186ff.

9. Ibid., p. 176.

10. P. Lorenzen, "Wie is Objektivität in der Physik möglich?" in *Methodisches Denken* (Frankfurt: 1968), pp. 142ff.

11. A. V. Cicourel, *Method and Measurement in Sociology* (Glencoe, IL: 1964), pp. 21ff.

12. Ibid., p. 19.

13. Ibid., p. 18.

14. W. I. Thomas, *The Child in America* (New York: 1928), p. 572, and Thomas, *Social Behavior and Personality*, ed. Volkart (New York: 1951), pp. 80ff. R. K. Merton calls the principle of the subjective interpretation of social action "the Thomas theorem."

15. W. Torgerson, *Theory and Method of Scaling* (New York: 1958), pp. 21ff.

16. C. Coombs, "Theory and Methods of Social Measurement," in Festinger and Katz, *Research Methods in the Behavioral Sciences* (New York: 1953), pp. 471ff.

17. C. Coombs, *A Theory of Data* (New York: 1964).

18. Cicourel (1964), p. 22.

19. Ibid., pp. 14ff.

20. Ibid., p. 171.

21. It does seem that transference phenomena cannot be completely excluded even under extreme conditions of objectification. The experimenter too is engaged in interaction with the experimental subjects. Aside from the measuring instruments themselves, which presuppose the intersubjectivity of traditional symbols and habitual interpretations obtaining between the researcher and his object, the *situation in which the measuring instruments are used* is also part of a cultural world shared by both parties. The experiments on experiments conducted primarily by Rosenthal and his colleagues confirm this. We have known for a long time that the socioculturally determined conception of the experimenter's sex, race, religion, social status, and personality characteristics have an effect on the performance of experimental subjects (experimenter attributes effects). The subtlety of transference phenomena, however, is especially evident in the influence of subjective variables: the performance of the experimental subject is dependent upon the experimenter's ability to solve the experimental tasks himself (experimenter modeling effects) as much as on the expectations and wishes of the experimenter regarding the outcome of the experiment (experimenter expectancy and data desirability effects). Rosenthal concludes his report "The Effect of the Experimenter on the Results of Personality Research" (in B. A. Maher, ed., *Progress in Experimental Personality Research*, New York and London: 1964, pp. 80ff) with the lines: "Perhaps the most compelling and the most general conclusion to be drawn is that human beings can engage in highly effective and influential unprogrammed and unintended communication with one another. The subtlety of

this communication is such that casual observation of human dyads is unlikely to reveal the nature of this communication process" (p. 111). What eludes observation is obviously the extremely fine-meshed screen of culturally binding conceptual schemata in terms of which the most inconspicuous events gain symbolic content. Cf. also Rosenthal, Kohn, et al., "Data Desirability, Experimenter Expectancy and the Results of Psychological Research," *Journal of Personality and Social Psychology* III (1960): 20ff.

22. Cf. Cicourel (1964), p. 223: "The sociological observer, therefore, who fails to conceptualize the elements of common-sense acts in everyday life, is using an implicit model of the actor which is confounded by the fact that his observations and inferences interact, in unknown ways, with his own biographical situation within the social world. The very conditions of obtaining data require that he makes use of typical motives, cues, roles, etc., and the typical meanings he imputes to them, yet the structures of these common-sense courses of action are notions which the sociological observer takes for granted, treats as self-evident. But they are just the notions which the sociologist must analyze and study empirically if he desires rigorous measurement. The distributions he now constructs relegate such notions to a taken-for-granted status or to some latent continuum. Therefore, the observations which go to make up a distribution of, say, types of cities, responses to questionnaire items, or occupational prestige categories are only half of the picture. The distribution merely represents the 'outer' horizon for which operational procedures have been devised. Yet the 'meaning' of the distribution relies upon common-sense knowledge which includes the observer's typification of the world as it is founded in his own biographical situation, and his formalization of the actor's typification which is inextricably woven into his response. Both sets of typifications must be objects of sociological inquiry. —The inner horizon of idiomatic expressions, course-of-action motives, institutional and innovational language, and the like remain unclarified in the sociologist's distributions. The observations which are coded into dichotomies, fourfold tables, ordinal scales, zero-order correlations, and distributions in general reveal only half of the story; the 'bottom half' has been taken for granted, relegated to a 'latent continuum', yet informs the observer's description and inferences about the 'top half' represented by 'rigorous' measurement devices. It is the lack of explicit conceptualization and observation on the 'bottom half' which makes measurement in sociology metaphorical and not literal. The difficulty is to be found in the lack of adequate conceptualization and the use of measurement axioms which do not correspond to the structure of social action."

23. (Vienna: 1932), 2nd ed. 1960. English: *The Phenomenology of the Social World* (Evanston, IL: 1967). See also A. Schutz, *Collected Papers*, Vols. I and III (The Hague: 1962, 1964).

24. Schutz (1967), p. xxxi; cf. also W. E. Muhlmann, *Max Weber und die rationale Soziologie* (Tübingen: 1966), pp. 21ff, and his "'Wertfreiheit' und phänomenologische Reduktion im Hinblick auf die Soziologie," in *Festschrift für K. Holzamer* (Tübingen: 1966), pp. 457ff.

25. Cf. the essays in *Collected Papers*, Vol. I, especially "Common-Sense and Scientific Interpretation of Human Action," "Concept and Theory Formation in the Social Sciences," and "Symbol, Reality and Society"; in the second volume there is an interesting piece that refers to Parsons: "The Social World and the Theory of Social Action."

26. Cf. *Collected Papers*, Vol. I, pp. 5ff: "If, according to this view, all scientific constructs are designed to supersede the constructs of common-sense thought, then a principal difference between the natural and the social sciences becomes apparent. It is up to the natural scientists to determine which sector of the universe of nature, which facts and events therein, and which aspects of such facts and events are topically and interpretationally relevant to their specific purpose. These facts and events are neither preselected nor preinterpreted; they do not reveal intrinsic relevance structures. Relevance is not inherent in nature as such, it is the result of the selective and interpretative activity of man within nature or observing nature. The facts, data, and events with which the natural scientist has to deal are just facts, data and events within his observational field but this field does not 'mean' anything to the molecules, atoms,

and electrons therein.—But the facts, events, and data before the social scientist are of an entirely different structure. His observational field, the social world, is not essentially structureless. It has a particular meaning and relevance structure for the human beings living, thinking, and acting therein. They have preselected and preinterpreted this world by a series of common-sense constructs of the reality of daily life, and it is these thought objects which determine their behavior, define the goal of their action, the means available for attaining them—in brief, which help them to find their bearings within their natural and socio-cultural environment and to come to terms with it. The thought objects constructed by the social scientists refer to and are founded upon the thought objects constructed by the common-sense thought of man living his everyday life among his fellow-men. Thus, the constructs used by the social scientist are, so to speak, constructs of the second degree, namely constructs of the constructs made by the actors on the social scene, whose behavior the scientist observes and tries to explain in accordance with the procedural rules of his science."

27. For a critique of Schutz, see E. Voegelin, *Anamnesis* (Munich: 1966), pp. 17–60.

28. Basing themselves on Schutz's phenomenology of the everyday world, and bringing in Mead's social psychology of ego-identity, P. L. Berger and T. Luckmann, in *The Social Construction of Reality* (New York: 1966), have undertaken the ambitious task of sketching the outlines of an anthropologically grounded theory of society in the form of a sociology of knowledge.

29. Schutz, *Collected Papers* I, p. 53.

30. H. Garfinkel, "The Perception of the Other: A Study in Social Order," doctoral dissertation, Harvard University, 1952, and Garfinkel, "A Conception of and Experiments with, 'Trust' as a Condition of Stable Concerted Action," in O. J. Harvey, ed., *Motivation and Social Interaction* (New York: 1963), pp. 187–238. The report is in Cicourel (1964), pp. 165–170, 204–208.

31. Cicourel (1964), p. 207.

32. Ibid., P. 169.

33. Cf. Goffman, *Asylums: Essays on the Social Situation of Mental Patients and Other Inmates* (New York: 1961), *Encounters* (Indianapolis: 1961), and *Stigma: Notes on the Management of Spoiled Identity* (Englewood Cliffs, NJ: 1963).

34. Goffman, *Encounters*, p. 93.

35. In Germany H. P. Bahrdt, in "Zur Frage des Menschenbildes in der Soziologie," *Archives Européennes de Sociologie* II (1961): 1ff, presented similar points of view in a discussion of Dahrendorf's model of *homo sociologicus*. Bahrdt is among the few who still maintain a phenomenological approach. On the problematic of role, see also H. Popitz, "Der Begriff der sozialen Rolle," *Recht und Staat* No. 331/332 (Tübingen: 1967).

36. "Role Distance," in *Encounters*, pp. 85ff.

37. Cicourel (1964), pp. 202ff.

38. Cf. Schutz, "Symbol, Reality and Society," in *Collected Papers* I, pp. 287ff.

39. Ibid., p. 296.

40. Peter Winch, *The Idea of a Social Science* (London: 1958), p. 126.

41. E. Stenius, *Wittgenstein's Tractatus* (Oxford: 1960), chapter 11: "Wittgenstein as a Kantian Philosopher," pp. 214ff; see also K. O. Apel, *Analytic Philosophy of Language and the Geisteswissenschaften* (Dordrecht: 1967), and Apel, "Wittgenstein und das Problem des hermeneutischen Verstehens," *Zeitschrift für Theologie und Kirche* 63 (1966): 49ff. My interpretation of Wittgenstein relies heavily on Apel's studies.

42. L. Wittgenstein, *Tractatus Logico-Philosophicus* (London: 1961), 4.002.

43. Ibid., 3.332.

44. Ibid., 4.12, 4.121.

45. Ibid., 5.6.

46. Ibid., 5.61.

47. Ibid., 6.13.

48. L. Wittgenstein, *Philosophische Bemerkungen*, 54.

49. Wittgenstein, *Tractatus*, 4.115.

50. Ibid., 5.632.

51. Cf. J. O. Urmson, *Philosophical Analysis*, 4th ed. (Oxford: 1965), especially pp. 130ff.

52. L. Wittgenstein, *Philosophical Investigations*, 3rd ed. (New York: 1968), 23.

53. Ibid., 31.

54. Ibid., 25.

55. Wittgenstein, *Philosophische Bemerkungen*, 3.

56. Wittgenstein, *Tractatus*, 4.113.

57. Ibid., 6.53.

58. Ibid., 6.42.

59. Ibid., 6.43.

60. Winch (1958), p. 42.

61. Ibid., p. 58.

62. Ibid., p. 62.

63. Ibid., p. 30.

64. Ibid., pp. 86ff.

65. "It must rather be analogous to the participation of the natural scientist with his fellow workers in the activities of scientific investigation" (ibid., pp. 87ff).

66. Ibid., p. 123.

67. Wittgenstein, *Philosophical Investigations*, 6.

68. Ibid., 7.

69. Ibid., 150.

70. Wittgenstein, *Philosophische Bemerkungen*, 3.

71. Wittgenstein, *Philosophical Investigations*, 6.

72. Ibid., 88.

73. Ibid., 98.

74. Ibid., 206.

75. Ibid., 241.

76. Ibid., 77.

77. Ibid., 7.

78. Ibid., 19.

79. Winch (1958).

80. Cf. the philosophical introduction to J. A. Fodor and J. J. Katz, *The Structure of Language* (1964), pp. 1ff; the editors' essays in this volume are contributions to a metatheory of grammar (pp. 400ff) and semantics (pp. 479ff, 519ff).

81. Fodor and Katz (1964), p. 19.

82. Ibid., pp. 1ff.

83. Ibid., p. 3.

84. Ibid., p. 4.

85. Ibid., p. 11.

86. Cf. P. Henle, *Language, Thought and Culture* (Ann Arbor: 1958), pp. 1–24, and D. W. Brown, "Does Language-Structure Influence Thought?" in *ETC, a Review of General Semantics* 17 (1960): 339–363.

87. N. Chomsky, "Current Issues in Linguistic Theory," in Fodor and Katz (1964), p. 80.

88. Fodor and Katz (1964), p. 17n.

89. Idem.

90. H. G. Gadamer, *Truth and Method* (New York: 1975), pp. 363–364.

91. Ibid., pp. 346–347.

92. Ibid., pp. 348–349.

93. K. Heinrich, *Versuch über die Schwierigkeit Nein zu sagen* (Frankfurt: 1964).

94. On Heinrich, see my review in *Philosophisch-politische Profile* (Frankfurt: 1981), pp. 445ff. This study demonstrates that the hermeneutic self-reflection of language proceeds easily to a dialectical theory of language. Bruno Liebrucks's planned six-volume work, *Sprache und Bewusstsein*, promises such a theory. Volume I, *Einleitung und Spannweite des Problems* (Frankfurt: 1964), and volume II, *Sprache* (Frankfurt: 1965), have already been published. Liebrucks's critique of Gehlen's anthropology (Vol. I, pp. 79ff) is important for the methodology of the sciences of action. Because Liebrucks advances a restricted notion of practice, which he reduces to instrumental action, however, he ends up with an abstract opposition between language and action. The portions of Liebrucks's work that have appeared to date do not do justice to the unique connection between language and practice, which Wittgenstein and Mead elaborated in terms of symbolically mediated interaction in language games and communicative action.

95. Gadamer (1975), pp. 271–273.

96. Ibid., p. 261.

97. Ibid., pp. 263–264.

98. Cf. Gadamer (1975), pp. 339–340.

99. Danto (1965), p. 142.

100. Gadamer (1975), p. 198.

101. Danto (1965), p. 169.

102. Ibid., p. 115.

103. Ibid., pp. 17ff.

104. Ibid., p. 142.

105. W. Dilthey, *Gesammelte Schriften*, Vol. VII (*Der Aufbau der geschichtlichen Welt in den Geisteswissenschaften*), p. 233.

106. Gadamer (1975), pp. 275–276.

107. Cf. especially *Nicomachean Ethics* VI, 3–10.

108. The comparison between *phronesis* and *techne* has acquired particular relevance since science, which was once reserved to contemplation, has become methodologically bound to the attitude of the technician.

109. Gadamer (1975), p. 289.

110. Ibid., introduction, p. xii.

111. Ibid., p. xxi.

112. Ibid., p. xvi.

113. Ibid., p. 258.

114. Ibid., p. xvii.

115. Ritter and Schelsky take up this thesis. Cf. section 2.1 above.

116. Gadamer (1975), p. 248.

117. Ibid., p. 269.

IV Sociology as Theory of the Present

1. Gadamer (1975), p. 420.

2. This is the point of view taken in K. O. Apel's critique of Gehlen's institutionalism. Cf. Apel, "Arnold Gehlens Philosophie der Institution," in *Philosophische Rundschau* 10 (1962): 1ff.

3. Cf. J. O. Hertzler, *A Sociology of Language* (New York: 1965), especially chapter 7, "Sociocultural Change and Changing Language."

4. W. Pannenberg saw this: "It is a strange spectacle to see how an intelligent and penetrating author has his hands full trying to keep his thoughts from running their natural course. Gadamer's book presents such a spectacle in his effort to avoid the Hegelian total mediation of present truth by history. This effort is very well grounded in his pointing to the finitude of human experience, which can never be raised to the level of absolute knowledge. But, strangely, the phenomena that Gadamer describes keep pushing in the direction of a universal conception of history, which he—bearing Hegel's system in mind—hoped precisely to avoid" (W. Pannenberg, "Hermeneutik und Universalgeschichte," *Zeitschrift für Theologie und Kirche* 60 (1963): 90ff). As far as I can see, in recent Protestant theology the reception of Bloch's work has provided the impetus to overcome the ontology of historicity (Bultmann, Heidegger) through reflection on the dependence of the transcendental preconditions of understanding on the objective context of universal history. In addition to Pannenberg's works, see also J. Moltmann, *Theologie der Hoffnung* (1964).

5. Cf. Don Martindale, *The Nature and Types of Sociological Theory* (London: 1961), pp. 285ff.

6. *Mirrors and Masks, The Search for Identity* (Glencoe, IL: 1959).

7. This tendency can also be seen in Strauss's collection of Mead's writings: *On Social Psychology* (Chicago: 1956).

8. Strauss, *Mirrors and Masks*, p. 38.

9. Ibid., pp. 38ff.

10. Cf. G. H. Mead, *Mind, Self, and Society*, pp. 197ff.

11. Strauss (1959), p. 51.

12. Ibid., p. 52.

13. A. J. Ayer, *Man as a Subject for Science* (London: 1964).

14. Ibid., pp. 12, 13.

15. Ibid., p. 24.

16. A. C. MacIntyre, *The Unconscious* (London: 1958).

17. Ibid., pp. 56ff.

18. Ibid., p. 87.

19. Ibid., pp. 97ff.

20. Ibid., p. 98.

21. When unconscious motives are attached to privatized symbols—symbols cut off from the public communication of everyday language—psychotherapeutic linguistic analysis has the task of replacing the repressed symbols in their public context through the use of the transference situation and thus bringing the private language of patient into correspondence with ordinary language. Alfred Lorenzer of the Sigmund Freud Institute in Frankfurt explained this conception of the psychotherapeutic process as linguistic analysis in a lecture using as an example a horse phobia of a small boy reported by Freud.

22. MacIntyre (1958), p. 61.

23. K. R. Popper, *The Poverty of Historicism* (London: 1957).

24. In his *Toward a Science of Man in Society* (The Hague: 1961), K. W. Kapp makes a noteworthy proposal for a categorial framework that includes the developmental perspective and takes into account the viewpoints of both philosophical and cultural anthropology. Kapp's functionalism is not biased by the program of a unified science or the principles of a general methodology: "In the first place the use of man and culture as integrating frameworks calls from the very outset for an explicit recognition of the distinguishing differences between physical and biological processes on the one hand and social processes on the other. Instead of a latent or implicit anthropology social analysis will be forced to bring its assumptions concerning man and society into the open, and no longer operate with tacit presuppositions concerning the alleged similarities between the structures of inanimate matter, living organisms, and human societies. The social, as a category, will thus find its final recognition and establish the social disciplines as distinct and yet related fields of inquiry alongside those of the physical and biological sciences. As long as the social disciplines fail or refuse to acknowledge the unique character of social processes, they jeopardize not only the validity of their generalizations but also their status as a distinct field of scientific inquiry" (ibid., pp. 179ff).

Index